D1176651

THE
SECRET
OF
THE
TEMPLE

About the Author

John Michael Greer (Western Maryland) has been a student of occult traditions and the unexplained for more than thirty years. A Freemason, a student of geomancy and sacred geometry, and a widely read blogger, he is also the author of numerous books, including *Monsters*, *The New Encyclopedia of the Occult*, and *Secrets of the Lost Symbol*. Greer has contributed articles to *Renaissance Magazine*, *Golden Dawn Journal*, *Mezlim*, *New Moon Rising*, *Gnosis*, and *Alexandria*.

John Michael Greer

THE
SECRET
OF
THE
TEMPLE

Earth Energies,
Sacred Geometry, and
the Lost Keys of Freemasonry

LLEWELLYN PUBLICATIONS
WOODBURY, MINNESOTA

First Edition
First Printing, 2016

Book design by Rebecca Zins
Cover design by Kevin R. Brown
Cover credits:
   iStockphoto.com/17364031/©_ultraforma_
   iStockphoto.com/68079155/©valentinrussanov
   iStockphoto.com/77292865/©Lava4images
   iStockphoto.com/15509209/©Man_Half-tube
Editing by Aaron Lawrence
Interior credits:
   Freemason symbol, square and compass, iStockphoto.com/45709994/©tschitscherin
   Temple front with columns, iStockphoto.com/57977690/©Askold Romanov
   Illustrations by the author and Llewellyn's art department

Llewellyn Publications is a registered trademark of Llewellyn Worldwide Ltd.

Library of Congress Cataloging-in-Publication Data
Names: Greer, John Michael, author.
Title: The secret of the temple : earth energies, sacred geometry, and the
   lost keys of freemasonry / John Michael Greer.
Description: Woodbury, Minnesota : Llewellyn Publications, 2016. | Includes
   bibliographical references and index.
Identifiers: LCCN 2016034706 (print) | LCCN 2016038336 (ebook) | ISBN
   9780738748603 | ISBN 9780738750552
Subjects: LCSH: Freemasons. | Geomancy. | Earth (Planet)—Religious aspects.
Classification: LCC HS395 .G8194 2016 (print) | LCC HS395 (ebook) | DDC
   133.3/33—dc23
LC record available at https://lccn.loc.gov/2016034706

Llewellyn Publications
A Division of Llewellyn Worldwide Ltd.
2143 Wooddale Drive
Woodbury, MN 55125-2989

www.llewellyn.com
Printed in the United States of America

CONTENTS

PART TWO: THE TECHNOLOGY

PART THREE: THE LEGACY

INTRODUCTION

This book has been many years in the making and had no single starting point. Over the course of decades of omnivorous reading about the folklore, mythology, and religious customs of many lands, I happened to notice unexpected similarities between traditions, far removed in space and time, that related to religious architecture on the one hand and agricultural fertility on the other. A long time passed, and much more research had to take place, before I began to suspect that those similarities fit into a single pattern, and even more time and study was required before I guessed what that pattern might once have been.

There have been plenty of attempts over the years to fit all the world's mythologies and folk traditions into some single theory. From solar mythology through the archetypes of the collective unconscious to ancient astronauts, there's no shortage of Procrustean beds into which, with enough stretching and lopping, any myth, legend, or tradition can be force-fitted. Thus it's probably necessary to point out that this book doesn't attempt any similar surgery. If anything has been learned from the last century and a half of comparative mythology, it's that myths, legends, and folk customs talk about many different things in many different ways, and no one scheme of interpretation makes sense of them all.

People tell stories and establish customs, in other words, for many different reasons. The hypothesis at the heart of this book is that certain people in a number of Old World societies told stories and established customs that, among other things, had to do with an archaic technology, centered on temples of certain specific kinds and kept secret by its possessors, that had beneficial effects on agriculture in the areas immediately around those temples. To judge by the traces of this technology in myth and folklore, it evolved very gradually in prehistoric times, flourished in many of the literate urban societies of the ancient world, and went out of use for a variety of complex historical reasons in the late Middle Ages or not long thereafter. While the actual mechanism behind the lost technology can't yet be determined with any certainty from the surviving traces and traditions, there's no reason to assume that the forces that underlie it are unknown to today's scientists, and nothing in those traces and traditions suggests that anything involved in that technology violates the laws of nature as presently known.

It's only fair to caution my readers that the investigation chronicled in this book is frankly speculative in places. That is unavoidable. Few tasks in any branch of scholarship are as difficult as trying to tease out, from fragmentary records, a secret that people in ancient times did their level best to conceal. I have followed a slender thread through the labyrinth that leads to the lost technology chronicled here, and that thread can be snapped readily enough by those who aren't interested in finding out where it leads. I can only hope that enough of my readers will find the quest as intriguing as I have, and so will follow it to its end.

For reasons that will become clear in the pages that follow, much of the research that led to this book was made possible by my membership in Freemasonry. I would therefore like to thank the officers and brethren of Doric Lodge #92, F&AM, Seattle, WA, where I was made a Mason in 2001; the officers and brethren of Queen City Lodge #131, AF&AM, Cumberland, MD, where I'm currently a member; and the officers and brethren of all the other grand lodges, lodges, and appendant and concordant bodies in the family of Freemasonry who have welcomed me as a member or visiting brother and very often given me clues and insights of critical importance to the adventure chronicled in these pages. My gratitude remains with all.

PART ONE

The Riddle

CHAPTER ONE

The Lost Word

Many paths lead toward the mystery this book attempts to unravel, and each of them begins in a different place. One path, though, points into the heart of the riddle a little more directly than most. You can begin it with a stroll through any American city that was built before the Second World War and hasn't suffered too drastically from urban renewal since then. Head for the old commercial district, and keep your eyes well above street level. Sooner or later, you're likely to spot a curious emblem, perhaps on a sign, perhaps on the facade, with or without words of explanation: a carpenter's square and a set of drafting compasses intertwined, with the letter G in the middle, the emblem of the Freemasons.[1]

The Most Worshipful Fellowship of Ancient Free and Accepted Masons, to give it the full dignity of its traditional title,[2] has been a perennial subject of fascination and suspicion for almost three centuries now, since the original Masonic Grand Lodge went public in London in 1717. Here in the United

---

1   The words "Masonry" and "Freemasonry" both refer to the same tradition and organization. This is one of many details that tend to confuse the outsider.

2   Masonry is remarkably diverse—in the United States, every state has its own independent Grand Lodge with its own rituals and practices—and so this title appears in different forms under different Masonic jurisdictions.

States, the Craft—that's what Masons call their brotherhood—has been a major cultural force since before the Revolutionary War. Its membership roll includes a litany of famous names reaching from Benjamin Franklin and George Washington to Apollo astronaut Edwin "Buzz" Aldrin and jazz great Louis Armstrong, along with millions of others who have found its rituals, fellowship, and charitable projects worth their participation. All through those same three centuries, though, Freemasonry has also been the target of lurid accusations of devil worship, political conspiracy, and worse.

The fascination Masonry exerts and the hostility it attracts both focus on its reputation as a repository of secrets. Are there secrets in Masonry? Of course there are; every Mason binds himself by a solemn promise not to reveal to any nonmember the details of the initiation rituals, the passwords and signs by which one brother Mason can identify himself to another, the private business transactions of the lodge, and any personal secret that another brother confides in him. You'll find much the same promises made to one another by members of college sororities and old-fashioned labor unions, though somehow these and the many other organizations that make similar pledges have been spared the wild accusations that beset Masonry.

In the minds of conspiracy theorists and ordinary citizens alike, though, the secrets of Masonry just mentioned aren't the secrets that matter. Exactly what the Masonic secrets that matter might be is a question that has exercised imaginations, filled bookstores, and lined the pockets of unscrupulous publishers ever since the eighteenth century. It's ironic to note, though, that during that same period, more or less accurate copies of Masonic initiation rituals have been available for sale to the general public, and anyone who reads those rituals will find out the single most important fact about the secrets at the heart of Masonry: the Masons themselves don't have those secrets anymore. There was once something of vast importance hidden at the heart of Masonry—the rituals make that clear—but the keys to the mystery have been lost.

The Legend of Hiram Abiff

To understand what follows, it's important to know that Masonry communicates its teachings by way of initiation rituals. These are considerably less lurid than the media likes to suppose. An initiation ritual is basically a dramatic performance in which the lodge members play parts in a traditional story—in Masonry, this is usually either taken from or inspired by some passage from the Bible—followed by a lecture or two in which some of the symbolic meanings of the performance are explained.

Well over a thousand initiation rituals have had a role in Masonry at one point or another in its history, but the vast majority of them are rarely if ever performed today. In the United States, maybe a hundred get conferred on a regular basis. The way these degrees relate to one another and to the various organizational bodies in Masonry confuses some Masons and nearly everybody outside the Craft. The chart on the following page may help make what follows a little less baffling.

The three Blue Lodge or Ancient Craft degrees of Entered Apprentice, Fellow Craft, and Master Mason are the foundation of Masonry. Every Mason has received these three degrees. Some brothers, after being "entered, passed, and raised" to the three Blue Lodge degrees, choose to go onward and become active in other Masonic bodies, while others are content with the Blue Lodge and don't pursue other degrees.

Those who go onward have their choice of various routes. In the United States there are two large organizations, the Scottish Rite and the York Rite, which confer further degrees on Master Masons. There's also a galaxy of smaller organizations, such as the Knight Masons and the Allied Masonic Degrees, that have degrees of their own to confer, as well as an assortment of "appendant and concordant bodies" that aren't part of Masonry, strictly speaking, but draw their membership entirely from the ranks of Master Masons and their families. All told, there are enough Masonic organizations of all these kinds that in any reasonably large city in the United States, if you're a Master Mason in good standing and enjoy initiation rituals and fellowship, you can count on being able to attend a Masonic meeting five or six nights a week.

Blue Lodge
1° Entered Apprentice Degree
2° Fellow Craft Degree
3° Master Mason Degree

Scottish Rite

4°–14°:
Lodge of Perfection

15°–18°:
Chapter of Rose Croix

19°–30°:
Council of Kadosh

31°–32°:
Consistory

York Rite

Royal Arch:
Mark Master
Most Excellent Master
Past Master
Holy Royal Arch

Cryptic Masonry:
Royal Master
Select Master

Knights Templar:
Order of the Red Cross
Knight of Malta
Knight of the Temple

Other Masonic Bodies
(hundreds of different degrees)

Scottish Rite Honors and Honorary Degrees
(*33°* and others)

York Rite Honorary and Invitational Degrees (many)

CHART OF MASONIC STRUCTURE

Despite this profusion of rites and degrees, one stands above them all. This is the Third Degree, the degree of Master Mason, the beating heart of Masonry. The first two degrees of the Craft are preparations for it, and all other degrees are additions to it. As with most other Masonic degrees, the narrative on which it's based is inspired by certain events in the Old Testament.

According to the seventh chapter of the first book of Kings, when King Solomon built a temple to the God of Israel, the brasswork was done by a man named Hiram, a skilled craftsman from Tyre, whose mother was a widow of the tribe of Naphtali and whose father had been a Tyrian. The fifth chapter of the second book of Chronicles repeats the same story with slight variations, but refers to Hiram the craftsman twice, curiously, as "Hiram his father."[3] In the older translations of the Bible that were available in the formative years of Masonry, the Hebrew word for "his father" was mistaken for part of the name and left untranslated, and so in these translations, the name of the craftsman became Hiram Abiff.

That's all the Bible has to say about Hiram the craftsman. In the Master Mason ritual, by contrast, Hiram Abiff appears not just as a brassworker but as the master builder of the temple, Solomon's architect and building contractor, who has control of every detail of the construction project. Even more significantly, he alone knows the Master's Word, the great secret of the builder's craft, and has promised to communicate it to his assistants, who are Fellow Crafts, once the temple is complete. A group of Fellow Crafts, however, decide to extort the Master's Word from Hiram by violence; when they threaten him with death, he refuses to give the Word to them, and they murder him, hide his body, and flee.

Because he alone knows all the details of the project, Hiram Abiff's disappearance brings work on the Temple to a standstill. Searchers are sent out to find him, and eventually discover his grave. His death has placed the entire Masonic community in jeopardy, since no one else can communicate the Master's Word and the secrets of a Master Mason. Solomon thus establishes

---

3   2 Chronicles 2:14 and 4:16.

a substitute Word and substitute secrets, which will be used by the Craft until the true Word and the true secrets are rediscovered. Those substitutes, according to Masonic tradition, are the ones that Master Masons still receive today.[4]

Has the true Word ever been found? That's a far more complicated question than it seems. Several other Masonic degrees claim to reveal the true Master's Word, but they disagree on what the true Word is. Masons who join the Scottish Rite in the Southern Jurisdiction of the United States, for example, can expect to be taught one version of the Master's Word in the Fourteenth Degree, a different one in the Eighteeenth, and yet another, different from both, in the Thirty-Second! It's understandable that authors of initiation rituals would take the discovery of the true Word as a promising theme, but the sheer abundance of different versions of the Master's Word in circulation within Masonry raises a reasonable doubt that any of them was the Word the original creators of the Master Mason degree had in mind.

Origins of the Masonic Craft

If there was once a secret knowledge hidden away in Freemasonry, the obvious place to look for clues about its nature is in the origins of the Craft itself. That may not seem like much help, since a fantastic amount of nonsense has been written about Masonic origins over the last three centuries or so. Go to a bookstore with a good selection of titles in the alternative history field and you can count on finding at least a dozen books claiming this or that exotic origin for Freemasonry. As we'll see, one of the most popular of those claims—the theory that Masonry descends in some sense from the medieval Knights Templar—may have some truth behind it, but many other theories have considerably less in the way of solid foundations beneath them.

Then there are the theories that go zooming off into the realms of utter nonsense. At least one popular author in the alternative history field, for example, has claimed that Freemasonry has been in existence on this plan-

---

4   See, for example, Gest 2007, 291, which paraphrases English Masonic ritual.

et since 11,500 BCE, when it arrived with refugees from the planet Mars.[5] Another popular New Age author has filled a number of books with claims that all Freemasons are actually evil reptilian aliens from a distant planet.[6] Compared to these flights of fancy—neither of which, it probably needs to be said, has a scrap of evidence to support it—the medieval Knights Templar seem positively tame.

Turn from these notions to reputable historical research, on the other hand, and the immediate origins of modern Masonry are no mystery at all. All the evidence, as well as the traditions of the Craft itself, traces the origins of Freemasonry to the stonemasons' guilds of the Middle Ages.[7] Across medieval Europe, practitioners of most trades formed social and economic organizations called guilds, which regulated prices and working conditions, maintained professional standards, and provided charitable assistance to members of the trade who had fallen on hard times. Each guild had its own patron saint, its own initiation rituals, and its own traditional secrets, and the stonemasons of medieval Europe were no exception.

Like most other guilds, the masons were divided into three levels based on technical competence. At the lowest rung of the ladder were apprentices, who served as unskilled labor while learning the rudiments of the trade. Capable apprentices eventually became fellows of the craft, who provided the bulk of the skilled labor force on a building project but had not yet learned enough to manage a project on their own or tackle the most demanding works of craftsmanship. Fellows of the craft who excelled at the builder's art finally became masters, who taught apprentices, hired fellows of the craft, and managed the entire process of design and construction from selecting the site and quarrying the stone to putting the final ornamentation on the finished building.

Stonemasons of all degrees distinguished themselves from mere day laborers—called "cowans" in Scotland—who lacked the skills to do more than the

---

5   This is one of a number of remarkable claims in Hancock 1995.

6   See, among others, Icke 2004.

7   See Knoop and Jones 1978 and Stevenson 1988.

most basic kinds of work with rough stone. The test of mastery of a medieval stonemason was his ability to work with freestone, the finely grained varieties of stone that could be fashioned into statues or used for the most structurally important parts of a building. A competent stonemason came to be known as a "freestone mason"—a phrase that eventually contracted into "freemason."

Due to the nature of their work, the stonemasons had to rework the basic guild structure in certain ways to cope with different working conditions. Where members of the grocers' or goldsmiths' guilds could set up their shops in any convenient place and let customers come to them, stonemasons had to travel to building sites, and very often a building project of any size would attract stonemasons from many different towns. In place of a single permanent guild organization in each town, as a result, stonemasons formed working groups that held their meetings on the worksite after hours. They met in makeshift wooden shelters called lodges, which were as standard on building sites in those days as storage trailers are today; it's for this reason that a local organization of Freemasons is still called a lodge.

With the end of the Middle Ages and the emergence of a new mercantile economy that made use of improved transportation technology, the local economies that supported the guild system were absorbed into larger regional and national economic networks, and as this happened, most guilds closed their doors forever. A few of the stonemasons' guilds, though, had a different destiny waiting for them. During the seventeenth century in Scotland and England, educated gentlemen who were interested in the symbolism and the geometrical lore taught in masons' lodges arranged to become "accepted" or, as we would now say, honorary stonemasons. They passed through the old initiation rituals, made the traditional pledges, and attended meetings, even though they may not have known which end of a stonecutter's chisel was which.

It became common practice in these years to refer to the practices of working with stone on building sites as "operative masonry" and the philosophical and moral symbolism that came to be attached to the mason's tools and activities as "speculative masonry"—the word "speculative" here had its old meaning of "contemplative." Over the course of the seventeenth century, as the economic functions of the medieval guild system fell apart and accepted members became a larger and larger fraction of the membership, the speculative side of Masonry gradually replaced the operative side, and the old stonemasons' lodges gradually evolved into lodges of Free and Accepted Masons.

The final step in the transformation began in 1717. In that year, four lodges of accepted Masons that had met in London "since time immemorial" organized the first Masonic Grand Lodge as an umbrella organization to standardize and regulate the Craft. According to surviving documents, the original group of four lodges only knew of the Entered Apprentice and Fellow Craft degrees of initiation. The Master Mason degree, and the legend of Hiram Abiff at its core, showed up around 1725 and was rapidly adopted by Masonic lodges. To this day, nobody knows where it came from.

Another event that would eventually have a great deal of influence on the history of Freemasonry happened in 1738. In that year the Roman Catholic Church issued the first of several formal condemnations of Freemasonry. The 1738 papal bull *In Eminente* is a very strange document. It notes that Masonry is a secret organization that has attracted a great many hostile rumors, and for this reason, "and for other just and reasonable motives known to us," Masonry was summarily condemned and proscribed; any Catholic who became a member was instantly excommunicated, and absolution could only be granted by the Pope himself.[8] Later papal condemnations insisted, in increasingly strident tones, that Freemasons worshipped the devil and engaged in a galaxy of other sins.

Exactly why the Catholic Church became so fixated on these latter claims is an interesting question, to which no one has yet offered a satisfactory answer. To begin with, anyone who has read or attended Masonic ceremonies knows that the claims in question are nonsense. Of course this hasn't stopped similar behavior before or since; an embarrassing number of

---

8   The text of *In Eminente* may be consulted online at *http://www.papalencyclicals.net/ Clem12/c12inemengl.htm.*

Christian churches seem to have forgotten that "thou shalt not bear false witness against thy neighbor" is one of the Ten Commandments, and the same logic that led good Christians not so long ago to insist that Jews made their Passover matzohs with the blood of baptized infants still gets used today to condemn Masons, among others, for crimes they haven't committed. Even so, the frantic intensity with which the Catholic Church denounced Freemasonry is remarkable—there are, for example, very few other sins that can only be absolved by the Pope himself.

The Pope's fulminations did little to stop the spread of Masonry across western Europe, though. In Catholic countries, there were plenty of people who objected to the reactionary political and social policies promoted by the Vatican at that time, and the Catholic ban on Masonic membership may actually have attracted more members than it drove away. In Protestant countries, meanwhile, Masons treated the Vatican's hostility as something of a badge of honor, and many Protestant churches quietly encouraged Masonic membership as one more way of distancing themselves from Rome. By the beginning of the nineteenth century, the Craft was firmly established in every country in Europe, and lodges were springing up throughout Europe's overseas colonies and the newly independent United States of America.

Masonic lodges by this time conferred the three degrees of Entered Apprentice, Fellow Craft, and Master Mason using rituals close to the ones practiced today, and regulated their affairs by rules and customs modern Freemasons would recognize at once. The fundamental ground rules of the Craft that Masons today call "the ancient landmarks" were in place, and Masonry began two centuries of dramatic expansion. The one part of modern Masonry that had not yet arrived were the degrees beyond Master Mason, and those were not long in arriving.

The High Degrees

A case can be made that the degree of Master Mason is the first of these "high degrees" since, as already mentioned, it was not part of the original two-degree system worked by the lodges that founded the Grand Lodge of

England. Once it was adopted into Masonry, though, other degrees quickly followed.

The first of these high degrees to appear was the degree of Scots Master. This is a mystery to modern Masonic researchers, as it first appeared in lodge records in England in 1733, flourished for a little more than two decades, and then apparently vanished.[9] The one evident trace it left behind was the habit of referring to some of the higher degrees of Masonry as Scottish. It may have left more behind than this, however, as contemporary records connect the Scots Master degree to one of the oldest of the high degrees to survive to the present, the degree of Knight Mason.

In 1737 Chevalier Andrew Ramsay made a famous and widely reprinted speech to his brother Masons in Paris in which he claimed that Masonry had originated with the knights of the Crusades. That claim came to be widely circulated and accepted among Masons. In 1745 a French book on Masonry repeated this claim, with an addition:

> During the Palestinian Wars, some of the Crusader Princes made a plan to rebuild the Temple of Jerusalem, & to restore Architecture to its original condition. But they were not really concerned with material construction; they wanted to build in a spiritual sense, & that, in the hearts of the Infidel. They assembled in this spirit & for purposes of recognition they took the name of Knights Free Masons.[10]

The Knight Masons, as they are now called, are still present in Masonry and have divided the ritual of the original Knights Free Masons into three degrees, Knight of the Sword, Knight of the East, and Knight of the East and West. Just as the three degrees of Ancient Craft Masonry are associated with the color blue, these three are the green degrees. Versions of the same rituals have also been adopted into both of the major American Masonic rites as the Illustrious Order of the Red Cross in the York Rite and the Fifteenth and Sixteenth Degrees of the Scottish Rite. All these rituals make use of a story

---

9   de Hoyos and Morris 2011, viii.

10   Quoted in Carr 1971, 236.

from the book of Esdras, one of the Hebrew books that didn't quite make it into the official Old Testament.

Long after the reign of King Solomon, according to the Bible, the Temple was destroyed by the Babylonians and the Jewish people were taken away into captivity in Babylon. Seventy years later, the Babylonians were conquered in turn by the Persians, and the Jews were allowed to return home. The Knight Mason degrees, and their equivalents in the York and Scottish Rites, tell of the journey of the Jewish prince Zerubbabel to the Persian court, as recounted in the book of Esdras, where he won permission for his people to rebuild the Temple.

According to the legend of the degree, the Knight Masons were first created by Zerubbabel himself to protect the Temple during its rebuilding, laboring with a trowel in one hand and a sword in the other. This is where the connection with the apparently lost degree of Scots Master comes in, because a 1744 French anti-Masonic tract refers the same story to the fourth or Ecossais (Scottish) degree.[11] For that matter, the very first exposé of the higher degrees of Masonry, published in 1766, treats Scots Master and Knight of the Sword (another early name for the original Knight Mason degree) as synonyms.[12] Thus it's at least possible that the Scots Master degree simply underwent a name change—not an uncommon thing at that time—and the Knight Mason degrees and their equivalents elsewhere in Masonry thus preserve variant forms of the oldest degree beyond Master Mason.

By the time the Knight Mason degree first appears under that name, however, an even more influential high degree had made its appearance. This is the Royal Arch degree, the keystone of what became the red degrees of Masonry.

The first apparent reference to the Royal Arch degree comes from an Irish newspaper article from 1743, which describes two "excellent masons" carrying the Royal Arch in a procession. Excellent Mason seems to have been another early high degree—a source from 1738 describes it as a degree above

---

11   Carr 1971, 197–198.

12   de Hoyos and Morris 2011, xxi and xxviii.

Master Mason—but as with Scots Master, nothing more is known for certain about it. In 1744 an account of the Masonic lodges in the town of York described a special assembly of Master Masons who had received the additional degree of Royal Arch.[13] Thereafter the Royal Arch quickly became an important part of nearly all high degree rites.

The Royal Arch degree, like the Knight Mason degrees, is set in the time of Zerubbabel, and relates to the rebuilding of the Temple after its destruction by the Babylonians. According to the legend of the degree, workmen clearing away the ruins discovered a chasm in the ground. Descending into the chasm, they found a hidden vault far beneath the Holy of Holies of the ruined Temple. In the secret vault was a treasure that had been placed there in the days of Solomon—a treasure that, among other things, included the Lost Word.

As with other Masonic degrees, the Royal Arch was soon rewritten in various ways, and details were changed to suit the tastes of their authors. The version of the Royal Arch degree currently included in the Scottish Rite, for example, backdates the story to the time of Solomon, relocates the vault to a site near the Temple, and has the treasure hidden away since the time of Enoch, who lived before Noah's flood. The version currently practiced in Ireland, on the other hand, moves the date to the reign of Josiah, a king of Judah in whose reign the Jewish religion was reformed and purified. Every version, however, retained the secret vault as a core element, and another degree soon appeared to explain how the treasure got into the secret vault. This is the degree currently called Select Master in the York Rite and Perfect Elu in the Scottish Rite—the word *élu* is French for "chosen" or "selected," so the two names mean much the same thing.

The legend of these two degrees, and their equivalents in other rites, focuses on a different way of reaching the hidden treasury beneath the Temple: a horizontal tunnel that ran from the innermost part of King Solomon's palace to the secret vault under the Holy of Holies. It was by means of this tunnel, in all versions of the degree, that the Lost Word was hidden away.

---

13   Quoted in Hughan 1874, 89.

The tradition of a secret vault inside the Temple Mount that can be reached by two routes—one vertically through ruins, one horizontally through a tunnel—may well be something more than the clever daydream of a ritual designer. It appears very early in the development of the higher degrees of Masonry; in fact, the first published high degree rituals, which saw print in 1766, include an explicit reference to the secret vault and the tunnel by which it can be reached.[14] What's more, as we'll see in a later chapter, the vault, the vertical descent through the ruins, and the tunnel all relate to specific, archeologically documented realities that cast an unexpected light not only on the origins of Freemasonry, but possibly on a far more ancient secret—the secret with which this book is primarily concerned.

An Operative Mystery

The initiation rituals, however, are by no means the only puzzles passed down to modern Freemasonry—nor the only ones that bear on the riddle at the heart of this book. Masonry, in fact, is full of remarkably odd details. To this day, for example, Masons routinely perform a ceremony at the laying of the cornerstones of public or Masonic buildings, in which the cornerstone has grain sprinkled on it and wine and oil poured on it.[15] Why? Plenty of ornate reasons have been suggested over the centuries, but when it comes right down to it, nobody in Masonry or outside of it knows for sure.

Even more obscure than the cornerstone ritual are the emblems and diagrams shown to newly made Masons in the course of their initiation. In the three Blue Lodge degrees, most of these appear on what are called "tracing boards."[16]

This term reaches back to the operative lodges of the Middle Ages. During the years when stonemasons' guilds built castles and cathedrals all over Europe, paper was unknown and parchment, which was made from scraped animal skins, was far too expensive to use for building plans. Instead,

---

14   de Hoyos and Morris 2011, 54–55.

15   Reed 1976, 118–119.

16   See MacNulty 1991, 44–45.

the master builder in charge of a project would have a large wooden board on which he would draw designs using chalk, charcoal, and clay to produce white, black, and red lines respectively, sketching out details of the day's work.

These were the original tracing boards. In early Masonic lodges, the symbols of the degree that was going to be conferred were drawn with chalk on the bare wooden floorboards of the meeting room, and the most recent initiate had the duty of washing the designs off the floor once the meeting was over. This habit gradually gave way to painted and printed boards with the relevant symbols on them, then to other ways of presenting the same symbols. These days, in up-to-date lodges, new initiates are as likely as not to encounter the symbols of each degree by way of computer graphics projected onto a screen on the wall.

Though the media have changed, the symbols have remained remarkably consistent down through the centuries. What makes this even more fascinating is that nobody today is really sure what many of the symbols mean. For example, according to Masonic tradition, every regular and well-governed lodge is supposed to have a curious diagram in it, consisting of a circle with a point in the center, placed between two parallel lines, which represent St. John the Baptist and St. John the Evangelist; see illustration on page 22.[17] Very often an open Bible is perched atop the circle, and nearly as often pictures of the two saints flank the two parallel lines.

In the Masonic rituals currently used in most North American lodges, this diagram is explained in purely ethical terms, as a guide to right behavior. Nearly all Masonic symbols have been given a moral interpretation of one kind or another. This is partly a reflection of the literary tastes of the eighteenth and nineteenth centuries, which delighted in moral allegories, and partly an inheritance from older sources—the moral interpretation of symbols was a standard feature of medieval and Renaissance culture. Since today's Freemasonry descends from the operative lodges of the Middle Ages, though, and the diagram of the point within the circle dates from the earliest

---

17   See, for example, Grand Lodge of Maryland 1935, 15–16.

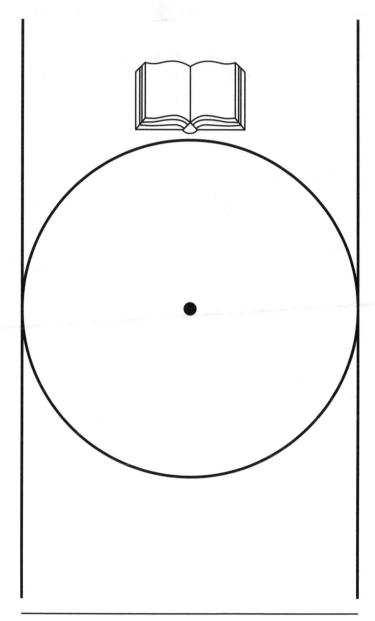

POINT IN CIRCLE

days of the Craft, it seems likely that this diagram once had an operative meaning—after all, however concerned the old operative stonemasons must have been about the moral character of their apprentices, they also had the practical tasks of the working builder's job in view.

Carl H. Claudy, whose introduction to the three Blue Lodge degrees is still presented to newly made Masons in many jurisdictions, made an intriguing suggestion along these lines.[18] He proposed that the diagram was used to try the builders' squares used by operative stonemasons and make sure they stayed at a right angle. It can certainly be used for that purpose, but his suggestion that this was the great secret of the operative Master Masons won't hold water. Anybody familiar with basic geometry—and geometry was one of the seven foundational branches of knowledge that every educated person in the Middle Ages learned—would have been able to figure out at a glance what was going on when the master builder in charge of a project ducked into the room where the diagram was kept with an armful of builders' squares and came back out knowing which squares needed to be fixed.

Researchers into Masonry are constantly falling into pitfalls of this kind and insisting that the grand secret of the Craft is some bit of information that was well known to most people in the days of the old operative lodges. That's not a prejudice unique to Masonic researchers, either. Modern popular culture loves to pretend that the Middle Ages were much more ignorant than they actually were. An astonishing number of people still believe, for example, that in 1492 everybody but Christopher Columbus thought the world was flat, even though a few keystrokes of online research or a few minutes in a decently stocked library are enough to prove that this simply isn't true.[19]

As we'll see in a later chapter, the diagram of the point in the circle has a straightforward explanation once it's examined in the context of the way medieval master builders laid out the churches of the time. In the same way, many of the other odd relics that make the symbolism and ritual of

---

18   Claudy 1931, 55–59
19   See Russell 1991 for a good summary of the evidence.

Freemasonry so fascinating to members make perfect sense once the realities of the old operative builders are kept in mind. Yet there remains, unexplained by the remaining fragments of the operative lore, the ancient legend of a tremendous secret that once lay at the heart of the Craft—a secret that has been lost, and that somehow related to the Temple of Solomon in ancient Jerusalem.

CHAPTER TWO

The Temple of Solomon

In the seventh year of his reign, according to the first book of Chronicles, King David captured the city of Jerusalem from the Jebusites, the Canaanite nation that had possessed it since time out of mind. Once the city was in Israelite hands, David moved the nation's capital there from Hebron and built a palace. Just north of the little walled city was a flat-topped hill owned by Ornan the Jebusite, who used it as a threshing floor—an outdoor space where grain was pounded with flails and then tossed in the air with a pitchfork so the grain fell straight down while the chaff went drifting away on the wind. Years after the conquest of the city, in response to a pestilence, David bought the hill from Ornan for fifty shekels of silver and built an altar there to make offerings to the God of Israel.

Some thirty centuries later, the threshing floor atop that flat-topped hill—or, more precisely, the vast complex of ruins built over and around the hill—is known to Jews and Christians as the Temple Mount, to Muslims as al-Haram al-Sharif, "the Noble Sanctuary," and to people around the world as one of the most intractable flashpoints in the bitter tensions between the nation of Israel and the Arab countries that surround it. This is nothing new in the Temple Mount's history. Over and over again since David's time, the mount and the sacred buildings raised upon it have been the focus of every kind of struggle and atrocity that religious, political, and ethnic passions can generate.

The symbols and rituals of Freemasonry include a great many references to the Temple Mount, the structures that have been raised and destroyed atop it, and the underground tunnels and vaults that traditionally lie beneath it. To understand the secret that may still lie hidden in Freemasonry's fragmentary traditions and enigmatic rituals, a glance back over the history of the Temple Mount will be crucial.

That history actually begins far to the south of the threshing floor of Ornan, on the slopes of Mount Sinai. According to the book of Exodus, that was the place where Moses received from the God of Israel a set of detailed instructions for the building of the first Jewish sanctuary, the Tabernacle. This was a sacred tent made of linen, divided by curtains into an inner sanctum, an outer space of lesser holiness, and a porch in front. The tent was surrounded by a screen of cloth supported on wooden poles, and inside the screen but outside the tent were a portable altar for sacrifices and a basin of water for purifications. Three chapters of the book of Exodus are given over to a painstaking description of the Tabernacle and its furnishings—detailed enough that more than one complete modern copy has been made.

To this day, nomadic peoples in various corners of the world have similar sacred tents, which they set up for worship and then take down and load upon their horses or camels when it's time to move to the next campsite. During their wandering years, the Israelites did much the same thing with the Tabernacle, and even after they settled down in what had previously been the land of Canaan and took up agriculture, the Tabernacle remained a center of Israelite worship for many generations. Only in the wake of sweeping political and cultural changes did it give way to a more permanent structure, the famous Temple of Solomon.

The First Temple

Open-air altars and sanctuaries of the sort King David established on Ornan's threshing floor were common all over the Middle East during the lifetime of that monarch and for centuries before and after his time. The Old Testament refers to them as "high places," as they were generally established on hilltops or other elevated locations. The Hebrew people had worshipped at such places for centuries before the First Temple was built. After the Hebrew conquest of Canaan under Joshua, as already noted, the Tabernacle remained a center of Hebrew piety, but it shared space in the religious life of the people with local high places, not all of which were consecrated to the God of Israel.

David and his son Solomon reigned during an era of centralization, when the eastern Mediterranean basin was in transition from a patchwork of independent tribes and city-states to a land of great kingdoms, and eventually of empires. One visible mark of that transformation was the emergence of the national temple: a holy place located in the capital of each kingdom, to which people from around the kingdom were expected to make pilgrimage and bring offerings at certain times of the year.

The Hebrews, as former nomads whose technology and culture lagged behind those of most of their neighbors, were latecomers to the process of centralization as well. Long before the Israelite tribes accepted their first king, Saul, powerful kingdoms and national temples were rising elsewhere in the region. When Solomon ordered work to begin on a national temple for the kingdom of Israel, therefore, one of his first actions was to bring in foreign craftsmen from the country of a more technologically and culturally complex ally.

According to the biblical accounts, the ally was Hiram, king of the thriving seaport of Tyre in what is now Lebanon. Hiram Abiff, the Tyrian master craftsman who plays so important a role in Masonic symbolism, was among the craftsmen the King of Tyre sent. These skilled workmen brought with them the knowledge obtained by generations of master builders in the eastern Mediterranean basin, and unsurprisingly, the temple they built for

Solomon had a great deal in common with other national temples in the region.[20]

The first thing that needs to be grasped in making sense of the Temple of Solomon is just how small it was: only about ninety feet long, thirty feet wide, and forty-five feet high.[21] Like the Tabernacle, the temple was divided into three parts—a porch (in Hebrew *ulam*) on the eastern end, some fifteen feet deep; the main room inside, the holy place (in Hebrew *heikal*), sixty feet long; and the *debir* or Holy of Holies at the western end, a perfect cube thirty feet on a side. To either side of the temple proper were narrow rooms used by the priests for storage and other purposes; see illustration on page 29.

Both the *heikal* and the *debir* were paneled with sheets of pure gold. The Ark of the Covenant, a wooden chest covered with gold that contained the most sacred treasures of the Jewish people, was kept inside the Holy of Holies under the wings of two wooden cherubim likewise covered with gold. In the main room were the sacred seven-branched candlestick, the altar of incense, and the table of shewbread, on which loaves of bread were placed as offerings.

Out in front were two huge pillars of brass, named Jachin (Hebrew for "he shall establish") and Boaz ("in strength"). Scholars disagree about whether they were part of the porch or freestanding structures; in either case, they were substantial—according to 1 Kings 7:15–22, they were 27 feet high; according to 2 Chronicles 3:15–17, their height works out to 47 feet 6 inches, and according to both sources, each pillar had a bronze capital on top, adding an additional 7 feet 6 inches to the total. In the courtyard in front of the temple was the so-called "brazen sea," a huge brass basin of water used for purification, and an altar of sacrifice, where animals were slaughtered as offerings to the God of Israel.

The biblical description is all that survives of the Temple of Solomon. The very limited archeological research that has been permitted on the Temple

---

20   See Lundquist 2008, 46–70.

21   The measurements cited in the Old Testament are 60 cubits in length, 20 in width, and 30 in height; the exact length of the cubit used in the building has been disputed, but it was somewhere around 18 inches.

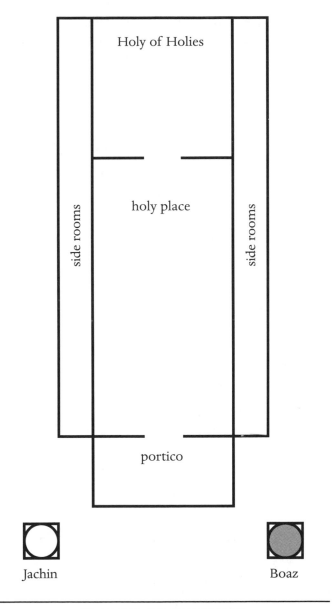

TEMPLE OF SOLOMON

Mount in modern times has turned up no single physical trace of it, and in fact evidence for the Hebrew kingdoms of Judah and Israel before the Babylonian conquest is very thin on the ground. Much has been made of this dearth of hard data in some circles, but the same shortage of evidence applies equally well to most of the little kingdoms of the ancient Near East.

A few good archeological sites in the region, a few caches of documents in Egypt and elsewhere, and the twist of fate that turned the traditional histories of one of the little kingdoms of that era into the holy scripture of one world religion and the Old Testament of another provide the little information about the First Temple that today's scholars have to go on. Not until the Temple of Solomon was leveled to the ground and a new temple rose in its place does documentation become more complete—and it is at this point that the inquiry central to this book finds its starting place.

The Second Temple

In the year 586 BCE, as commemorated in several of the Masonic rituals described in chapter 1 of this book, a Babylonian army besieged and captured Jerusalem, destroyed the city and the temple, and deported its population. In 539 BCE Babylon fell in its turn to the armies of Cyrus, king of Persia. Among the new ruler's first acts was to terminate the Babylonian policy of deporting conquered populations, and the Jews were among the beneficiaries.[22] Many of the exiles returned to Jerusalem, and under the leadership of their prince Zerubbabel, they began the long and difficult process of building a new city and temple on the ruins of the old. Despite political troubles with the Persian authorities and conflicts with the local population, the new temple was completed in 516 BCE.

The Second Temple, as this structure is called, was built on the pattern of the Temple of Solomon, and in all likelihood on the same foundations. It was a considerably less lavish structure than its predecessor had been—Solomon's temple was the focus of worship for an independent and prosperous

---

22   This decision of Cyrus is documented outside the Old Testament; see Lundquist 2008, 71–72.

nation, while the Second Temple was merely one of many ethnic religious centers in a huge and polyglot empire. The gold that played such a massive role in Solomon's temple was in considerably shorter supply in Zerubbabel's, though Cyrus ordered the return of the temple furnishings that had been looted by the Babylonians and presented as trophies of victory to the temples of Babylonian gods.

Certain things present in the Temple of Solomon were absent in the Second Temple. The most important of them was the Ark of the Covenant, which apparently did not survive the Babylonian conquest—there is no record of it in the Bible or any other written source after that point. Throughout the history of the Second Temple, though the traditional furnishings of the *heikal* (main hall) were recovered or replaced, the *debir* (Holy of Holies) was empty. The two pillars Jachin and Boaz, which came to play such an important part in Masonic symbolism later on, were also missing in the time of the Second Temple. There is no discussion of the reason for their absence; they simply weren't replaced.

The new building campaign brought considerable changes to the Temple Mount. The Babylonians apparently tore down the retaining walls and left behind only a mass of rubble. The builders of the Second Temple rebuilt the retaining walls, making the Temple Mount larger than it had been in Solomon's day. According to the *Letter of Aristeas*, one of the few surviving writings that describe the Second Temple before the time of Herod, the rebuilding also involved putting in drainage channels for the blood from sacrificed animals and a network of cisterns and tunnels that provided an ample supply of water for priestly use.[23]

The Temple of Herod

Zerubbabel's temple remained the center of Jewish religious life for well over four centuries. Toward the end of that time, it had become something of a national embarrassment, a small and shabby building in an age of great architecture. That was the situation when Herod the Great became the king

---

23   Lundquist 2008, 83–84.

of Judea. Herod was not even Jewish in origin—he was an Idumaean, from the eastern side of the Jordan valley—but he was a supremely talented politician. When King Antigonus II of Judea tried to shake off Rome's overlordship with the help of the Parthians farther east, Herod managed to get himself appointed king of Judea by the Emperor Augustus, and conquered the country with Roman help.

He then set out to conciliate his new subjects by rebuilding the Temple Mount complex on the grandest scale possible. This was a complicated project, not least because worship and sacrificial offerings had to continue on the site straight through the rebuilding process—this is why, in Jewish tradition, the temple of Herod isn't considered the third temple but counts as a continuation and expansion of the second. Difficult as the project must have been, Herod accomplished it with aplomb, and the temple and its surrounding courtyards, porches, and buildings counted thereafter among the architectural wonders of the ancient world.

The whole complex covered some 36 acres, surrounded by massive retaining walls topped by porticoes supported by a forest of Corinthian columns. This was a huge area by the standards of the age, twice as large as the Forum in Rome and more than four times as large as the Acropolis in Athens. Inside the greatly expanded Temple Mount, additional cisterns, drains, and channels for water were built, along with underground storage rooms for priestly use. Ten gates in the retaining walls, with tunnels behind them, provided access to the Temple complex.

The largest of the porticoes, on the south, was where the moneychangers had their booths—Jews from around the Mediterranean world came to the temple and were expected to pay a temple tax in the local currency. Inside the porticoes, courtyards divided the Temple Mount into areas with progressively more restricted access—the Court of the Gentiles, the Court of the Women, the Temple Court, and the Court of the Priests, surrounding the temple itself.

Herod's temple used the same foundations as the temples of Solomon and Zerubbabel but placed a massive facade in front, a hundred cubits high and wide—that is, around a hundred and fifty feet each way. The side rooms were greatly expanded, and an upper story was added atop the *heikal* and *debir*, with rooms accessible by a spiral staircase in the temple's northeast corner. The whole structure was faced with white limestone and sheets of gold, which must have shone brightly enough to hurt the eyes when the sun rose and sparkled on the eastern facade.

The rebuilding project got under way in 20 BCE, and work was still proceeding on some of the outlying parts of the complex when the Jewish revolt against Rome in 66 CE made the whole point moot. When the city fell to the Romans in 70 CE, the temple was demolished. After a second revolt in 132 CE, the Temple Mount itself was systematically destroyed, the upper sections of the retaining walls toppled over into the valleys to either side, and a temple to Jupiter built atop the ruins. That was leveled in its turn when the Roman Empire was Christianized in the fourth century CE, and from then until Jerusalem was conquered by Muslim armies in 638 CE, the Temple Mount was a ruin.

The destruction of the temple has been a central theme of Jewish thought and practice ever since the fall of Jerusalem in 70 CE. Among the immediate consequences of that national catastrophe was the creation of the Mishnah, the compilation of scholarly tractates that forms the core of the Talmud. Much of the material included in the Mishnah consists of details of the temple and the ceremonies that were practiced there,[24] and cherished memories of the temple and lamentations for its loss appear all through the Mishnah and its commentaries. Curiously, though, one of the things most fondly remembered and most bitterly lamented was the temple's power to make crops flourish.

---

24   Lundquist 2008, 130.

The Temple as a Source of Fertility

Perhaps the strangest thing about the Temple of Jerusalem, in fact, is the traditional insistence that it was a source of agricultural fertility. The accounts of the temple and the temple service in the Mishnah testify to this in no uncertain terms:

> And so you find that all the time that the service in the Temple was per-
> formed, there was blessing in the world, and the prices were low, and
> the crop was plentiful, and the wine was plentiful, and man ate and was
> satisfied, and the beast ate and was satisfied, as it is written: "And I will
> send grass in thy fields for thy cattle that thou mayest eat and be full."[25]

Over and over again, in the Talmud and other collections of Jewish tradition and folklore, the temple is held to have functioned as a source of fertility. The rock on which the temple stood, at the heart of what is now the Temple Mount, was believed to be the first solid land created by God, around which the rest of the world took shape. Far beneath it lies the Tehom, the primal abyss of waters that rose up during the flood, and subterranean channels spread out in every direction from the Temple Mount to every part of the world, giving each country the power to grow its proper agricultural products.[26]

The functions of the Temple were believed to extend even to weather modification. Before the Temple was built, according to a Talmudic midrash (commentary) on the book of Genesis, torrential rains fell on the land of Israel for forty days each year, causing great destruction.[27] The erection of the Temple of Solomon put an end to the torrents. When the Second Temple was destroyed, the torrents did not return; instead, the south wind, which used to bring rains while the temple stood, ceased to do so and has never brought rains since that day.[28]

---

25   Cited in Patai 1967, 123; the Scriptural quote is from Deuteronomy 11:15.
26   Patai 1967, 85–6. I have cited Patai's book here as an accessible English language source on the Talmudic literature concerning the traditional lore surrounding the Temple.
27   Ibid., 121.
28   Ibid., 125.

According to the Talmud, the destruction of the temple cut off all the structure's beneficial influences on soil and weather and was therefore a disaster not only for the Jews but for every people in the world: "Rabbi Joshua ben Levi said: Had the nations of the world known how beneficial the Temple is to them, they would have surrounded it by camps in order to guard it."[29] The prophesied restoration of the temple in the time of the Messiah, in turn, is expected to bring about an extraordinary change in the world: twelve streams of water will rush forth from underneath the Temple Mount and flow in all directions, and these will cause even barren fields and vineyards to bear fruit.[30]

An interesting disagreement between different accounts of the temple's miraculous effect on fertility relates to the actual source of those powers. According to some Jewish legends, the powers exercised by the temple centered on the Ark of the Covenant, which is called the Life of the World in these accounts. So powerful was the Ark, claimed one story, that when it was first brought into Solomon's Temple, the very cedar beams of the structure became green and brought forth fruit.[31]

Yet the fertilizing powers of the temple were held to have resumed as soon as the Second Temple was built. In the second chapter of the book of Haggai, the prophet asks the people rhetorically how they fared "before a stone was placed upon a stone in the Temple of the Lord"; the answer, of course, was that they had lived under the constant threat of famine, but since the laying of the cornerstone of the Second Temple, the fertility of the land had improved dramatically.[32] This is all the more startling in that, as we have seen, the Ark of the Covenant was long lost by the time the exiles returned from Babylon and began work, and the Holy of Holies of the Second Temple, throughout its history, contained nothing at all. In this tradition, at least,

---

29   Cited in Patai 1967, 127.

30   Ibid., 88.

31   Ibid., 91.

32   Lundquist 2008, 76.

it was not the Ark that brought fertility to the land of Israel, but the temple itself.

Here, as elsewhere, it's crucial not to reduce the richness and complexity of human religious life into any single factor. The Temple of Solomon and its successive structures had many different roles in the life of the ancient Jews, and the most important of them were religious in the same sense that word generally has today—that is, the temple was a place where Jews prayed to the God of Israel, sought his forgiveness for their sins, and invoked his blessings on every aspect of human life. The temple was a spiritual phenomenon first, in other words, and its relation to fertility came second to that.

Agricultural fertility was only one of the many things that people prayed for when they went to the temple to make offerings or simply faced it from a distance in order to pray to the dwelling place of God on earth. Agricultural fertility was also only one of the miraculous things that are said to have occurred while the temple was still standing; for example, a number of Jewish legends and certain passages in the Old Testament[33] claim that at certain times the temple became filled with a luminous cloud so brilliant and blinding that the priests could not perform their duties.

Thus it's fascinating that Jewish legend and tradition place so much repeated emphasis on the temple as a source of agricultural fertility, as distinct from its other religious functions and traditional miracles. What makes this focus all the more curious is that elsewhere in the world, wherever temples of a design more or less similar to the Temple of Solomon were in use, traditions assign them a similar power. As we'll see, there are reasons to suggest that there may be an unexpected reality behind these remarkable parallels.

---

33   See, for example, I Kings 8: 10–11.

CHAPTER THREE

The Temple Tradition

It has been an item of faith in Judaism since ancient times that the Jewish religion and its God are uniquely true, and whatever pertains to them is equally distinct from the religions of the world's other peoples. Whether or not this is correct in a theological sense is an issue I don't propose to explore here. For the purposes of this book, the relevant point is that in any historical or architectural sense, it's hard to find anything about the Temple of Solomon, or its successive structures in the days of Zerubbabel and Herod, that was unique in any way. Quite the contrary, the Temple of Solomon was for all practical purposes just another temple of the national deity of another Levantine kingdom, and the structures that followed it were no more distinctive in their own times. The one thing that sets them apart is the traditional exclusion of all other deities from the Jewish Temple, and even that has counterparts elsewhere.

One of the many things that the Temple of Jerusalem has in common with other temples, though, is its legendary power to increase the fertility of crops and livestock. Far from being unique to Solomon's structure, this claim appears wherever you find temples like the one in Jerusalem. Scholarship on temples repeats this point again and again. In his study of the Jerusalem

Temple, to cite only one example, John M. Lundquist notes, "This [associa-tion of temples with agricultural fertility] is a universal idea among temple-building peoples, and relates to my observation that 'The temple is associated with abundance and prosperity, indeed is perceived as the giver of these.'"[34]

It's important to understand what's being said here. Scholars of compar-ative religion not that many decades ago used to lump all faiths other than Christianity, Judaism, and Islam into the arbitrary category of "fertility reli-gions," and some traces of that attitude still linger in the holes and corners of the modern imagination. It's true that many ancient religions placed a high value on the fertility of their fields and crops, but the same is true of modern Christianity—go to any church service next Sunday in any part of rural America that's being hit by drought, for example, and you're very likely indeed to hear the preacher and congregation alike praying to God with all their might for rain and a bountiful harvest.

What's more, different religious traditions use different methods to ask the beings they worship for help with fertility. The "increase ceremonies" performed by Australian aborigines don't have much in common with the prayers for rain in a Baptist church in Kansas, say, or with young couples making love in the fields to bring good crops—this used to be common prac-tice in much of rural Europe—or, for that matter, with the sacrifices and prayers that were standard practice at the Temple of Solomon. Rather than some vague association between religion and fertility in general, in other words, what's being discussed here is something much more concrete: a spe-cific set of architectural design elements and ritual practices that consistent-ly has a traditional reputation for improved harvests in nearby agricultural areas.

Nor do these parallels show up randomly at various places and times around the planet. The design elements and ritual practices under discussion can be traced from country to country and age to age, following the same channels of cultural transmission that brought many better documented

---

34   Lundquist 2008, 76.

legacies from one age and people to another. Variations in design and practice appeared as the basic concepts moved from culture to culture, and some of these were then taken up elsewhere and modified in their turn. All in all, the spread of the patterns discussed here resembles nothing so much as the way that technical innovations such as the arch, steelmaking, or the printing press migrated around the world.

Thus we can speak of a temple tradition: a particular body of knowledge and practice that appears to relate to temples and their traditional effects on fertility. This tradition seems to have originated in prehistoric times and spread over much of the Old World, only to be abandoned in Europe and the Middle East for religious reasons, and then largely obscured throughout the world during the centuries of Europe's political and cultural dominance over the rest of the planet. A thorough survey of the temple tradition would fill many volumes the size of this one. In this and the following chapter, I will be providing a very brief overview, focusing on those cultures and temple designs that are particularly well-documented and have had a significant impact on the tradition as a whole.

The survey that follows falls naturally into two parts. In this chapter, we'll consider temples in what might best be called traditional religions—those faiths that had no one historical founder, but descend from the distant past. In the next, we'll consider the transformations of the temple tradition in what can be called prophetic religions—those faiths that were founded by historical individuals. The Pagan faiths of ancient Egypt and classical Greece, as well as such surviving religions as Hinduism and Shinto, belong to the first category, while religions such as Buddhism, Christianity, and Islam belong to the second.

While the temple tradition, as a later chapter will show, seems to have its roots in prehistoric times, the oldest known civilization to practice it is that of ancient Egypt. Our survey, therefore, will begin on the banks of the Nile.

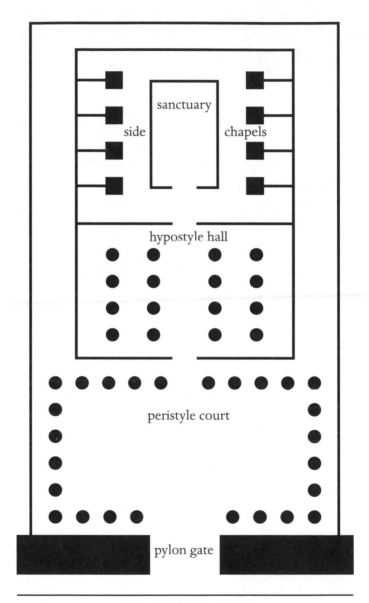

EGYPTIAN TEMPLE

Egypt

When they encountered Egyptian culture in its twilight years, Greek and Roman writers remarked admiringly on the vast number of temples that stood on the banks of the Nile and the centrality of religion to Egyptian life. According to contemporary archeologists, they were not exaggerating. No other culture, ancient or modern, produced temples in such numbers, and the vast sacred precinct at Karnak, near Thebes in Upper Egypt, is still the single largest temple complex on the face of the planet.[35]

Traditionally, modern archeologists divide Egyptian temples into two classes—divine temples, dedicated to deities, and mortuary temples, dedicated to the honored dead. The relevance of the distinction has been challenged by some recent scholars, who note that the ancient Egyptians themselves drew no such distinction.[36] Even granting the division, though, there is enormous diversity among Egyptian temples. During the more than three thousand years that ancient Egyptian civilization flourished, many different designs came and went. Only in the Middle Kingdom did something like standard patterns begin to emerge, and even those saw spectacular variations now and then as Egyptian history continued; see illustration on page 40.

In the later centuries of Egyptian history, however, it becomes possible to talk about a standard design for an Egyptian temple, especially when talking about the smaller sanctuaries of provincial towns and the shrines of the non-royal dead. These were rectangular stone structures, usually oriented so that their entrances faced the eastern horizon, with a series of courts and halls of increasing sanctity leading up to an innermost sacred space that functioned much like the Holy of Holies in the Temple of Solomon.

The best way to envision an ancient Egyptian temple is to imagine following a festival procession from the world outside to the innermost sanctuary. As you approached the main entrance of the temple, the first thing you would encounter is the massive pylon gate, a soaring structure with four or more flagpoles rising against its face, bearing the fluttering banners that

---

35   Wilkinson 2000, 154.
36   Haeny 1997, 86–90.

since earliest times were the ancient Egyptian emblem of divinity. Beyond the pylon gate you would enter an open courtyard called the peristyle court, surrounded by a pillared portico. This was open to ordinary worshippers during the many festivals of the Egyptian calendar, and many temples have hieroglyphic signs on pillars to mark the places where the *rekhyet*, the common people of Egypt, were supposed to stand.[37]

Further in, beyond the peristyle court, lay one or more hypostyle halls, broad roofed rooms with massive stone pillars supporting the roof, where the lesser priests and priestesses carried out their part in the temple rituals. Beyond that lay the innermost part of the temple, where only the senior priests and priestesses went: the sanctuary of the god or goddess, containing a consecrated image that filled roughly the same role in Egyptian religion that the Ark of the Covenant did among the Jews. This was very often surrounded by a series of side chapels dedicated to other deities, each with its own sacred image.

Animal sacrifice along the lines practiced at the Temple of Solomon had no part in traditional Egyptian religion. Instead, banquets were prepared in a kitchen outside the temple itself—bread, beef, poultry, onions, fruit, milk, beer, and wine, all the things that pharaohs and rekhyet alike loved to eat—and served to the deity as part of the regular temple service. Over the course of the day for that service, priests and priestesses treated the statue of the deity as servants treated a pharaoh: waking it in the morning, bathing it, dressing it, serving its meals, entertaining it with music and dancing, and managing the affairs of its household.

On occasion, especially during festivals, the image of the deity would be taken out of the sanctuary and placed in a traveling shrine to visit other deities or attend important ceremonies outside the temple complex. As boat travel on the Nile was the most common mode of transport in ancient Egypt, the traveling shrine usually looked like a model boat covered with gold and precious stones, with poles along the sides so it could be carried on the shoulders of priests. In these vehicles, the images of the gods would visit

---

37   Bell 1997, 164–67.

one another—the sacred image of the goddess Hathor at Dendera, for example, would travel every year to the temple of her husband, the god Horus, at Edfu, so that their lovemaking would bring fertility to the fields.[38]

These ritualized activities had little in common with the sacrifices and prayers offered to the God of Israel at the temple in Jerusalem. Nor, for that matter, did the exuberant diversity of the Egyptian pantheon or the elaborate Egyptian theory of personal immortality through mummification share much common ground with the very different religious traditions of the Jews. Thus it's all the more intriguing that Egyptian temples shared so many design features in common with the Temple of Solomon and its successors—and, as already noted, the traditional conviction that the temple and the worship performed there would improve agricultural fertility.

There was one major exception to the pattern of Egyptian temple religion sketched out here, and that was the short-lived solar monotheism of Akhenaten, Egypt's famous heretic pharaoh. As part of his attempted religious revolution, Akhenaten ordered the temples of all the traditional gods and goddesses of Egypt closed, desecrated, and in many cases demolished, and he replaced them with temples of a very different design—temples devoted to his sole god, the Aten or sun-disk. The temples of the Aten were basically large halls in which people gathered to pray to the Aten, without any of the ceremonies, offerings, or other activities that were part of the rich texture of traditional Egyptian faith. Later in this book, the same pattern—the transformation of religious architecture from a specially designed sacred space for making offerings to a hall used solely for communal prayer and readings from scriptures—will appear more than once. For the time being, it may be worth mentioning that one of the troubles that afflicted Egypt during the last years of Akhenaten's reign, and helped bring his religious revolution to a sudden stop after his death, was widespread agricultural failure.

---

38   Wilkinson 2000, 96.

Mesopotamia

The broad valley of the Tigris and Euphrates Rivers, in present-day Syria and Iraq, was called Mesopotamia—"the land between the rivers"—by the ancient Greeks, and it boasted civilizations as old as Egypt's. Cities, writing, and the other foundations of civilized life emerged there about the same time they appeared on the banks of the Nile. The temple tradition discussed in this book, though, did not appear in Mesopotamia until it was brought there by the armies of Alexander the Great. The Sumerians, Babylonians, Assyrians, and other peoples of the Tigris-Euphrates valley built lavish structures for their gods and goddesses, to be sure, but the core elements of the temple tradition shared by Egypt and ancient Israel did not appear there.

Mesopotamian temples were as diverse as religious structures in other cultures, but broadly speaking, there were two basic types.[39] The most common type derived from palace architecture and, in fact, differed from the palaces of local kings only in minor details. There was no Holy of Holies in such a temple—in fact, it was a common practice for worshippers to be brought into the presence of the divine statue in the innermost chamber of the temple by priests or priestesses in exactly the same way that a king's servant might bring a petitioner into the presence of the king.[40]

Less common than these palace-temples, but considerably more spectacular, were ziggurats, artificial mountains of mud brick with small temples on top. Most Mesopotamian cities had a single ziggurat, which was the residence of the city's deity, for each city in the Land Between the Rivers had its own divine patron: Marduk, for example, was the patron god of Babylon, and the moon god Nanna was the patron of Ur.

The ziggurat and the temple atop it might face any direction. The vast ziggurat of Babylon faced south-southeast, for example, while that of Ur faced northeast.[41] The temple itself was usually a single large room with an image of the god or goddess inside it. The linear structure of Jewish and

---

39   Curatola 2006 provides a good overview.

40   King 1976, 210–16.

41   Curatola 2006, 212 and 266.

Egyptian temples, moving inward along an east-west line from an outer door flanked with pillars or pylons to a Holy of Holies inside, does not appear in Mesopotamia.

Mesopotamian religion did have a strong focus on agricultural fertility, and the ziggurats played an important role in ceremonies relating to that purpose. As we'll see, the ziggurat was at the center of a different tradition—more precisely, a different technology—which pursued the same goal as the temple tradition but used alternative methods to achieve it. This tradition seems to be older than the one at the heart of this book's project, and as we'll see, traces of it can be found in certain cultures over a remarkable fraction of the world.

Greece

Ancient Greece, by contrast, was in the mainstream of the temple tradition, which reached the Greek peninsula from Egypt in the seventh century BCE. Egypt was at that time experiencing the last flowering of its ancient culture. The pharaohs of the twenty-sixth dynasty, whose capital was at Sais in the Nile delta, presided over the systematic revival of old religious practices and temple cults, and sacred texts, such as the Book of the Dead, which had once been reserved for the political and religious elite, became accessible to any literate Egyptian. At the same time, Egypt needed trading partners and military allies against the rising powers of the Tigris-Euphrates basin farther east, and the Greek city-states were full of ambitious merchants and some of the toughest soldiers in the eastern Mediterranean. As trade increased and Greek mercenaries found steady work and good pay under the pharaohs, cultural exchanges blossomed, and the temple tradition was among the many things that crossed the sea to the isles and rocky peninsulas of Greece.

Before the arrival of the temple tradition, Greeks went to outdoor sanctuaries—the Greek word for such an outdoor place of worship was *temenos*—to sacrifice to their gods or simply made offerings at their homes or in other public places. Another set of religious customs, dating from very ancient times, focused on cairns—that is, heaps of loose stones marking pathways and boundaries, to which every passerby added another stone. Hermes, the god of travelers, merchants, and thieves, was originally the guardian spirit of the cairn.[42] These cairns were later replaced by pillars of stone carved to resemble erect penises or schematic statues with the god's head on top and an erect penis farther down.

By the eighth century BCE, as trade with the eastern Mediterranean coast brought new ideas and inspirations to the nascent city-states of the Greek peninsula, some Greek communities built simple temple structures made of wood and sun-dried brick, with thatched roofs, in established *temenoi*. As late as 600 BCE, the main temple at the important pilgrimage center of Olympia was built of these same humble materials. By that time, though, Egyptian architectural knowledge was becoming widespread, and the first stone temples were already rising elsewhere in Greece, as part of a general cultural flourishing that also kickstarted the rise of Greek philosophy and science.[43]

The temples that came out of this transformation took several forms, but the one relevant to our purposes is the *naos*, the classic Greek colonnaded temple. The naos was reserved for a handful of divinities; of the 142 Greek naoi whose presiding god or goddess is known, 90 belonged to just 5 deities—Apollo, Athena, Zeus, Artemis, and Hera—with Apollo accounting for no fewer than 29.[44] Sparta, the most conservative of the Greek city-states, never built a naos at all, and even in Athens, where naoi were common, one of the city's holiest shrines—the Erechtheum—was built to a completely different design.

There seems to have been a specific logic behind the religious attributions of naoi, which is anything but irrelevant to the theme of this book. Four of the five deities just listed have significant connections to the religious dimension of Greek agriculture: Athena was the goddess of the olive groves, Zeus ruled the sky and thus the rains that made the grain flourish, Artemis

---

42   Burkert 1985, 156.

43   Spawforth 2006, 20–25. See Hahn 2001 for an overview of the cultural flowering that created the classical Greek naos.

44   Ibid., 98.

governed the fertility of animals, and Hera governed human fertility among other things. The reason that Apollo was patron of so many naoi is less clear, but his role as god of reason and the sun suggests that he may have been seen as the patron of the temple tradition itself.

The diversity of temple types in ancient Greece was in large part a consequence of the disunity and diversity of classical Greek culture. The unification of the Greek peninsula and the expansion of Greek culture across the eastern Mediterranean world in the wake of the conquests of Alexander the Great changed that dramatically, leading to a standardization in favor of the naos design. When Greek ideas were spread across the Mediterranean world and western Europe under the aegis of the Roman Empire, the naos became the standard form of temple over a vast geographical region. At the peak of the naos' popularity, around the beginning of the Common Era, temples built to this pattern could be found across the ancient world from Britain to southern Egypt and from Morocco to Afghanistan, the widest geographical expansion of any single outgrowth of the temple tradition.

Whether or not it was a naos, each Greek temple—and each temple built in the Greek style, whether it stood in Roman Britain or in the Greek-influenced kingdoms of the Silk Road far to the east—stood within a temenos, surrounded by a wall, and the entrances were flanked by vessels of water for purification. Very often—especially in rural temples, or in the shrines of deities associated with the natural world—the precinct was full of trees and other vegetation that was sacrilege to cut down. Toward the center was the naos itself, usually but not always oriented with its main door facing some point on the eastern horizon; see illustration on page 48.

Every naos differed from every other, but the diagram shows the most common general layout. The columns around the exterior support the roof, which extends well out from the inner building. The front porch gave access to the inner building; the back porch was a place where people assembled to listen to poetry, music, and the like—Herodotus is supposed to have read his *Histories* aloud to an audience for the first time from the back porch of the

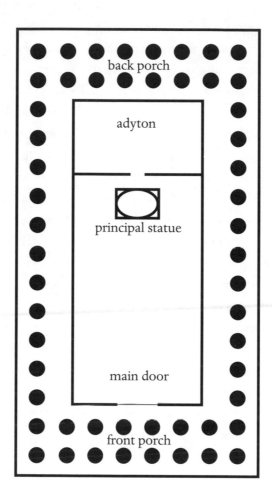

GREEK TEMPLE

temple of Zeus at Olympia.[45] Inside the inner building was the main stat-ue of the deity facing the door, anything up to several dozen incense burn-ers, and a table on which barley cakes and other bloodless offerings were placed—animal sacrifices, which were as central to ancient Greek religion as they were to the worship at the Temple of Solomon, always took place out-side the temple at an altar under the open sky, just as they did in Jerusalem. Inside there might also be statues of other deities, votive gifts, and works of art lining the walls, but these were of less importance to the temple and its cult than the main statue.

Some Greek temples included spaces set apart where ordinary worship-pers did not go—close equivalents, in other words, to the Holy of Holies in the Temple of Solomon. The Greek term for such a space was *adyton*, literal-ly "not to be entered." In some cases the adyton of a temple can be identified in the ruins—it was fairly common to have an inner room behind the main statue of the deity, for example, while other temples had underground crypts reached by stairways.

One thing the Greeks didn't borrow from Egypt was the linear structuring of space by which processions toward the inmost part of the temple moved through progressively more sacred zones—an arrangement the Egyptian temples shared, as we've seen, with the Temple in Jerusalem. The more egalitarian ethos of Greek culture required a less structured approach to sacred space. As already noted, every temple was surrounded by a temenos, a sacred enclosure of the kind that had been used before the first temples were built. Worshippers ritually purified themselves with clean water before entering the temenos.

Individuals who were considered impure for one reason or another were not allowed to enter. Most of these impurities had nothing to do with moral issues; women who had just given birth, for example, were not supposed to enter a temple precinct until some days had passed and a ceremonial cleans-ing had been performed. Once inside the temenos, though, the entire temple

---

45   Spawforth 2006, 94.

and its surroundings were open to the public, except for an adyton if there was one.

The relationship between the temple and agricultural fertility in ancient Greek religion was nuanced, but very important. As already noted, many of the principal Greek gods related directly to some part of the agricultural economy—thus Zeus ruled the life-giving rain, Demeter the soil, Athena the olive groves, Bacchus the vineyards, Artemis the forests, and Pan the uplands where sheep and goats grazed. Many of the religious festivals in the ancient Greek year celebrated events in the agricultural cycle.[46] Then there were the Mysteries, which deserve special attention in terms of this book's investigation.

The ancient Greek Mysteries were secret initiatory ceremonies in honor of deities closely linked to the soil and the agricultural cycle. The most famous were celebrated every autumn in Eleusis, a small town close to Athens, but there were many others. Some were celebrated all over the ancient Greek world, others were local rites unknown outside of a single town or rural district.[47] It has been noted by many writers down through the years that the Mysteries filled roughly the same role in Greek society that Freemasonry fills in the modern Western world, though there was one consistent difference: unlike Freemasonry, initiation into the Greek Mysteries was open to women as well as men.

Exactly what was taught and enacted in the Greek Mysteries remains almost completely unknown. One Gnostic writer states that the central act of the Eleusinian Mysteries was the reaping of a single stalk of grain in perfect silence. Of the Mysteries of the Great Mother we know a little more, thanks to a description in On the Gods and the World by Sallust, a Pagan writer of the fourth century CE.[48] In these Mysteries, which were celebrated at the time of the spring equinox, initiates fasted and dressed in mourning garments to commemorate the death of the god Attis, then made incisions

---

46   Parke 1977 is a good introduction to the Greek ritual calendar.
47   Burkert 1985, 278–81.
48   Sallust 1976, 21–22.

of some kind in a tree, then drank milk, and finally donned festive garments and crowns to celebrate Attis's resurrection. Sallust explains these events in terms of his own austere Neoplatonist philosophy; what might have been taught to the initiates in the ritual itself remains, in every sense of the word, a mystery.

The Greek Mysteries were not associated with naoi. Some were celebrated in private homes, others had their own ceremonial buildings. At Eleusis, the Telesterion (hall of initiation) was a vast structure that could hold several thousand people at a time. In the center was a stone building, the Anaktoron, resting on an outcropping of unworked rock. It was quite literally the Holy of Holies of the Eleusinian Mysteries, and into it only the Hierophant, the high priest of those Mysteries, was allowed to go. The Telesterion itself faces southeast, toward the midwinter sunrise, though the Mysteries themselves were celebrated near the autumn equinox, and none of the surviving records explain the divergence.

During the nocturnal ceremony that completed the process of initiation at Eleusis, the Telesterion blazed with light so brilliant that the illumination from its clerestory windows could be seen from many miles away.[49] Most modern scholars assume without evidence that the "great light" that appeared at the climax of the Mysteries must have been merely torches or a bonfire, but it's at least remarkable that there should be so close a parallel with the light or fire that blazed mysteriously in the Temple of Solomon on certain occasions.

India

The temple tradition found its way to India somewhat after it reached Greece; estimates vary, but a date around 500 CE for the first classic Hindu temples would fit the evidence well. The Vedas, immense collections of ancient hymns and ritual texts, are the oldest strata of Hindu religious teaching, dating from sometime before 1000 BCE, and according to their testimony, the gods were worshipped at that time on a fire altar in a sacred open-air

---

49   See Plutarch 1937, 18–19.

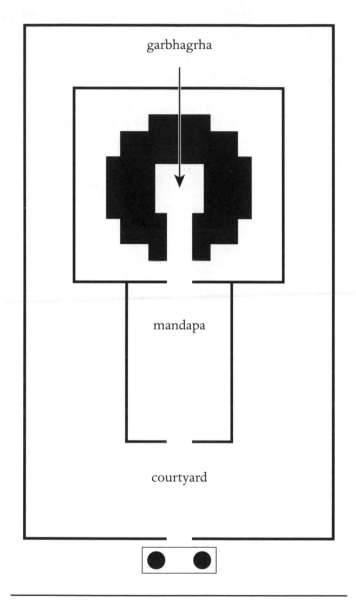

HINDU MANDIRA

enclosure not unlike a Greek temenos. Though the Vedas are still honored wherever the gods and goddesses of the Hindu faith are worshipped, the old open-air enclosure has long since been replaced in most uses by the *mandira*, the classic Hindu temple (see illustration on page 52), which combines the exuberant richness of India's architectural and artistic heritage with a set of elements that will be familiar already to readers of this book.[50]

As with temples and other religious buildings everywhere, mandira vary significantly from place to place in India and throughout the Hindu diaspora. There are important regional differences, and the creativity of individual architects and builders also plays a part. In general, though, a mandira is surrounded by a low wall, with an open space between wall and temple all the way around to allow the practice of the Hindu rite of circumambulation—that is, walking clockwise around a holy place as a sign of reverence. The main entrance through the wall is often marked by an arch supported on pillars, and richly carved; outside it will be a pool where worshippers can cleanse their hands and feet in fresh water.

Inside there will usually be one or more courtyards, each entered by its own ornate arch. Farther in, beyond a veranda, is at least one *mandapa* (pillared hall) where worshippers gather and sacred dances and hymns are performed. Beyond the innermost mandapa is the *garbhagrha*, the innermost shrine or Holy of Holies, where the deity of the temple is believed to be present. Around the garbhagrha is a passage allowing devotees to circumambulate in the immediate presence of the god or goddess, but the garbhagrha itself is entered only by a single opening, and only the presiding priest is permitted to go there. Above the garbhagrha, finally, stands the most visible dimension of the mandira—the *shikhara*, a stone tower or symbolic mountain covered in ornate carvings.

While scholars trying to figure out how Egyptian and Greek temples were designed and laid out have to rely on guesswork, fragmentary records, and the ambivalent results of archeology, the mandira is quite another matter. Hinduism is very much a living tradition, with countless temples in use

---

50   Wangu 2009, 96–97.

today. What's more, detailed writings, the Shilpa Shastras, cover every detail of the process of setting out and building a temple, from the selection of the site to the final consecration of the sacred images.[51] According to these documents, once the site is selected, the ground is cleared, seeds are planted on it and allowed to grow through an annual cycle to determine if the soil is of sufficient quality, because a temple can only be built on fertile ground—a more direct indication of the link between temples and agricultural fertility is hard to imagine.

Then the ground is smoothed, a pole set up in the center, and its shadow is used to determine the cardinal directions. From this center, using ropes and stakes, a complex geometrical pattern is laid out by the master builder, and the mandira rises on the foundations defined by the plan. Most mandira are aligned with all the gates and arches on a straight line from the door of the garbhagrha—the same arrangement we have already seen in Jerusalem and Egypt and will see again in other expressions of the temple tradition.[52]

Animal sacrifice was once an important element of Hindu worship but has been set aside by nearly all of the many traditions of the faith. Instead, as in ancient Egyptian temples, food is prepared and placed before the deity of the temple as a banquet, then taken away and consumed by priests and worshippers as an act of communion with the deity. Requirements of personal purity that are more or less parallel with those that surrounded Greek temples, or for that matter the Temple of Solomon, can also be found in Hindu practice—as, of course, can the traditional link between temple worship and agricultural fertility.

China

With China, as with Mesopotamia, we come to a radically different style of temple with its own distinctive traditions of orientation and design. Since very ancient times, Chinese temples have been built according to the pattern of the traditional Chinese house, a walled compound with the door facing

---

51   Wangu 2009, 94–96.
52   Huyler 1999, 131.

south and the most important rooms on the north side.[53] For well over two thousand years, this indigenous pattern has remained dominant across the entire lively spectrum of Chinese religion to such an extent that Buddhist temples in China have the same form as the temples of clan ancestors or traditional Chinese gods.

A Chinese temple is a facility for offering prayers and incense to one or more holy beings, a broad category that can include deities, Buddhist saints, clan ancestors, and revered figures of the past, such as Confucius. Any religious group too poor to afford a temple simply has a large incense burner that is kept in the house of one of the members and brought out for ceremonies, which can be held in any convenient space. There is no Holy of Holies in a Chinese temple—in fact, it is not uncommon for less prominent temples, which are only used for occasional festivals, to have a very poor family living there for want of better shelter, so the deity's altar and incense burner share the space with household goods and the family chickens.[54]

The Chinese temple was just as central to the traditional Chinese community as its equivalents were to the communities of other cultures, but these social and religious functions were not combined, as elsewhere, with the agricultural dimension explored in this book. Worshippers at Chinese temples prayed for good harvests, to be sure, as religious people do in every agricultural society, but the concept of the temple as a generator and amplifier of the productivity of farms and fields does not seem to be found there. The logical conclusion is that the temple tradition central to this book's inquiry was not present in the formative periods of Chinese religion, and it seems to have left few traces on Chinese soil.

What does appear in traditional Chinese religion is another kind of sacred space that serves a function closely related to the temple tradition. Before the Communist takeover in 1949, every community in China had—apart from temples for locally revered deities, temples for clan ancestors, Buddhist temples, and the officially mandated civil temple for Confucius and the

---

53   Thompson 1975, 62–66.
54   DeGlopper 1974, 54.

leading figures in Confucian philosophy—an outdoor altar for the gods of land and grain. This was in a courtyard of its own and consisted of a square, raised area of pounded earth, reached by a flight of three or more steps. At the center of the altar a stone pillar was buried in the packed earth so that its rounded upper end protruded from the ground. Worshippers approached this altar from the east and faced west while performing the rites that guaranteed agricultural fertility.[55]

The altar for the gods of land and grain resembles nothing so much as a miniature version of the Mesopotamian ziggurat, with a standing stone at the center. As we'll see later on, there are good reasons to think that the altar and the ziggurat are independent developments out of the same prehistoric tradition, shaped by the very different religious and cultural patterns of China and Mesopotamia respectively. The Chinese version also incorporates a standing stone, which has been used in other parts of the world as a focus for fertility ceremonies. The reasons for this focus will become clear when we turn to the technology behind the tradition.

Southeast Asia

East of India and south of China, the diverse nations of Southeast Asia have enriched their indigenous traditions with influences borrowed from one or both of their mighty neighbors. Where Chinese influence predominated, as in Vietnam, the temple tradition discussed in this book left few if any traces. Where India's cultural heritage has been a major influence, on the other hand, temples built in some variant of the Hindu form are common, and some of these are among the most spectacular buildings ever to embody the temple tradition.

The temples of the ancient Khmer capital of Angkor, in what is now Cambodia, are a case in point. Angkor Wat, the largest of the temples of old Angkor, was built in the early twelfth century CE when the Khmer state religion was a blend of Hinduism and traditional Khmer beliefs. It is among the largest and most elaborate expressions of the Hindu version of the temple

---

55   Thompson 1975, 80–81.

tradition ever attempted. Like temples all over India, it was carefully orient-ed to the compass points, with the route from the innermost sanctuary to the outermost gate running, as usual, straight along the main axis from east to west, and lavishly ornamented stone galleries around the sanctuary to allow for the ritual of circumambulation. Above the innermost garbhagrha rises a soaring stone shikhara, visible for miles around. The geometries and proportions of the great structure are so precise that a recent study of Ang-kor Wat has been able to decode the symbolism of the entire temple com-plex on purely mathematical grounds.[56]

The other temples of old Angkor are laid out to a similar plan, if not on so lavish a scale. The reflections of Hindu temple architecture are precise enough that it's clear that at least one of the Shilpa Shastras came east across the Bay of Bengal along with other aspects of Hindu tradition. In the century following the building of Angkor Wat, however, the Khmer people convert-ed to Buddhism, and the temple tradition lapsed not long after, only to be replaced by the very different religious architecture of the Buddhist tradition.

Some sense of the change can be seen today in the innermost sanctuary of Angkor Wat, which was walled off on three sides once the local religion changed from Hinduism to Buddhism. A tall stone statue of the Buddha stands before each of the sealed doorways. On the fourth, while the door-way remains open, another statue stands in the way, blocking whatever fer-tilizing influences might once have flowed from the Holy of Holies down the axis of the temple.[57]

Korea

Located just east of China and well within the Chinese sphere of cultural and political influence, Korea absorbed Buddhist and Confucian traditions from its huge neighbor but has also retained a rich indigenous tradition of village rites and folk shamanism.[58] Korean Buddhist and Confucian temples

---

56   Mannikka 1996.

57   Ibid., 14–17.

58   See Kim 1996 for a good overview.

thus resemble their equivalents in China, and like them, lack any of the distinctive signs of the temple tradition. It's in the village rites and sacred spaces that traces of an archaic fertility magic appear, and as in China, these derive from the older tradition found also in Mesopotamia—but with elements we've already seen in a surprising place.

Traditionally, each Korean village has a *sŏnang*, or guardian deity, who dwells in a shrine at the entrance to the village or on a hillside nearby. The *sŏnangdang* or sŏnang shrine is either a cairn of stones, a tree with a rope tied loosely around it, or a combination of the two. Villagers offer food and wine to the sŏnang at specific dates in the Korean lunar calendar. A more routine form of veneration is practiced whenever a villager passes the sŏnangdang: adding a stone to the cairn—the same rite as in ancient Greece—or tying a bit of cord around the tree.

The ancient Greek parallels aren't limited to sŏnangdangs. Stone phalluses rise from the ground all over rural Korea; some have faces carved on them and look for all the world like ancient Greek herms. Their positions are chosen by traditional geomancers in order to influence the subtle currents of energy that, according to Korean geomantic lore, flow through the soil and can bring fertility to the fields if managed correctly.[59]

Japan

Like Korea, Japan lies within China's sphere of influence and combines traditions imported from the Asian mainland with its own unique cultural forms. Surprisingly, though, Japan received the temple tradition in something close to its standard form. In the religious structures of the indigenous Japanese religion of Shinto, so much of the temple tradition remains intact that it comprises one of the most extensive surviving bodies of information relevant to the subject of this book.

The explanation for this curious fact is simple if surprising. Until the ninth century CE, Shinto, Japan's indigenous religion, had few sacred buildings, and those served mostly as storehouses for sacred properties. Worship

---

59   Kim 1996, 168 and 184–85.

normally took place either in ordinary homes and public places or outdoor enclosures in places of traditional sanctity—identical, for all practical purposes, to the temenoi of early Greece or the sacred enclosures of Vedic India. These holy places were set apart from the profane world by rice-straw ropes hung with strips of cloth or *shide*—strips of rice paper folded in a zigzag pattern that look, to Western eyes, remarkably like stylized lightning bolts.

The straw ropes and zigzag shide can still be seen at every Shinto holy place in Japan, and so can many of the practices once performed within the sacred precincts that were marked out in that way. Starting in the sixth century CE, though, Shinto came to share space in the Japanese religious consciousness with Buddhism, which was imported from Korea at that time. After a brief period of religious conflict, partisans of the two religions worked out a compromise that allowed room for both.

The ninth century CE saw a new influence arrive: esoteric Buddhism, enriched with a lavish heritage of ritualistic, meditative, and magical practices from Buddhist schools in India and China. Two major schools, the Shingon and Tendai sects, were responsible for introducing esoteric Buddhism to Japan. Both were founded by Japanese monks who traveled to China and, as noted in the next chapter, both these monks had access to the temple tradition by way of a remarkable chain of connections. An important difference distinguished the esoteric schools from earlier forms of Japanese Buddhism: where the earlier schools by and large held Shinto at arm's length, the esoteric schools actively pursued alliances with the traditional faith and brought Shinto deities and practices into their own traditions.

This habit of creative borrowing had been a core element of esoteric Buddhism from its earliest days. Historians of religion have traced certain Japanese esoteric Buddhist practices back through this route to surprising sources: for example, the *goma* fire-offering ritual practiced by Shingon and Tendai priests was originally practiced by the Zoroastrians of Persia, borrowed from them by early esoteric Buddhists and passed from there all the way to Japan.

The temple tradition seems to have made much the same journey. As we have seen, it was received and elaborated in India early on and thus would have

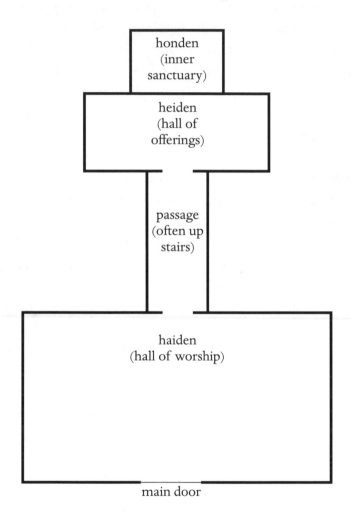

honden
(inner
sanctuary)

heiden
(hall of
offerings)

passage
(often up
stairs)

haiden
(hall of worship)

main door

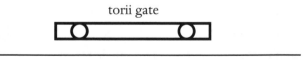

torii gate

SHINTO SHRINE

been available to esoteric Buddhist scholars and mystics from the beginning. For reasons to be explored in the next chapter, Buddhist practice had few points of contact with the temple tradition and the important philosophical and spiritual differences with the religions that preserved it, and so the tradition found only a few tentative expressions in Japanese Buddhist architecture. Shinto was another matter. Over the course of the ninth century, many art forms borrowed from esoteric Buddhist sources found a home in Shinto, and at the same time structures clearly modeled on the traditions explored in this book began to appear at Shinto holy sites.[60] Ironically, the Japanese word for these sacred structures—*jinja*—is normally translated "shrine" in English, while the word "temple" is reserved for Buddhist structures that have little in common with the temple tradition this book discusses.

Shinto architecture is extremely diverse, drawing on local architectural forms and fitting closely to the local landscape, so it's difficult to define any single pattern or geometry. A remarkable custom has kept that diversity fixed in place: until recently, most important Shinto shrines were rebuilt every few decades, but the new shrine building was a precise copy of the old one, raised next to it—the few shrines that are still regularly rebuilt have two sets of foundations set side by side, and the location of the actual shrine alternates from one to the other with each rebuilding. That said, the floorplan shown on page 60 is a more or less approximate fit to the layout of many Shinto shrines. As so often in the temple tradition, the usual design elements remain standard, but the details of their relationship go through an assortment of changes.

Approaching a Shinto shrine, the first thing the visitor encounters is one or more *torii*—two pillars joined at the top by an elaborate superstructure, forming a gateway.[61] In most cases, the outermost torii marks the formal entrance to the shrine grounds, which are normally full of greenery—in

---

60   Kageyama 1973, 15–18.

61   The following description is based in part on Tsubaki America Shrine, Granite Falls, WA, where I attended ceremonies from 2002 to 2004. I am grateful to Rev. Koichi Barrish, chief priest of the shrine, for the opportunity to experience a surviving form of the temple tradition in its natural habitat.

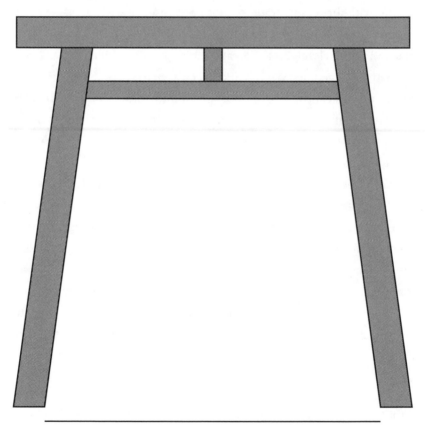

ONE COMMON STYLE OF TORII,
THE CEREMONIAL GATEWAY TO A SHINTO SHRINE

urban or suburban shrines, this typically takes the form of a formal garden, while rural shrines are generally surrounded by native forest. The route that worshippers follow from the outermost torii to the shrine doors sometimes runs straight along the axis of the shrine, but in a great many cases it deliberately avoids doing so because the line that extends from the heart of the shrine straight out to the outermost torii is sacred; its Japanese name is *sei-chu*, and worshippers are permitted to cross it but should never walk along it or stand upon it. For this reason, many of the more important shrines have two routes extending from the main doors—a wandering route taken by human beings, and another route that runs dead straight along the seichu until it ends at a river or the sea.

At the main doors of the shrine, worshippers ceremonially cleanse their hands and mouths in clean water before entering or addressing the *kami*, the gods and goddesses of Shinto. Under ordinary circumstances, worshippers at a Shinto shrine simply pray at the outer door, make an offering of money in the offertory box, and go on their way. During regular services and festivals at a shrine of any size, however, as many worshippers as will fit inside proceed to the outermost room of the shrine, the *haiden* (hall of worship). This is where the public ceremonies of the shrine take place.

Further in, usually separated from the haiden by a passage that may involve a flight of stairs, is the *heiden* (hall of offerings), where offerings are placed before the kami of the shrine. An ancient Egyptian who was suddenly transported to modern Japan would find this part of the worship completely familiar, as the offerings in most shrines consist of food and drink, which is placed before the kami and then taken away to be served to the priests and priestesses of the shrine, as well as respected members of the lay community.

Behind the heiden, finally, is the *honden* (inner sanctuary), which is forbidden to all but the most senior priests, and it serves the same function as the Holy of Holies in the Temple of Solomon or its equivalent in other forms of the tradition. It contains one or more objects called *goshintai*, which are held to contain the *tama* (soul) of the kami who inhabit the shrine.[62] Most of

---

62   Nelson 1996, 30.

the time, the doors to the honden remain tightly shut; on special occasions, the doors may be opened or the goshintai may be taken out by the priests and placed in a traveling shrine to go out among the people—another detail of Shinto practice that an ancient Egyptian would have understood at once.

Not all Shinto shrines are large enough to have a full-time priest. There are many small neighborhood shrines that are open once a year on the date of a festival, though worshippers may pray privately there at any time. Smaller still are stones all but identical to ancient Greek herms, complete with phallic shape, which can be found in rural Japan by the thousands marking the route of old roads; farmers make offerings there to the local agricultural kami, who is usually but not always some form of the rice kami Inari.

As this may suggest, fertility plays a large role in Shinto thought and practice. Like the believers of every faith, worshippers at Shinto shrines have the normal human diversity of needs to bring into the presence of the divine, but agricultural fertility is a central theme in a vast number of Shinto rituals—more important in the overall scheme of the faith, perhaps, than any other factor beside the core Shinto concept of purification. Shrines dedicated to the rice kami Inari or to a galaxy of other agricultural kami are found in profusion all over Japan, and ceremonies meant to help bring bountiful harvests play a significant role at most Shinto shrines. The traditional Jewish belief that the Temple in Jerusalem made the fields bear abundant crops would cause no surprise at all among believers in Shinto; according to their tradition, that's one of the most important things that shrines and shrine ceremonies are meant to do.

Africa

Africa, it bears remembering, is a continent, not a country, and traditional African religions are as richly complex and diverse as those of any of the world's other continents. The sacred spaces that play a role in the religious lives of African peoples are just as diverse. Some traditional African religions make use of temples and other sacred buildings; others worship in sacred groves or at open-air altars; others worship primarily in the home.

One common thread to be found all throughout traditional African religions, though, is that these faiths experience the presence of the divine everywhere, not merely in sacred spaces. In his widely acclaimed book *African Religion and Philosophy*, John S. Mbiti notes:

> Again we see that to African peoples, this is a deeply religious universe whether it is viewed in terms of time or space, and human life is a religious experience of that universe. So, African peoples find or attribute religious meaning to the whole of existence.[63]

This focus on the omnipresence of the divine means that spaces set apart for sacred use are relatively less important in traditional African religions than in many other faiths. To the African religious imagination, the divine is everywhere and can be worshipped in any setting.

Thus it may not be accidental that the temple tradition explored in this book seems to have left few lasting traces in traditional African religion. During the heyday of ancient Egypt, temples in the Egyptian style spread south along the Nile into the kingdom of Nubia, and the Ethiopian Christian church appears to have its own variant of the modified temple tradition that was adopted by other branches of Christianity. Other African cultures, as China did, maintained their own traditions of religious architecture and sacred space and made no use of the temple technology.

Native America

In the New World, finally, rich and complex temples with elaborate ceremonial uses emerged in the belt of urban civilizations that extended from the Mississippi Valley through Mexico and Central America to the Andes. Those traditions, though, have very little in common with the temple tradition central to this book. Surprisingly, they share a great deal of common ground with another tradition discussed briefly in an earlier section of this chapter: the older tradition found in Mesopotamia, which centered on the ziggurat.

---

63   Mbiti 1990, 73.

The great religious structures of Native America, though they're normally called pyramids by modern people, are actually ziggurats of the classic Mesopotamian type. Like the great ziggurat of Babylon and its many equivalents, they rise from the ground in a series of great steps, and a stairway allows ascent to the summit, where a temple is perched high above the ground. None of these features are found in the great Egyptian monuments from which pyramids take their name.

The "pyramids" of the Aztecs, Mayans, and other Mesoamerican people, the great earthen mounds of the so-called Mound Builder peoples of the Mississippi basin, and equivalent structures elsewhere in pre-Columbian North and South America all follow the Mesopotamian pattern, not the Egyptian one. It's interesting to speculate whether the ziggurat tradition, as we may as well call it, got to the Americas somehow from the Old World, or whether it appeared as a result of independent invention by the Native peoples of the Western Hemisphere. The first traces of it known so far are in the ruined settlements of the Olmecs, the New World's first known urban civilization, dating from before 1000 BCE; this is well after the ziggurat tradition reached its full flowering in Mesopotamia, but well before the kind of maritime technology needed to cross the Atlantic seems to have been available.

What makes the traditions of the New World of central importance to the theme of this book is that a few of the old Mesoamerican ziggurats are still being used today by native peoples as places for activities meant to improve the fertility of their fields and crops. These traditions—along with experimental evidence collected by researchers into their practices—offer crucial insights into the nature of the ziggurat tradition, as well as the temple tradition central to this book. We'll discuss that evidence in a later chapter.

CHAPTER FOUR

The Changing of the Gods

Most versions of the temple tradition surveyed in the previous chapter belong to faiths that have passed through many centuries of eclipse. Hindu temples and Shinto shrines still thrive, to be sure, and not only in their original homelands, while here and there individuals and small groups are struggling to resurrect the ancient faiths of Egypt, Greece, and Rome. Between these surviving or revived traditions and their ancient equivalents, though, lies an immense and almost wholly unexplored historical transformation—a religious revolution whose echoes still resound through the thinking of much of the modern world.

Though its implications are vast and complex, the revolution itself is simple enough to describe. Beginning around 2,500 years ago, most people in literate societies across the Old World stopped worshipping the old gods and goddesses of nature and started revering abstract creator gods and dead human beings instead. The first stirrings of this religious revolution were in Persia, where Zarathustra preached the gospel of the one god Ahura Mazda sometime in the second millennium BCE, and Egypt, where Akhenaten's short-lived solar monotheism had its day between 1370 and 1350 BCE. In India, the religious revolution got started around 500 BCE and is associated with the names of Siddhartha Gautama, later known simply as the Buddha, and Mahavira, the founder of the Jain faith; in China, the relevant name is that of Zhang Daoling, who transformed Taoist philosophy into an ascetic religion in the second century BCE; farther west, the names of Jesus and Muhammad are the most widely known figures of this kind.

Even those religions that stayed more or less intact through the great transformation underwent massive change. Judaism is a particularly relevant example here. The scholar Raphael Patai has argued on the basis of a great deal of evidence that the Jewish faith did not become monotheistic until the aftermath of the Babylonian captivity (586–539 BCE) when it absorbed important influences from Persian Zoroastrianism and rewrote its sacred scriptures to suit.

Patai demonstrates that the official religion of the Israelites during the era of the First Temple included the worship of two goddesses as well as the God of Israel in addition to many of the same rites and customs—many of them oriented toward agricultural fertility—as their Caananite neighbors.[64] In the wake of the religious revolution, the goddesses were expelled from the religion and their worship redefined in retrospect as the terrible sin for which the nation of Judah was destroyed. Meanwhile the God of Israel himself underwent a change at least as drastic—from the crusty tribal deity of the Old Testament's earliest strata to an abstract creator of the cosmos whose special relationship with one small Middle Eastern people landed later theologians in any number of perplexities.

Gods of Life, Gods of Death

Though the revolution centered on a change from worship of nature deities to reverence for prophets and saints, it had broader implications. One of these involved a complete reversal in attitudes toward nature, sexuality, and biological existence. In religious festivals in ancient Greece, large wooden penises were paraded down the streets as emblems of the abundant life and joy the gods of nature brought into the world without anyone being the least

---

64   Patai 1990.

embarrassed by the custom. You can find nearly identical wooden penises being paraded through the streets of Japanese towns during some Shinto festivals today, in exactly the same spirit. To the prophets and heirs of the religious revolution, by contrast, the idea of sexual delight as a divine gift to be celebrated in public was unthinkable. Holiness, to them, required the renunciation of sex, not its celebration; at most, it might be grudgingly permitted for the sake of reproduction, but never enjoyed and never treated as sacred.

At the same time, attitudes toward death and the corpses of the dead underwent an equal and opposite reversal. Though there were exceptions—the ancient Egyptian cult of the dead comes to mind—most of the old nature religions had very strong taboos concerning contact between dead things and holy things. To bring a corpse into an ancient Greek temple would have been the kind of impious act that would leave devout pagans waiting for Zeus to throw a thunderbolt. In exactly the same way, nothing connected with death can be brought into a Shinto shrine to this day without rendering the place and everyone involved in that act dangerously impure. The new prophetic religions, by contrast, gave the relics of the dead a central role in their theology, their ceremonial life, and above all in their architecture. Christian churches from before the Reformation are thus surrounded by churchyards full of tombs. Sites where some part of the Buddha's body is enshrined are among the core holy places of Buddhism, while the tombs of Sufi shaykhs attract the devotion of many Muslims.

Similar changes reshaped attitudes to every other aspect of biological existence. In the old temple cults, priests and priestesses might fast from specific foods and abstain from sexual activity during certain periods in order to attain a state of ritual purity appropriate for some special ceremony. After the religious revolution, by contrast, these customs were applied to the whole of life, backed up by the insistence that anybody who failed to abide by what were once priestly disciplines of ritual purity would be tortured in the afterlife for their sins.

More broadly, where life in its full, richly biological reality was central to the older worship of the deities of nature, the prophets of the religious revolution turned their backs on life—in that robust sense—to focus attention on an idealized otherworld on the far side of death. The Buddhist insistence that life is suffering, the Christian devaluation of physical existence in favor of the imagined delights of heaven, and equivalent rhetorical strategies in other prophetic faiths all flow from and feed into the rejection of concrete biological life that defined the new vision.

It's important to realize that the transformation we're discussing was not some kind of universal shift in consciousness, which certain modern theorists like to imagine. While it spread over much of the Old World, its reach was never total. In sub-Saharan Africa, many nations retained their traditional religions in spite of pressure from missionaries of prophetic faiths; in Japan, political factors forced one of the new faiths to accept the persistence of an older tradition; in India, although Buddhism swept all before it in the centuries immediately after the Buddha's time, the tide turned in the fifth century CE, and thereafter Hinduism resumed its place as the dominant religion on the Indian subcontinent.

In the New World, the new faiths had no presence at all until imported at European gunpoint after 1492. Legends surrounding the career of the Toltec prophet-king Ce Acatl Topiltzin, who reigned in the tenth century CE and was later identified with the gods Kukulcan and Quetzalcoatl, suggests that an attempt at something like the Old World's religious revolution may have taken place in Mesoamerica. If so, however, its legacy was quickly reabsorbed into the existing framework of native Mesoamerican religion.

The causes and consequences of this massive changing of the gods could occupy a much larger book than this one. For our present purposes, though, the relevant point is the impact that the religious revolution had on the temple tradition sketched out in previous chapters. Wherever the temple tradition existed in ancient times, it had become deeply interwoven with the old religions of the gods and goddesses of nature. The prophets and apostles of the new religions accordingly denounced temples and everything done in them as an element of the old ways, which had to be brushed aside to make room for the newly revealed truth.

The entire matter might have ended there. In some places and times, it did end there. Orthodox Sunni Islam, for example, seems to have eliminated the temple tradition root and branch in the process of imposing its own distinctive religious vision on the lands where it predominates. Most branches of Buddhism have erased the tradition nearly as completely. Here and there, though, in the wake of the religious revolution, elements of the temple tradition crept back into some branches of the newly founded prophetic religions. We've already seen how esoteric Buddhism in Japan became a vehicle by which the temple tradition found its way into Shinto—although that story has further complexities, which will be detailed below. Processes of the same kind seem to have occurred elsewhere in a few other faiths, as people aware of the temple tradition's secret technology worked out ways to combine the old practices with the new religions.

The most dramatic example of all took place in Western Europe. There, despite the bitter hostility dividing the local prophetic religion and the older, nature-centered faiths that it supplanted, the entire toolkit of the classic temple tradition seems to have found its way nearly intact into medieval Christianity. The process by which this transition took place was complex and involved at least two distinct processes of transmission—one of which, as we'll see, left definite traces of its presence in the traditions of Freemasonry.

During the high Middle Ages, as a result of this complex history, Christian churches across Europe were built according to the same principles as the Pagan temples of an earlier time. Many of them, in fact, were built on the same locations, faced the same directions, and celebrated festivals on the same dates. So extensive were the borrowings from the temple tradition that accounts of medieval church design and ceremony—together with the churches themselves and the immense body of traditional folklore that gathered around them—are among the most important sources of information from which the overall pattern of the temple tradition can, however tentatively, be reconstructed.

The Zoroastrian Foreshadowing

A transformation of the same kind, by which the temple tradition was adopted for a time by one of the new prophetic religions, also happened in Persia in the fourth century BCE. Until that time, the Zoroastrian religion had no temples. Greek writers noted with amazement that their Persian adversaries worshipped without temples or altars, and the Zoroastrian scriptures take it for granted that the worship of the Zoroastrian god Ahura Mazda takes place in the open air.[65]

After the Persian conquest of Mesopotamia, though, the mother goddesses who had long been worshipped by the native peoples of the conquered lands became popular among their new Persian overlords as well. The Zoroastrian priesthood responded by finding a *yazata* (subordinate deity), the goddess Anahita, who more or less corresponded to Ishtar, Astarte, and the other great Mesopotamian goddesses, and permiting Mesopotamian styles of worship to be offered to her.[66] Readers familiar with the history of Christianity will recall the way that worship once paid to Pagan goddesses in Europe was redirected into reverence for the Virgin Mary; the parallels with the rise of Anahita worship in Persian-occupied Mesopotamia are very close.

Along with worship of the yazata Anahita, the Zoroastrians in Mesopotamia seem to have adopted some version of the classic temple tradition, and this appears to have spread back into the Zoroastrian mainstream in Iran. The oldest known remains of a Zoroastrian temple at Seistan in southeastern Iran follow a plan that will be familiar to readers of this book. It was built atop an isolated hill and featured a large hall with a smaller square hall off one end, and beyond that a third space, smaller still, seems to have filled the role of Holy of Holies. The original temple probably dates to the third century BCE; it was rebuilt at least twice thereafter following the same plan.[67]

Whatever spiritual and philosophical compromises led to this fusion of Zoroastrian monotheist religion and the old temple tradition, though, the

---

65   Boyce 1979, 6, 46, and 60.
66   Ibid., 61–62.
67   Hamblin and Seely 2007, 103.

fusion itself did not endure. The great temples of the Zoroastrians were wrecked and abandoned after the Muslim conquest of Iran, and many of the more complex priestly practices went by the boards in the struggle to preserve the essential core of the Zoroastrian faith. When Zoroastrian communities in India and elsewhere established temples of their own in later centuries, those did not follow any version of the temple plan explored in the earlier chapters of this book. This trajectory of adoption and abandonment proved to be prophetic, for much the same thing happened in the Christian faith between the fall of Rome and the aftermath of the Reformation.

The Temple Tradition and Buddhism

As mentioned in chapter 3, esoteric Buddhism seems to be the vehicle by which the temple tradition made its way to Japan. The presence of the temple tradition in any Buddhist source is surprising, to be sure. The Buddhist faith is focused on winning salvation for all beings from the wheel of rebirth and the suffering inherent in existence, and its early architecture focused on two kinds of structures unrelated to the temple: on the one hand was the monastery, which was simply a dwelling for monks, and on the other was the *stupa*, a structure containing a relic of the Buddha himself or a Buddhist saint, where the faithful gathered to pray, meditate, and circumambulate.

One complexity in tracing the temple tradition's connection to Buddhism is that the original homeland of the Buddhist faith, India, returned to Hinduism in the early Middle Ages, and trying to piece together ancient and medieval Indian Buddhism from its surviving traces and the small Buddhist communities that remain in India itself is a very challenging process. Elsewhere in Asia, Buddhism very quickly picked up local architectural traditions among many other things; architecturally speaking, as a result, a Buddhist monastery in Tibet has almost nothing in common with a Buddhist monastery in Vietnam.

A second complexity is that the esoteric school of Buddhism, the branch that seems to have picked up the most information about the temple tradition, went extinct not only in India but in most of the rest of Asia as well.

It remains active today mostly in Japan on the one hand and in Tibet and regions such as Mongolia that received cultural influence from Tibet on the other. Adding to the complexity is the fact that the Japanese and Tibetan versions of esoteric Buddhism are radically different from one another.

The literature on Tibetan Buddhism is immense, and only a small portion of it has been translated into any Western language. The sources available to me, however, have not shown any trace of the temple tradition in Tibetan Buddhism. There is some reason to believe, rather, that only the Japanese traditions of esoteric Buddhism had contact with the temple tradition—and that they got it from a surprising source.

The founders of esoteric Buddhism in Japan were two enterprising monks, Saicho and Kukai, who made what was then a long and difficult journey from Japan to the imperial Chinese capital at Chang-an in 804 CE. One of the leading Buddhist masters with whom they studied was an Indian monk named Prajna. Prajna is well known to scholars of Chinese religion as an important translator of Buddhist scriptures into Chinese, but he did not produce his translations alone. Rather, he worked with a Chinese-speaking Persian who had adopted the Chinese name Ching-ching and was a famous translator in his own right, as well as a bishop in the Nestorian branch of Christianity.[68]

The Nestorian Church is one of the forgotten success stories of early Christian history. In the year 431 CE, Nestorius, Patriarch of Constantinople, was deposed from his position by the Council of Ephesus for theological irregularities. Undaunted, he organized an alternative church in Syria. Persecution by the established church drove the Nestorians, as his followers came to be called, out of Roman territory into the rival Persian empire, where they became the most influential of the various Christian sects.

By 631 CE, the Nestorian movement had spread all the way across Asia to the Chinese Empire. Four years later, according to a famous monument in Chang-an, the emperor Tai-tsung reviewed the teachings of the Nestorian Church, found them acceptable, and authorized the newly arrived church

---

68   Jenkins 2008, 15–16.

to seek converts throughout the Chinese empire. The "Religion of Light," as the Nestorian faith was called in China, gained a substantial following in the century or so that followed and was still a significant force in the Chinese religious scene when Saicho and Kukai arrived.

By the time he began working with Prajna, Ching-ching (Bishop Adam as he was also called) had already translated thirty books of Christian scripture and teaching into Chinese, including the Gospels, the epistles of Paul, and the Psalms. Saicho and Kukai both stayed in the Buddhist monastery in Chang-an, where Prajna and Ching-ching worked, then returned to Japan with copies of the seven volumes of Buddhist sutras the two men had translated. Then, after Saicho and Kukai established the two esoteric sects of Japanese Buddhism and cordial relations with the indigenous Shinto faith, shrines that appear to make use of the classic temple tradition suddenly became an important part of Shinto practice, replacing the open-air enclosures that had been standard up to that time.

The logical conclusion is that information about the temple tradition passed from Ching-ching to Saicho and Kukai and from them, by way of the schools they founded, to Shinto. Exactly how the lore reached Ching-ching in the first place is a complex question. As we'll see, there is some reason to believe that detailed information concerning the temple tradition may have survived in heretical Christian circles in the Middle East, but the Nestorian church also established an enduring presence in India, which could have absorbed the necessary lore there. The fact that Ching-ching apparently felt no qualms of conscience about helping a missionary from a different religion translate his scriptures into Chinese suggests that he was a man of unusually tolerant opinions, a point that broadens the possible range of sources even further.

Whatever Ching-ching may have bequeathed to Saicho and Kukai found little place in the esoteric Buddhist sects these latter two founded. Like the rest of Japanese Buddhism, the esoteric sects adopted the standard Chinese approach to Buddhist architecture for their own use and adapted it to

Japanese conditions.[69] There were good reasons why this should have happened. In Japan, broadly speaking, Shinto is the religion of life and nature, and Buddhism is the religion of the afterlife and the supernatural. A Japanese person's religious life begins in a Shinto shrine, where he or she will be presented to the kami not long after birth, and ends in a Buddhist temple, where the funeral and the offerings to the ancestral spirits take place. Thus it makes sense in terms of the Japanese religious imagination that the temple tradition, with its links to life and fertility, was assigned to Shinto early on, and Buddhist temples and monasteries followed different design principles, acquired different legends—and had different practical effects.

The Rebuilding of the Temple

Christianity, finally, came into being in a society crammed with temples, and Herod's Temple in Jerusalem, in particular, was a massive presence in the first days of the newborn faith. Some of the major events in the life of Christ as depicted in the four officially approved gospels took place in or near the Temple. Among them are the appearance of the archangel Gabriel to Zechariah announcing the birth of John the Baptist,[70] the first recognition of Jesus as the Messiah,[71] Jesus teaching the elders at the age of twelve,[72] the flogging of the moneychangers,[73] the prophecy on the Mount of Olives overlooking the temple,[74] and the rending of the veil of the Holy of Holies at the moment of Christ's death.[75]

As the new religion began to define itself in contrast to Judaism and the Pagan faiths of the Hellenistic world, however, many early Christian writers deliberately distanced themselves not just from the temple in Jerusalem but from temples in general. Much early Christian writing draws a hard

---

69   Kidder 1964.

70   Luke 1:5–25.

71   Ibid., 2:22–38.

72   Ibid., 2:41–52.

73   Matthew 21:12, Mark 11:15, and Luke 19:45–46.

74   Matthew 24 and Mark 13.

75   Luke 23:45.

contrast between the physical temple of Jewish worship and an assortment of metaphorical temples "not made with hands" that were to be central to Christian faith. Thus the promised New Jerusalem of the last two chapters of the book of Revelation, unlike the material city familiar to the earliest Christians, has no temple in it at all, "for its temple is the Lord God Almighty and the Lamb."[76] Along the same lines in the third century, the church father Minucius Felix could state categorically, "We have no temples; we have no altars."[77]

These distinctions were not simply a matter of language. Christians in the early centuries of their faith's history refused to engage in any practice too closely reminiscent of the surrounding temple cults. Their refusal to practice animal sacrifice or to eat meat offered to Pagan deities is well attested in Christian and Pagan sources. Less widely known, though just as significant, was their refusal to use incense in a religious context, not only in Pagan ceremonies but in their own sacraments as well.[78]

All this changed dramatically when Constantine's Edict of Milan abolished the legal proscription of Christianity and brought the new faith under imperial patronage and control. In place of the remodeled houses and catacombs Christians used for worship during the era of persecution, substantial church buildings as large as Pagan temples rose in urban centers around the empire. The new churches didn't use the temple architecture the Roman world inherited from the Greeks, partly because that architecture was too deeply intertwined with Pagan tradition to be acceptable to Christians and partly because the differences between Christian and Pagan ritual required a different kind of building—one that could accommodate large congregations inside to witness the ceremony of the Mass and the other sacraments.

The design that became standard was based on the basilica, the standard Roman design for government facilities meant for public use. In its secular form, the basilica was a long rectangle divided by a double row of pillars into

---

76   Revelations 21:22.

77   Jones et al. 1992, 529.

78   Ibid., 486.

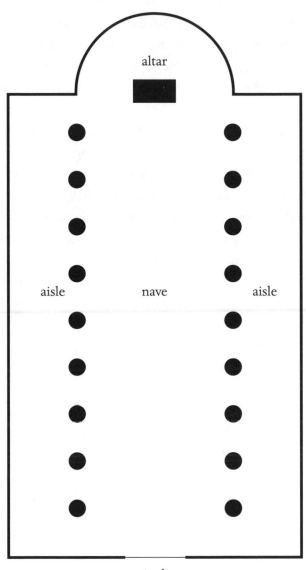

EARLY CHRISTIAN BASILICA

a wide central space and two aisles extending up the sides. The doors were at one end; at the other end, often set in a semicircular apse, was a dais with a throne for the presiding official. Place an altar on the dais and decorate the walls with mosaics on Christian themes rather than secular ones, and you have the standard design of a Christian church during the last centuries of the Roman world; see illustration on page 78.

Inevitably, concepts and symbols from the older temple traditions began to slip back into Christian practice the moment the new churches began to rise. Eusebius, Constantine's Christian adviser, launched this process by using biblical texts about the building of Solomon's Temple to provide a symbolic frame for church construction. His speech at the dedication of the church at Tyre compares the bishop of that town to Bezaleel, Solomon, and Zerubbabel, the builders of the Tabernacle, First Temple, and Second Temple respectively.[79]

Rhetoric along those lines had an inevitable impact on the more practical dimensions of church design. It's surely not an accident, for example, that the baptismal font in Christian churches from the time of Eusebius to the Reformation was almost always placed in roughly the same location relative to the main body of the church that the brazen sea had in relation to the Holy Place of Solomon's temple—either just inside the entrance of the church and over to one side, or in a separate baptistery building just outside the church proper—or that the font itself routinely resembled nothing so much as a small-scale replica of the brazen sea itself.

Other examples of borrowing from the older temple tradition are less easily explained from biblical sources. As Christian churches spread across Europe, for example, it became standard practice to surround them with a churchyard, a sacred area into which certain classes of people were not supposed to enter until cleansed with the appropriate ritual. Women who had recently given birth, for example, were not supposed to return to regular attendance until they had been "churched," that is, blessed by means of a traditional service. Every member of the congregation was expected to purify

---

79   Lundquist 2008, 156–7.

himself or herself with holy water before entering the church, and incense came to play an important role in the services. All these were straightforward borrowings from Greek Pagan practice.

Borrowings of the same kind took place at a far more profound level as well. In the centuries following the Edict of Milan, a great many Greek and Roman intellectuals who became Christian brought with them the same Neoplatonist philosophy that Sallust and his peers had applied to the Pagan Mysteries, and these intellectuals came to conceptualize Christianity as a mystery tradition along the same lines as the Mysteries of Eleusis or Cybele. Some of the products of this fusion ended up being adopted enthusiastically by the leadership of the new faith—for example, the writings of a sixth-century Christian Neoplatonist who wrote under the pseudonym of Dionysius the Areopagite became central to Christian theology for most of a millennium after his time, and still have that status in the Eastern Orthodox churches—while others strayed outside the boundaries of orthodoxy in various directions.

Quite a bit of material from the old Mysteries seem to have come across into Christian practice through these channels. David Fideler's intriguing study *Jesus Christ Sun of God* has shown that the rich Greek tradition of cosmology and number association with the half-legendary figure of Pythagoras found a home very early on in Christianity and kickstarted a tradition of numerical and geometrical symbolism in the Christian church that remained a living source of inspiration for well over a millennium thereafter.[80] It may well have been through these connections that the temple tradition first found its way into Christian practice—though, as we'll see, it received at least one, and probably two, substantial inputs from other sources later on.

The Temple Tradition in Christianity

One of the things that makes it difficult for many modern people to notice the continuities between Christianity and the older Pagan faiths is that the Christianity practiced in most of the world today has little in common with

---

80   von Simson 1962, 21–50.

ancient and medieval Christianity but the name. Ask a devout Christian in today's America about the basic elements of his faith, for example, and odds are you'll be told that Christianity is about having a personal relationship with Jesus Christ, and its central practices are prayer, Bible study, and weekly attendance at church services that include prayer, congregational singing, and listening to a sermon. All these are standard elements of modern Christianity, but they came in with the Reformation, when much of what had previously been standard Christian belief and practice was discarded.

If you could ask a devout Christian in early medieval Europe about the basic elements of his faith, by contrast, you'd get a completely different answer. At that time, for most people the thought of having a personal relationship with Jesus Christ was rather like an ordinary American citizen expecting to have a personal relationship with the president; most people's personal spiritual relationship was with one of the saints, who was their link with the Church as the mystical Body of Christ. Bible study was an esoteric branch of scholarship mostly of interest to theologians, and while prayer had an important role in daily spiritual life, the heart of religion was the sacramental rituals practiced at every church in Western Christendom.

Those rituals had a dimension that's not widely known these days outside of the more traditional Christian denominations. To this day in the Roman Catholic and Eastern Orthodox churches alike, Mass can only be celebrated properly if the altar contains part of the corpse of a dead saint. In earlier times before the Reformation, the relics of the dead were even more central to Christian faith and practice. All those who could afford to do so had at least a minor relic of some local saint in their homes as a focus for private devotion; churches vied with each other for possession of the most extensive collection of relics of the holy dead, and the idea of being buried somewhere other than a churchyard or, better still, in the church itself, was all but unthinkable—so dire a fate was reserved solely for the worst of unrepentant sinners.

In those days the sacraments of the church and the cult of the dead formed the center of religious life in ways that would seem profoundly alien

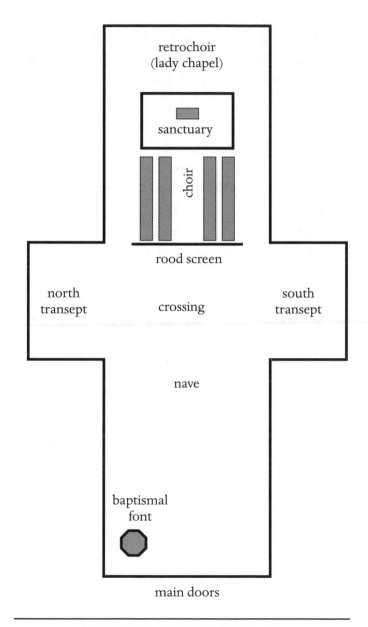

MEDIEVAL PARISH CHURCH

to modern believers. If you were an ordinary parishioner in the Middle Ages, you might well not attend Mass more than once a year, and then only after the austerities of Lent had purified you to the point that you could risk contact with the perilously holy divine presence in the communion wafer. It was the grace conferred by your baptism, the powerful assistance of your patron saint, the blessings conferred by devotion to relics and the sacraments, your own avoidance or repentance of mortal sin, and the final help of the last rites that would help you escape the traps laid out for you by God's sworn enemy, the fallen angel Sathanas, and make your way to safety in heaven.

The church you attended—whether it was a great urban cathedral, the abbey church connected to a monastery, or a humble parish church—was the spiritual powerhouse behind the whole system, the place where a priest ordained by the heirs of Christ's apostles spoke the words and performed the rites that renewed the descent of Christ into the fallen word of matter. When you went to church, if you lived in the countryside, you generally got to your destination along a set of straight tracks that radiated out across the parish and were used only for going to church for worship or taking the dead there for last rites and burial. At the end of the track, you passed through a gate in the low wall surrounding the church, crossed a churchyard full of tombstones and ancient trees, and came to the door set aside for ordinary use, which was usually a side door—very rarely the main doors at the far end of the church; see illustration on page 82.

Inside, if you were going to attend a High Mass, the most elaborate form of the Church's central sacrament, your place was usually in the nave, the main body of the church to the west of the choir and sanctuary. (The word *nave* comes from the Latin word for "ship," the same word that yields English words such as "naval" and "navigation;" an ancient and complex symbolism lies behind the term.) You would sit or stand there, depending on your social class, and look toward the rood screen, so called because it carried a large image of Christ on the Cross; *rood* was the Middle English word for "cross." The rood screen was a barrier of wood or stone that sheltered you from the sacred Mysteries being enacted beyond it in the sanctuary. People in the Middle Ages thus spoke of hearing Mass rather than attending it.

If you weren't there to hear High Mass, where you went depended on what your purpose was. If a child was to be baptized, that was performed at the font in the west end of the church. If a wedding was to be performed, that took place at the porch by the entrance most often used—the matrimonial Mass now performed by Catholic priests came in after the Reformation. Other sacraments often didn't take place at the church at all—priests usually performed the last rites in the homes of dying parishioners, and confession and absolution could be accomplished in any relatively private place.

If you were there to pray to your patron saint, on the other hand, you would go to the chapel set aside for that worthy, which might be in one of the two transepts or in the aisles to either side of the nave and the choir. If your patron was the Virgin Mary, on the other hand, her chapel—the Lady Chapel, as it was called—was most often in the retrochoir, the eastern end of the church beyond the sanctuary. Low Masses would be celebrated in the chapels from time to time, especially for the souls of the dead and other worthy causes. Curiously, it was not in any way inappropriate for the ordinary faithful to watch the Mass when it was performed in a chapel. Only the High Mass performed in the sanctuary of the church had to be hidden by the protective rood screen from all but ordained clergy.

Those of my readers who have been paying attention will already have noticed the close parallels between these arrangements and the temple traditions already surveyed in this book. Like the Temple of Solomon, the core ritual space of churches built between the early Dark Ages and the Reformation was divided into an area for worshippers—indoors rather than outdoors, due to the colder and wetter climate of Europe—a place for ordinary clergy, and an innermost space for the presiding priest. Like the temples of ancient Egypt, the inmost sanctuary was surrounded by smaller chapels dedicated to other holy beings, where ceremonies of secondary importance took place. Like the temples of ancient Greece or the shrines of contemporary Shinto, the entire structure was surrounded by a sacred enclosure and a galaxy of ceremonial taboos that are hard to explain in terms of Christian theology but easy to understand in terms of the surviving traditions far more ancient than Christianity.

And the role of agricultural fertility in the medieval European church? To understand that, it's necessary to look at a different body of evidence—the collection of strange and luminous legends that seem to blend Pagan and Christian motifs and center around that enigmatic object, the Holy Grail.

CHAPTER FIVE

The Secret of the Grail

In or around the year 1190, a man named Chrétien de Troyes dipped a quill pen in an inkwell and began to write:

> He who sows sparingly, reaps sparingly, but he who wishes to reap plentifully casts his seed on ground that will bear him fruit a hundredfold.[81]

It was an auspicious line—more auspicious, in fact, than the author had any way of knowing. This is the opening sentence of *Le Conte del Graal*, the first known story of the quest for the Holy Grail, and the seed Chrétien sowed with those words would bear fruit a hundredfold and more over the decades and centuries to come.

Le Conte del Graal was Chrétien's last work, and he died before completing it. His earlier work includes four other tales—*Erec et Enide*, *Cligés*, *Lancelot*, and *Yvain*—which invented Arthurian romance as we know it. Geoffrey of Monmouth had launched Arthur and his knights into lasting fame in 1136 with his *History of the Kings of Britain*, and Breton and Welsh storytellers had retold and reshaped their own traditional tales of Arthur for newly appreciative audiences across Europe thereafter. It was Chrétien, though, who

---

81   Chrétien de Troyes 1991, 381.

set the old stories in a world compounded partly of contemporary chivalry and partly of timeless wonder and created the atmosphere that defined the Arthurian legends ever after.

Chrétien's story of the Grail is cut from the same cloth as his other Arthurian tales.[82] It tells of a young man of noble birth, Perceval, who has been raised in the forest by his widowed mother, isolated from the world of war and chivalry. A chance encounter with knights on a forest road sends him on his way from home, and the rest of the tale recounts his education in the ways of knighthood, love, and the world. In the course of his travels, he finds his way to a mysterious castle where lives the wounded Fisher King, and he is received hospitably. Just before dinner is served, a strange ceremony takes place.

First, a page enters the room carrying a spear that bleeds drops of red blood from its point. After him come two more pages with candlesticks, and following them, a maiden bearing the Grail in her hands. The Grail is made of pure gold and set with many precious stones and shines so radiantly that the candles in the candlesticks lose their brightness. After her comes another maiden carrying a silver platter. All these file past and go into another room. Perceval wonders about the ceremony, but he has been taught by another character earlier in the story not to ask too many questions, and so he says nothing.

The meal is served, the Fisher King departs, and Perceval is taken to a chamber and sleeps through the night. The next morning the castle is deserted, and when he rides out over the drawbridge, it suddenly closes behind him, shutting him out. Later the same day, he learns from a weeping maiden in the forest that if he had asked about the meaning of the ceremony, the Fisher King would have been healed. Since he remained silent, however, much suffering will befall Perceval and many others. Hearing this, Perceval vows to find his way back to the castle of the Fisher King. More adventures follow; Gawain, Arthur's nephew and one of his most valiant knights, ends

---

82   A good English translation is Chrétien de Troyes, 1991, 381–494.

up on a quest for the spear Perceval saw in the Fisher King's castle; as he rides in search of it, he encounters still more adventures, and then ...

The story ends in the middle of a sentence. We never learn how Perceval found his way back to the Fisher King's castle and the Grail.

It was common enough at that time for a good rousing story to be picked up and retold by other writers, but what happened to the story of the Grail was very nearly unprecedented.[83] Over the next four decades, four different authors wrote lengthy continuations to Chrétien's story, and two more wrote prologues. By 1210, Robert de Boron had penned a trilogy—*Joseph of Arimathea*, *Merlin*, and *The History of the Grail*—that claimed to give the real story behind Chrétien's romance, and another anonymous author had produced a completely different retelling, *The High Book of the Grail*, in which the protagonist's name was changed to Perlesvaus and the whole affair was transported to the countryside around the great shrine of Glastonbury in Britain. In the following decades, other Grail romances appeared: Wolfram von Eschenbach's great German version, *Parzival*, by 1220; the sprawling Vulgate Cycle in French, and Heinrich von dem Türlin's *The Crown* by 1240; the awkwardly labeled Post-Vulgate Cycle by 1250.

These further developments of the story enrich Chrétien's original tale considerably. Perceval is joined in his quest, or replaced entirely, by other knights: Bors, Gawain, Lancelot, and Galahad take part in the search for the Grail and achieve or fail to achieve the quest in their own distinctive ways. New adventures and new marvels are added to the original; the Grail changes shape and takes on new meanings freighted with Christian theology; the tale stretches back to the life of Christ, the court of King Solomon, or the Garden of Eden. In the Vulgate Cycle, the longest of the Grail legends, the parade of wonders reaches its peak; the solitary journeys of the questing knights culminate in a sea voyage by Bors, Percival, and Galahad aboard the Ship of Solomon, which was launched onto the seas by King Solomon himself and bears the knights to the mysterious city of Sarras, where the Grail knights finally meet their strange and splendid destinies.

---

83   Barber 2004, 27.

Then, suddenly, the torrent of Grail romances stopped. After 1250, the next significant Grail narratives to be written were Ulrich Fütrer's *Lanzelet* and Thomas Malory's *Le Morte d'Arthur*, both of which appeared in the late fifteenth century. No one knows why.

The Secrets of the Grail

We can start finding our own way through the wilderness that surrounds the Grail castle with an examination of the word itself. It was originally spelled *gradal* and was a medieval French word for an expensive serving dish, the sort of thing on which a large fish might be served at a banquet.[84] It was never a common word, but it occurs now and then in surviving medieval documents from centuries before Chrétien's time. Once he used it in *Le Conte del Graal*, it quickly dropped out of use in most other contexts, though variants of it are still used in some regional dialects of French for serving dishes and the like.[85]

Among the many mysteries surrounding the Grail legend is the speed with which this straightforward meaning was shaken off by the writers of Grail romances and replaced by others. To Robert de Boron, the Grail was still a serving dish, but it was the very dish from which Jesus and the apostles ate at the Last Supper and in which Joseph of Arimathea collected the blood that flowed from Jesus's wounds when his body was cleaned for burial. *The High Book of the Grail* describes it instead as a chalice of the sort used for the celebration of the Mass but says mysteriously that this is only the last of five forms, the other four of which may not be named. The Vulgate Cycle, which drew its raw material from several earlier sources, wavers between dish and cup in its description.

The most original description in the first great wave of Grail romances was Wolfram von Eschenbach's. In *Parzival* the Grail is a magical stone, "the perfection of paradise ... which surpasses all earthly perfection."[86] It mirac-

---

84   Carey 2007, 11–13.

85   Barber 2004, 95–96.

86   von Eschenbach 1961, 129.

ulously feeds the company of Grail knights at the castle of Muntsalväsche, heals wounds, gives the legendary phoenix its power of rejuvenating itself through fire, and displays in mysterious writing the names of those who are summoned to its service. It also has a secret name, *lapsit exillis*.

While an amazing range of interpretations have been offered for it, this phrase is relatively straightforward Latin. *Lapsit* is the normal poetic contraction of *lapsavit*, "he, she, or it fell," very slightly misspelled. (The correct spelling would be *lapsat*;[87] minor garblings of this kind are so common in medieval manuscripts that it's rare to find a text without them.) The second half of the phrase, *exillis*, is actually two words, *ex illis*, "from among them." As every first-year Latin student learns, *ille* and its declensions imply "famous, well-known," and the like;[88] "it (or he, or she) fell from among *them*" catches something of the flavor of the phrase.

Wolfram's curious name for the Grail is far from the only secret associated with the legend. From Chrétien's version onward, in fact, the Grail is surrounded by mysteries.[89] In the *Conte du Graal* itself, Perceval is counseled by a holy hermit, who teaches him a prayer full of secret names of Christ that should never be uttered aloud except in the greatest peril. In the continuations of Chrétien's *Conte*, there are constant references to the secrets of the Grail, "which no man can hear without shivering and trembling, changing color and going pale with fear."[90] Robert de Boron refers to the secrets of the Grail repeatedly. Here is a typical passage from *Joseph of Arimathea*:

> Then Jesus spoke some other words to Joseph which I dare not tell you—nor could I, even if I wanted to, if I did not have the high book in which they were written: and that is the creed of the great mystery of the Grail.[91]

---

87   Greenough et al. 1992, 91.

88   Ibid., 178.

89   References to secrets of the Grail are helpfully summarized in Barber 2004, 161–66; ironically, Barber then attempts to explain these references away, without much success.

90   Barber 2004, 163.

91   Cited in Barber 2004, 42.

Similar passages appear in the Vulgate Cycle and elsewhere among the legends. In all the original Grail romances, in fact, the Grail is said to embody a tremendous and terrifying secret, which can be communicated to the questing knight only under very specific conditions.

The role of secret knowledge in the original Grail romances and the extent to which many of those romances amount to the story of how a given knight of Arthur's court was prepared for contact with the Grail suggests that one of the things that may be tangled up in these strange and haunting stories is some form of initiatory ceremony. This was the theory proposed in the early twentieth century by Jessie Weston, who was among the most thoughtful and interesting of all modern students of Grail lore. Weston argued that behind the Grail romances as we have them is a garbled account of a ritual of initiation related to the initiations of the ancient Mysteries and to certain traditions in that complex and generally misunderstood movement called Gnosticism.[92]

Perceval's first visit to the Fisher King's castle, Weston proposed, represents a failed initiation in which his unwillingness to ask a question at the right time marked his unfitness to proceed. (Masonic rituals to this day likewise require the candidate to answer certain questions correctly at certain points of the ceremony, on pain of being removed from the lodge and barred from membership; the details are different but the principle is much the same.) On his second visit to the castle, Perceval makes good his error and successfully passes through the initiation process. It's an intriguing hypothesis and one that has much to offer to this book's project, as a later chapter will show.

That said, there was more involved in the successful completion of the Grail quest than the personal initiation of the questing knight, and this further dimension was also central to Weston's thesis. If the question was not asked, according to most of the original Grail stories, and the Fisher King not healed, a terrible misfortune would come upon the land. Chrétien is vague about what that misfortune might be, but his successors are not. The Fisher

---

92   Weston 1983 is the best introduction to her ideas.

King has been struck through the genitals (or, euphemistically, through the thighs) with a spear, and while he remains unhealed, the countryside around his castle is barren, unfruitful, and uninhabited. Only if the right question is asked and the Fisher King healed of his wound will the curse that lies upon the Waste Land be lifted.

The Waste Land

The theme of fertility—the common thread this book has traced through temples and churches across much of the world—is also close to the heart of the Grail legend and becomes steadily more important to the original Grail romances as these develop the themes that Chrétien de Troyes first sketched out. In all its forms, the Grail is a source of food. Chrétien does not introduce this theme—the Grail is simply carried past the Fisher King and the baffled young knight Perceval as dinner is served—but it appears in full flower shortly thereafter. In Wolfram's *Parzival*, the Vulgate Cycle, and most of the later texts, one of the distinctive miracles of the Grail is that it provides every knight with the food he loves best:

> As the maiden passed in front of the dining table, each knight knelt before the holy vessel and the tables were at once replenished with all the delightful foods that one could describe; and the palace was filled with delicious odors as if all the spices in the world had been scattered there.[93]

This miraculous provision of food is only one of the Grail's wonders, though, and a more important factor is the Grail's relation to the Waste Land. From Chrétien on, the unhealed wound of the Fisher King and the unasked question are linked to the devastation of the lands surrounding the Grail castle, and as the legend develops, the nature of that devastation comes more and more to relate to a failure of crop and livestock fertility. The Grail has many aspects, but one of its essential roles is as a talisman of fertility. Thus in Robert de Boron's *Joseph of Arimathea*, the first table of the Grail is

---

93   Cited in Barber 2004, 54.

established to end a famine,[94] and in Heinrich von dem Türlin's *The Crown,* Gawain's success in asking the Grail question restores the Waste Land to fertility and breaks the spell that holds the Fisher King in an enchanted semblance of life.

What caused the desolation of the Waste Land is less clear in most of the original texts. In Chrétien, Perceval's failure to ask the question is at fault. In the later tradition, from the Vulgate Cycle onward, the Dolorous Blow that originally caused the Fisher King's wound is at fault. In between, though, a strangely detailed account appears in a text usually called *The Elucidation,* which is found in a handful of manuscript copies of other Grail narratives from the thirteenth and fourteenth centuries.[95] As the title suggests, *The Elucidation* purports to be an explanation of the Grail stories, though it's at least as puzzling as any of the texts it claims to explain. The story it recounts, though, points straight to the concealed meaning of the Grail legend— though following that track requires careful attention to a number of factors not usually included in scholarly studies of the Grail, among them the points already raised in this book.

Long ago, *The Elucidation* tells, the land of Logres was green and fertile, full of the wealth of all the world, and blessed with a special magic, for there were wells throughout the land and maidens who dwelt in them. If any traveler desired food or drink, he could stop by one of these wells, and a maiden would come out of the well with a golden cup in her hand and served him whatever food he most desired. One time, though, the wicked king Amangon raped one of the maidens and took her golden cup from her, and his vassals followed his example and did the same to the other maidens. Thereafter, the maidens no longer appeared, and the land was laid waste, so that there were no longer leaves on the trees or water in the rivers, and the fields and flowers withered. From then on, no one could find the court of the Fisher King, from which abundant wealth once came.

---

94   Barber 2004, 42.
95   Carey 2007, 181–88.

A long and bitter age later, Arthur became king of Logres and called every good knight to his fellowship of the Round Table. They were the best champions of the world, and they swore to restore the wells, guard the maidens, and destroy the lineage of those who had harmed them. The knights rode forth on this quest and found maidens wandering in the wild lands, each guarded by a knight, who would do battle with any who approached. It was Gawain who first vanquished one of the knights and sent him, in the manner of the time, to King Arthur's court.

That knight was named Blihos Bleheris, and he explained to Arthur and his court that the wandering maidens and knights were descended from the maidens of the wells whom Amangon and his vassals had raped. They must wander and the land would remain blighted until the court of the Fisher King could once again be found. That, in turn, was what began the great quest for the Holy Grail, in which seven champions in all found the Fisher King's court.

Gawain was the first to accomplish the quest, and when he did so, the waters flowed again, fields and woods became green, and the land of Logres was repopulated. Once this happened, however, an unknown evil folk came forth from the wells and established their own rule over the land, making war on King Arthur. After many battles, quests, and wonders, they were finally vanquished by the knights of the Round Table, and the court of the Fisher King was found and freed from its enchantment.

Near the end of *The Elucidation*, the anonymous author includes these riddling words, hinting yet again at a profound secret hidden in the stories of the Grail:

> And the one who made the book
> (So I tell you, one by one)
> Wishes to show to each of you
> Why the Grail served.
> For the service which it performed
> Will be revealed by the good master.
> And it was not known, but hidden,

The good which it served;

For he will freely teach it to all people.[96]

Scholars who have wrestled with *The Elucidation* have offered varied theories to explain it; some have considered it an important key to the mysteries of the Grail, while others have dismissed it as an irrelevant oddity. For reasons that may already be clear to my readers, I consider it to be crucial if it's understood correctly, but its meaning—like the meaning of the Grail tradition as a whole, and the broader secret with which this book is concerned—has to be put in its proper context.

Solving the Grail Riddle

The nature of that context was traced out by an American philologist, Urban T. Holmes, in his 1948 study *A New Interpretation of Chrétien's Conte du Graal*. Scholarly studies of the Grail legend prior to that time centered on one of two theories: one tracing the legend to archaic Celtic roots, the other deriving it from the theology of the Mass in the medieval Christian church. Both theories had their strengths and weaknesses; each could explain certain things about the Grail texts but failed to explain other things. As we'll see, both of them account for part of the broader explanation to be attempted here.

Holmes, though, chose a different path in his quest for the Fisher King's court. He noted that a great many details of the Grail Castle in Chrétien's *Conte del Graal* came from an easily identified source: passages in the Bible and the Talmud that relate to the Temple of Solomon and the priestly ordinances surrounding it. Thus the Fisher King wears a garment with a purple fringe, as required for priestly use in Numbers 15:38, and his lameness parallels that of the patriarch Jacob; the Grail's capacity to strike down the sinful closely parallels the similar power of the Ark of the Covenant; furthermore, Holmes pointed out, the Waste Land of the Grail romances is prefigured in

---

96   Carey 2007, 187; the translation is Carey's.

such biblical passages as Isaiah 6:11 and Jeremiah 44:22, which prophesy that Israel would become a waste land.

On this basis, Holmes argued that Chrétien was probably a converted Jew who had studied the Cabala in the famous Jewish school at Troyes, headed by Rabbi Solomon ben Isaac, who is traditionally known as Rashi. While this is possible, it goes considerably beyond what the evidence requires. Rashi and his school received patronage from the influential Christian nobleman Hugues I, Count of Champagne, whose court was at Troyes, and the presence of Rashi and his students in that town helped spark a general flowering of Hebrew and Aramaic studies in the region, among Christians as well as Jews.[97] As we've already seen, Jewish traditions surrounding the Temple of Solomon were adopted into Christianity as early as the third century CE. By the twelfth century, the traditions Holmes traced in Chrétien's work were the common property of Jewish and Christian traditions alike.

Nonetheless, Holmes was right to point out that references to the Temple of Solomon can be found in the Grail legends. What lies behind those references could have been discovered in another way had enough attention been paid to the differences between medieval and modern thought. People in the Middle Ages made extensive use of a mode of thinking—typological thinking—that has fallen entirely out of use in recent centuries, and the riddle of the Grail can be solved surprisingly easily once its typological role is understood.

What is typological thinking? In simple terms, it's the habit of thinking in terms of concrete metaphors rather than abstract concepts. Consider the traditional titles of the Virgin Mary in medieval religious writings. There are scores of them: "sealed fountain," "seat of wisdom," "tower of ivory," "mystical rose," "star of the sea," "tabernacle of the Lord," "walled garden," and so on. Each of these is a precise metaphor communicating some part of the role that the Virgin Mary plays in the Gospel story and in Catholic theology and legend. Such metaphors, or as they were called by medieval thinkers, types, played an important and familiar role in every kind of thinking in the

---

97   Ralls 2003, 38.

Middle Ages, filling many of the roles that abstract concepts and categories have in our thinking today.

If the central images of the Grail mystery are understood as types, their meaning is not hard to find. Imagine those images, for example, as a medieval riddle: "It is a spear borne before a vessel; it is a chalice glowing with light; it is a dish that will not serve the sinful, but gives the virtuous the food they love best; it is a ship that Solomon set sailing on the seas of time; it is the Temple of Solomon itself. What is it?"

The answer, of course, is a church of the high Middle Ages. The tall central steeple rising from the body of the church west of the sanctuary is the spear standing upright before the chalice of the Mass; stained-glass windows and myriads of lamps make it a container glowing with light; the Masses celebrated in it are forbidden to those who are guilty of mortal sins but provide the virtuous with spiritual food; the nave of a church, as already mentioned, gets its name from the typological metaphor of a ship, and the equation of the church with the Temple of Solomon has already been discussed at length.

The essential powers of the Grail, in turn, are the same powers that we've seen associated with temples across much of the world and include as a central theme the power to bring fertility to an otherwise barren land. There's a crucial difference, though, between the way that power is manifested in the Grail narratives and the way the same powers appear in the older temple cults. In the temples of old and the lore that surrounds them, the gifts of agricultural fertility and inner transformation are envisioned as established realities, subject only to the proper maintenance of certain customs and rites. In the Grail legend, by contrast, the same powers are in eclipse and the land lies waste, waiting for a specific and unusual form of deliverance.

In his book on the Grail legend, Richard A. Barber comments on the startling originality of the theme of the Grail question. "There are many stories in folklore and literature which revolve around the finding of an answer to a question, but stories where the crux is the asking of the question in the first place are rare in the extreme."[98] Not any question will do, though; it has to be the right question, asked of the right person, at the right time.

What has to be asked varies slightly from one source to another. In Chrétien, the questions Perceval fails to ask are why the lance bled, where the Grail procession was going, and who was to be fed from the Grail. The authors of the Continuations ring various changes on these themes, and in most of the other narratives, the question is simply, "Whom does the Grail serve?" The central theme of the question is not simply what the Grail is, but what it does. Only when that question has been asked can the Fisher King be healed and the Waste Land made green.

The same question might well be asked concerning all the material covered up to this point: the puzzling symbolism of Freemasonry, the traditional lore of the Temple of Solomon, the vast geographical spread of parallel temple traditions, the curious borrowings of Pagan practice by the medieval Christian church, the legends of the Grail, and the thread that connects all these—a thread that connects sacred buildings and agricultural abundance in a manner that baffles the modern mind, though it seems to have been something close to common sense not that many centuries ago. Like the strange and luminous objects carried past the knights in the Grail Castle, these things are meaningless marvels until the right question is asked.

It's far from coincidental that the question is also the same that had to be asked about the Grail: "What do these things mean?" In the pages ahead, I will propose a tentative answer.

---

98   Barber 2004, 109.

PART TWO

The Technology

CHAPTER SIX

The Temple Technology

The puzzling traditions summarized in the first part of this book have been explained in many ways. Nearly always, though, they have been approached in isolation from one another. That temples all over the Old World share a common set of structural elements unrelated to their obvious function as places of worship; that these same structural elements crop up in Christian churches in the Middle Ages; that Masonic traditions dating back to the Middle Ages retain enigmatic scraps of lore related to those structural elements; that these elements and the temples that embody them are so constantly associated with the renewal of agricultural and ecological fertility; that this same theme of fertility also plays a central role in that most mysterious of medieval legends, the narrative of the Holy Grail: these points have been addressed piecemeal, not together, and the connections linking them have been dismissed as mere coincidence when they've been noticed at all.

The hypothesis at the heart of this book is that the connections between the themes just listed aren't coincidences—that they point to an extraordinary and largely unsuspected reality. I propose, in fact, that ancient temples and medieval churches did exactly what the legends claimed they were able to do: they caused a significant increase in local agricultural and ecological productivity when they were built and operated according to certain principles.

The effects thus produced, furthermore, have nothing to do with magic or miracle. They were physical phenomena generated by physical forces that are most likely well known to today's science, but they were put to work in ways that happen to be unfamiliar to us today. The principles, design features, and practices that generated and made use of these effects can best be understood as the elements of a technology that used relatively simple but carefully chosen means to produce surprising results. These means, taken together, comprise what this book will call the temple technology.

I'm aware that these are sweeping claims, and some of my readers will doubtless reject them out of hand. On the one hand, even in an age that's used to wireless Internet service, a surprising number of people still have a hard time remembering that physical effects can radiate outward from a central point to affect an area surrounding it. The temple technology, if the hypothesis at the core of this book is correct, involves exactly such a physical effect, which is generated and broadcasted by structures built and operated according to specific principles. As we'll see shortly, there are at least two known physical phenomena that influence agricultural fertility and are known to function in this way, so the basic concept is by no means impossible.

On the other hand, it's unfashionable these days to suggest that ancient cultures could have made what contemporary society considers advanced scientific and technological discoveries, even when all the evidence points to that conclusion. What tends to be forgotten, amid all the cheerleading for today's technology, is that people in ancient times might have lacked our current theoretical understanding of nature, but they were perfectly capable of noticing what worked and what didn't, drawing rational conclusions on the basis of experience, and trying out new techniques to expand their ability to work with natural phenomena—even when their theories about the nature of those phenomena strike us as primitive or absurd.

One crucial difference between modern science and the lore of ancient societies needs to be kept in mind as we proceed. Our science is analytical: it takes apart every phenomenon into the factors that account for it, and repeats the process on the factors, until analysis finally stops with a small number of simple processes as the foundation beneath it all. That's an extraordinarily powerful approach, but it's a very recent one in historical terms.

The sciences of older societies were synthetic rather than analytical. Instead of taking phenomena apart, synthetic sciences put them together, treating similar effects in very different spheres of nature as though they were manifestations of a common pattern. This can be seen clearly in surviving ancient sciences such as feng shui, the traditional Chinese science of landscape and architectural placement. Some rules of feng shui relate to physical phenomena—for example, the rule that houses in the northern temperate zone should be built on south-facing slopes, so they will get as much sunlight as possible in the winter months. Some rules relate to psychological phenomena—for example, the rule that fences and other psychological barriers can be used to screen out unwanted influences. Others relate to cultural phenomena—for example, the rule that nothing relating to the traditional Chinese symbolism of death should have any place in houses for the living— and many others fuse these categories in ways that very often seem to make little sense to the modern mind.

To the practitioners of the old synthetic sciences, the tradition at the heart of this book was and is no mystery. Back in the fourth century CE, Iamblichus of Chalcis discussed standing stones and similar monuments in his famous work *On the Mysteries*, noting that "the erection of the phalli is a certain sign of prolific power, which, through this, is called forth to the generative energy of the world."[99] In the same way in the twentieth century, the Austrian mystic Rudolf Steiner advised gardeners to plant vegetables in raised beds, because any piece of ground raised above the ordinary level of

---

99   Iamblichus 1984, 53.

the soil attracted a subtle influence that resulted in increased vitality and growth of plants.[100]

Both of these pieces of advice are echoed in important expressions of the temple tradition. Still, the question that occurs first to the modern mind— what causes these reported effects?—is a question that the old synthetic sciences are poorly equipped to answer. Lacking the concept of an analytical science, it never occurred to people in ancient societies to try to pick apart the complex phenomena of nature to figure out exactly how they worked. What often gets forgotten, though, is that the lack of analytical science did not prevent them from getting remarkable results by careful observation and experiment.

There are plenty of examples. One that's relevant to the present case is the process by which modern food crops were bred out of ancestral wild plants. The grains that provide most of humanity's food today all descend from various species of wild grass, all of which provide fewer grains and far less food value than their cultivated descendants. Scientists exploring the way that wild grasses became domesticated grains have tracked the process by which ancient farmers brought about that transition, using selective breeding and hybridization to encourage traits they wanted in their crops and get rid of traits they didn't want.

What makes this especially interesting is that the scientific basis behind their activities wasn't figured out until the late nineteenth century, when Gregor Mendel carried out the epochal experiments with pea blossoms that founded the science of genetics. Thousands of years before, though, farmers and breeders had figured out through trial and error and careful observation how to make use of the unknown laws of genetics to reshape plants and animals to meet human needs.

In the same way, the founders of the temple technology, lacking scientific knowledge of the laws of nature that made the technology function, were still able to use the same skills of observation and experiment to get equally remarkable results. They had no idea what forces they were using,

---

100   Steiner 1974, 68.

and since the very existence of the temple technology has remained unnoticed and unsuspected by contemporary scientists, the specific forces used by the temple technology can't yet be identified with any kind of certainty. Some branches of recent scientific research, however, suggest two likely candidates: two forces well known to today's physicists have known positive effects on agricultural fertility, and which can act over the modest distances that separated, say, an ancient Greek temple or a medieval church from the surrounding fields.

Terrestrial Electricity and Magnetism

One possible medium by which the temple technology could have worked is the beneficial effect of weak electrical charges on plant growth, which was extensively researched and documented in the late nineteenth and early twentieth century before chemical fertilizers came into widespread use. Professor Selim Lemström of the University of Helsingfors in Sweden carried out extensive experimental research on this effect and found that a weak electrical current applied to the soil, or an electrostatic field in the air, increased plant growth by an average of 40 percent.[101]

Electroculture, as this effect came to be called, became widely known in the decades that followed—enough so that in the early twentieth century how-to manuals meant to teach farmers about electrical appliances routinely included a chapter about electroculture among discussions of electric irrigation pumps and automatic milking machines.[102] Only with the arrival of chemical fertilizers and pesticides, marketed relentlessly by the chemical industry, did electroculture drop out of use, becoming one of many orphan technologies that never had the chance to fulfill their early promise.

More recently, John Burke and Kaj Halberg have spent many years documenting connections between ancient religious sites, terrestrial electricity, and food crops.[103] Burke's background as an inventor in the agricultural

---

101   Lemström 1904, 10; see the detailed results in the pages following.
102   See, for example, Allen 1922.
103   Burke and Halberg 2005 is a good summary of their work for general audiences.

technology field brought him into contact with intriguing research into the effects of electric charges on seeds. When seeds are exposed to a strong electrical field before planting, the plants that grow from them are consistently more productive and more resistant to stress than seeds of the same kind that don't get the same treatment. That was an interesting data point and nothing more until Burke realized that certain kinds of ancient monuments are well designed to produce exactly the sort of electrical field that will provide the electron-shower treatment.

At Tikal, one of the great ruined cities of the Maya, local farmers still take their seed corn and beans to the top of one of the surviving pyramids, leave them there for the duration of a ceremony, and then take them back down for planting.[104] The custom was apparently common throughout the ancient Mayan world; the old Mayan name for their pyramids, in fact, translates literally into English as "corn mountain."[105] Similar customs are reported from all over the world and, in particular, wherever holy places take the shape of ziggurats or raised mounds. For reasons of simple physics, such structures attract electrical fields from the ground and sky that are strong enough to provide seeds with the necessary stimulus.

Some places, due to a galaxy of complex geological and physical reasons, are better suited to this effect than others. Burke and Halberg found that far more often than not, important sacred sites where some form of the electrical-charge treatment seems to have been used are located atop conductivity discontinuities in the Earth: places, that is, where the flow of natural electricity through the ground is disrupted. A mound, pyramid, or raised platform placed over such a discontinuity will generate a much stronger electrical field than the same structure located somewhere else.

How did ancient peoples, without the benefit of advanced technological equipment, locate these spots? This is, in some ways, the most fascinating dimension of Burke and Halberg's research. A significant fraction of people, they have pointed out, are sensitive to electrical and magnetic fields and can

104   Burke and Halberg 2005, 39–45.
105   Ibid., 43–44.

perceive them directly. Research carried out over many decades by Canadian researcher Michael Persinger, in fact, has shown that many experimental subjects exposed to a pulsing magnetic field begin to hallucinate, and a much larger fraction experience less dramatic changes in consciousness.[106] The fields Persinger used were considerably stronger than those that appear in most places on the Earth's surface, but quite a range of factors can concentrate electric and magnetic fields in specific places, to the point that effects of the sort Persinger found become possible.

Terrestrial electricity thus apparently provides a straightforward explanation of the ziggurat tradition discussed in chapter 3, as found in Mesopotamia, China, and the New World. Whether or not this is the only thing ziggurats and the rituals associated with them were meant to do is another matter. One of the consequences of the synthetic approach to knowledge pursued in ancient times is that many different factors can feed into any one practice or tradition, since the intellectual tools needed to tease out different causal mechanisms hadn't been devised yet. Much more research needs to be done, and traditional customs surrounding the "corn mountains" of the Maya and Chinese earth altars carefully studied, before any but the most tentative conclusions can be drawn.

The temple tradition at the center of this book's inquiry is less easy to link directly to the specific use of terrestrial electricity explored by Burke and Halberg. Electroculture, the use of electrostatic charges to enhance plant growth directly, is another matter. If ancient temples were located in places where terrestrial electricity builds up relatively strong charges, as their research suggests, the lore surrounding the Temple of Solomon takes on a new and remarkable meaning. The lore cited in chapter 2, boiled down to its basics, claims that streams of water flowed out from a hidden spring underneath the Temple Mount to fertilize the countryside, and that the presence of the Temple caused changes in the weather near Jerusalem.

These claims make perfect sense if they're understood as fragmentary memories of the lost temple technology. The Jews who passed on these

---

106   Persinger and Lafreniere 1977; see also Burke and Halberg 2005, 25–28.

stories knew no more about the physical forces behind the temple tradition than any other ancient people; they knew, at most, that something flowed out from beneath the temple and brought unexpected fertility to fields along the routes of flow. They had no way of knowing that the currents they could track though their effects on greenery were currents of terrestrial electricity, not of water. To dwellers in a dry land, the thought that there must somehow be underground streams associated with the burgeoning of the fields would have been an obvious guess.

In the same way, a strong electrostatic charge built up on high ground attracts corresponding electrostatic charges in the atmosphere, making lightning more likely. Top the high ground with a stone building with plenty of metal on it, and two huge brass pillars in front of it, and the effect will be considerably amplified. In arid countries, thunderstorms are welcomed for the rain they bring—it's no accident that many of the thunder gods of cultures in the world's arid belts are also gods of fertility—and Jewish scholars in the centuries immediately following the destruction of the Temple, when folk memories of the change in the weather were still keen, would have had reason to note down the change in the frequency of storms.

It's entirely possible that some of the specific weather effects those scholars recorded, such as the torrential downpours in the time before the First Temple and the rains brought by the south wind during the era when the Temples stood, were the product of natural climate change rather than results of the temple technology. That's one of the drawbacks of research into the old synthetic sciences: it's often impossible to tell, without extensive research, when some detail included in the traditional lore is there for reasons of raw coincidence. In this case as in many others, and for reasons that will be explored later in this chapter, any attempt to carry out that research faces significant challenges.

Low-Frequency Infrared Radiation

More speculative but potentially just as relevant to the temple technology are the discoveries of entomologist Philip S. Callahan, whose pioneering studies of the effect of infrared radiation on insects and plants offer glimpses of an otherwise unexplored realm of ecological interactions. Callahan served as a radio technician during the Second World War before embarking on a scientific career studying insects, and his background in radio engineering enabled him to recognize something about night-flying moths that other researchers had missed: their antennae pick up radiation in the part of the electromagnetic spectrum where microwaves and infrared light overlap.[107]

To make sense of his discovery and its implications, it's necessary to know at least a little about electromagnetic waves. The crucial point is that the only difference between radio waves, microwaves, infrared light, visible light, ultraviolet light, X-rays, and gamma rays is their wavelengths—quite literally, the distance the waves cover between one peak and the next as they move past at the speed of light. Radio waves from an AM station can have wavelengths of half a mile; wavelengths from an FM station have a much shorter wavelength, around a yard; the waves a microwave oven uses to cook with have wavelengths around five inches, and so on up the scale to gamma rays, which have wavelengths less than a millionth of an inch. Wavelength has nothing to do with how far an electromagnetic wave can travel—a gamma ray with a wavelength of a half millionth of an inch can travel from one end of the galaxy to the other if it doesn't run into anything en route—but waves of different wavelengths have different effects on matter, including the matter that makes up living things.

The retinas of your eyes, for example, contain cells full of compounds that are sensitive to a narrow band of wavelengths of electromagnetic radiation—the wavelengths we call "light." Other wavelengths a little shorter or longer than light don't make the compounds in your retinas react, and so you can't see them. What Callahan discovered is that the antennae of many insects can sense electromagnetic radiation with wavelengths around a

---

107   Callahan's research on insect communication and the infrared spectrum has been published in more than two dozen papers in peer-reviewed journals; see Callahan 1975, 229–234 for a list of papers. I have cited his book for the general public here, as it is considerably more accessible to those readers who don't have access to a well-stocked research library.

thousandth of an inch long, on the border between microwave and infrared radiation. He showed that certain species of moths will come from miles around to an antenna radiating these wavelengths, and slight shifts in wavelengths change the way the moths behave—for example, when certain wavelengths are broadcast, male moths of a particular species frantically attempt to mate with the antenna.[108]

Further experiments showed that the interactions between insects and electromagnetic radiation in the microwave-infrared region of the spectrum are even more complex than Callahan originally guessed. Most insects, like most other living things, emit pheromones—chemical signals that can be smelled by other members of the same species and influence their behavior—and the pheromones of most species of moths, like those of many other insects, have a remarkable property: under certain conditions, they glow in very precise wavelengths in the microwave and infrared part of the spectrum.

A great many organic compounds will do the same thing at one wavelength or another. The laser in your computer's DVD drive works that way: a trickle of electricity flowing through a laser diode makes an organic compound in the diode give off light at a single frequency. What Callahan found is that under natural conditions, moth pheromones do exactly the same thing, absorbing energy from the background radiation of the night sky and releasing it in the form of infrared beacons at specific wavelengths that other moths can pick up with their antennae.[109]

Moth antennae can sense infrared and microwaves because they have very fine spines called sensilla, too small to be seen without a microscope, which are covered with a layer of wax. Their shapes and the wax coating allows them to function very efficiently as what physicists call dielectric antennas.[110] What Callahan noticed, as he pursued his research, is that insects are not the only living things that have wax-covered spines well suited to function

---

108   Callahan 1975, 69–90.

109   Ibid., 163–178.

110   Ibid., 96–100.

as dielectric antennas. Nearly all plants have equivalent spines, called tri-chomes, and nearly all plants emit aromatic compounds that absorb energy from various sources and release it in specific wavelengths at various points on the electromagnetic spectrum.

All this offers a glimpse into a dimension of nature that human beings, with our narrow senses, can never experience firsthand. Imagine a mead-ow at night. In place of darkness, the air is filled with shimmering veils of color—not just the narrow range of colors our eyes can see, but a spectrum many times broader, as complex and nuanced as scent. Every insect flying through the night air and every plant in and around the meadow is attuned to the dance of colors through their sensilla or trichomes, and each of them contributes to the spectacle by emitting pheromones and aromatic com-pounds that glow when stimulated by movement, sound, or the background radiation from the night sky. Millions of years of evolution have tuned each species to perceive those wavelengths that matter most to them. Each type of moth, for example, catches the gleam that means a fertile mate of its own species is near, and each species of plant reacts to the presence of parasites by producing protective compounds—and the parasites, in turn, sense the protective compounds and zero in on those plants that produce them least effectively.

Now imagine a structure set up to influence this unseen realm using a technology evolved over thousands of years of trial and error methods. A building is set up in a carefully chosen location where a strong charge of ter-restrial electricity builds up due to the shape of the terrain and the presence of conductivity discontinuities in the ground. Incense is burnt to fill the air inside the structure with a complex mix of volatile aromatic compounds that absorb certain infrared wavelengths and radiate others. Movement, sound, and background radiation—the same things that stimulate infrared emis-sions from insect pheromones and aromatic compounds from plants—pro-duce similar effects inside and around the structure, saturating the local envi-ronment with a distinctive set of infrared wavelengths. What effect would this have on nearby plants, insects, and ecosystems? Nobody knows, because the research that would be needed to answer these questions has never been done.

That, ultimately, is the central challenge that will have to be faced to make sense of the temple tradition. The research that would be needed to track down the effect at the heart of the temple technology is well within the reach of today's science. It would be a relatively straightforward research project, for example, to use currently available technology to check for unusual electrical charges and infrared radiation in and around surviving temples and temple ruins. The difficulty is that while this would be easy to do, it wouldn't be cheap; the equipment that would be necessary is complex and expensive, and many hours of fieldwork would be needed to do even the most elementary research. Nor is this a branch of study that the scientific mainstream is by and large interested in exploring, or funding.

The Dragon Project

Some measure of the challenges involved in any such research project can be found by paying attention to the one really sustained attempt to carry out a similar investigation, Britain's Dragon Project.[111] Beginning in 1977 under this label, a network of volunteers invested their own time and money to carry out a program of scientific research at a number of stone circles and other megalithic sites in northwestern Europe. Their focus differed significantly from the more orthodox archeological research at the same places: they were attempting to follow up on reports of puzzling energy effects surrounding these ancient sacred spaces.

There was (and is) no shortage of such reports. Hundreds, perhaps thousands, of people have experienced what felt like an electric shock when touching ancient standing stones. Strange magnetic phenomena, such as dramatic deflections of compasses, have been reported from these sites at least as often, and there were also scattered reports of unusual effects involving high-frequency sound waves and electromagnetic radiation around ancient sites. Anecdotal evidence of this kind proves nothing, at least in the eyes of

111   Devereux 1990 is an accessible survey of the Dragon Project's results.

contemporary science, but it very often points out subjects worth research-ing. That was exactly what happened in this case, with one difference: the institutions that have the funding, staff, and equipment to carry out the research weren't interested, and so the volunteer staff of the Dragon Project were left to pursue their investigation with their own resources.

The Project's findings were fascinating but ultimately inconclusive. Strange ultrasound phenomena, sharp swings in the terrestrial magnet-ic field, and unexplained interference with radio signals were all detected around the Rollright Stones, the site most closely studied by Dragon Project investigators.[112] Other sites, though they received much less attention due to lack of funding, also showed remarkably odd phenomena: there are several standing stones in Britain, for example, that reliably cause compass needles to swing round at sharp angles to their normal alignment.[113] Due to a lack of funds and staff, though, it was never possible to maintain a constant record of ultrasonic, magnetic, and electromagnetic effects—or even any one of these—at any one site for an extended period. Such research as the Project was able to carry out was constantly hampered by difficulties with equip-ment that a very modest research grant would have prevented.

Research grants, however, aren't generally available for investigations of the kind the Dragon Project was trying to carry out. Nor are they likely to be available for research into the temple technology this book attempts to sketch out. I've already mentioned the common modern prejudice against any suggestion that ancient peoples might have known anything that we don't. For a variety of complex historical reasons, the scientific community these days is even more deeply committed to that prejudice than public opin-ion in general. While that prejudice endures, a great many interesting and potentially useful legacies from the old synthetic sciences will go unnoticed or remain in the hands of the few people willing to ignore today's dogmas and explore the old sciences on their own terms.

---

112   Devereux 1990, 69–94.

113   See, for example, Devereux 1990, 96–99.

There is at least one other major difficulty that any such exploration will have to overcome, though. For all of its ancient and medieval history, the temple technology explored in this book has been closely associated with religion. One of the chief reasons why the scientific community these days is hostile to investigations like those carried out by the Dragon Project, not to mention those that would be necessary to confirm or challenge the hypothesis at the center of this book, is the widespread scientific antipathy to religion. Nor can religious institutions be expected to welcome such investigations with open arms, for reasons that unfold from the same unfortunate and unproductive rift between the sciences and the world's religious traditions.

Religion and the Temple Technology

One of the least useful consequences of the secularizing fever of modern times is the habit of trying to redefine religion as something other than what it is: the body of traditional teachings and practices through which human beings relate to those transcendent powers that we may as well call "divine." It's unfashionable these days to notice that a great many human beings have had, and continue to have, experiences that they describe as interactions with such powers by way of the teachings and practices just mentioned, and so scholars in a baker's dozen of disciplines and more have busied themselves coming up with other things that religion must "really" be about. Suggest that some dimension of religious practice has practical results in some other aspect of human life and it's tolerably common for people to take the practical results as the real point, purpose, and meaning of religion.

Thus it's probably necessary to say in so many words that the temple technology is not the real point, purpose, and meaning of religion. It's one set of design elements and practices, particularly beneficial to agricultural societies, that were adopted into the toolkit of certain religions and embodied in some religious buildings. The members of many other religions, and in some cases other branches of the same religions, have carried on equally devout religious lives without reference to the temple tradition.

Perhaps the best way to think of the temple technology in its religious context is to compare it to religious music or some similar art or craft. Many religions accompany their ceremonies with music of some sort, and in some, musical accompaniment is an essential part of worship. It's quite common for religious buildings to be adapted in various ways for the sake of music, whether this involves finding a place for an electric organ or a choir or the use of far-reaching design features that shape the acoustic properties of the entire building. At the same time, the fact that hymns are sung and organs played in many churches does not prove that churches exist to provide venues for musical performances.

In exactly the same sense, the traditions explored by this book have historically been put into practice in a religious context by priests, monks, and other religious professionals and incorporated into certain aspects of religious life. Nonetheless they remain, like religious music, one part of the much broader phenomenon that is religion as a whole. Just as certain aspects of religious music can be found across a remarkably broad range of faiths, in turn, the traditions studied in this book can be traced in a great many religious traditions of past and present, leaping straight across even the most profound differences in theology and practice; just as all religious music has to conform to the laws of acoustics, equally, the temple technology may be understood in various ways in different religious traditions but must ultimately conform to the laws of physics, biology, and ecology.

It's probably also necessary to discuss here the relationship between the temple technology and recent disputes in the field of religious architecture. Many of the ideas that have been fashionable among church architects over the last century or so have come in for heavy criticism of late, and it's fair to say that much of that criticism is well justified. During the course of the twentieth century, modernist and postmodernist architects threw out traditional principles of religious architecture as often as they could get away with it, and the resulting buildings were hailed as innovative, daring, exciting, and so on through the avant-garde's litany of praise.

Now, with the benefit of a few decades of hindsight and experience, other terms generally come to mind: dated, dismal, dysfunctional, and just plain ugly. Architectural critics such as Michael S. Rose have anatomized the failures and the implicit agendas that left so many congregations in America and Europe burdened with aesthetically bleak and spiritually barren structures that look more like high school gymnasiums or third-rate shopping malls than holy places.[114] In response, revivals of older and arguably more fitting traditions of religious building are under way in many faith communities.

All this is relevant to the state of religious architecture and of religion, more generally, in today's world. Once again, though, the temple tradition and the technology at its heart is something distinct from the issues these arguments have addressed. Many churches built after the temple technology dropped out of use are still beautiful and fitting places of worship. In the same way, a vast number of religious structures built for the use of faith communities that never encountered the temple tradition are still appropriate and beautiful sacred spaces.

The design features necessary to the functioning of the temple technology, in other words, are distinct from esthetic or religious fitness, though they're not contradictory to either of these things. The temple technology itself is something distinct from, though not opposed to, religion: a way of directing physical forces to improve crop yields that was once wielded by the clergy of many faiths but has been forgotten in modern times. While that technology seems to have been originally developed by priesthoods in ancient times and put to work in the context of religious buildings all through its heyday, it is an open question whether a revival of the temple tradition will take place under religious auspices or not—and that question will be decided, as it should be, by the clergy and congregations of each faith community.

---

114   Rose 2001 is a good example of this literature.

CHAPTER SEVEN

Location and Orientation

A mystery thus stands at the heart of the ancient temple technology. Exactly what set of physical effects causes the enhanced agricultural fertility that temple-building cultures expected from their temples remains unknown for the time being. It might have been something related to terrestrial electricity, or to the complex realm of ecological interactions between plants, insects, volatile organic compounds, and low-frequency infrared radiation. It might also have been something else entirely, and until a great deal of research is done, the question remains open.

There is at least one other way of exploring the subject, though. The builders of ancient temples and medieval churches didn't have access to electrostatic voltmeters, infrared-sensitive CCD cameras, and the like. They got the effects they did with hand tools and natural materials. Whether or not the cause of the temple effect can be identified, at least some of the methods that were used to generate the effect can be learned from the remains of the temple tradition itself. The next four chapters will sum up some of what can be learned from that source.

One of the basic rules of the old temple tradition is that not every place was suited for a temple. Legends in every culture that participated in the tradition tell of holy places whose sites were revealed directly by God or the gods through all the usual means of religious folklore: here a god or an angel is said to have pointed out the proper location to an awed worshipper; there the oxen pulling a cart full of sacred relics suddenly set out across country for three days and nights without stopping until they reached the proper place, from which they could not be budged once they arrived, and so on. Read any collection of local folklore in a place where the temple tradition flourished and you're likely to find plenty of stories of the same kind.

The historical accuracy of these tales is beside the point. What they communicate in the usual symbolic language of myth and folktale is that the locations proper for important temples or churches are chosen by something other than mere human preference or convenience. The exact details of the ancient art of siting temples for maximum effect are mostly lost at this point, but it may be possible to recover some of them by a careful study of surviving sacred places, as discussed below.

Once the temple site is determined, its groundplan needs to be laid out in the right orientation. This is one of the few places where surviving documents, existing sacred places, and the fragmentary legacies embodied in Freemasonry all point toward the same body of knowledge with enough exactness that the principles can be worked out in detail. This, too, will be discussed below.

Finally, temples and churches built to make use of the effect at the heart of the temple tradition tend to have a distinctive set of surroundings, which can be found in one form or another across the entire geographical reach of the tradition. Here, too, it's possible to put together enough knowledge from the temples that survive in different regions that a fairly complete idea of the principles can be obtained, and the last two sections of this chapter will explore what can be known or guessed about this aspect of the temple technology.

One crucial point to keep in mind as we proceed is that not every temple or church—not even among those built in times and places where the temple tradition was in full flower—made use of the full toolkit of the secret technology. The buildings that embodied the tradition were all primarily places of worship, and in places where people wanted and expected to worship but the necessary location, orientation, and surroundings weren't available, a temple or a church went in anyway and served the needs of local worshippers without having any of the functions explored in the previous chapter.

This was especially true of temples and churches constructed in cities, where whatever rules of urban planning and land ownership might be in force took precedence over the secret knowledge of initiates and master builders. On the other hand, in rural areas where land was readily available, and especially at traditional holy places, as well as monasteries and other establishments that could be located wherever conditions were right, the full panoply of the temple tradition could be, and was, employed to good effect.

Location

One thing that makes it hard to work out the principles behind temple siting is that ideas concerning the proper location for temples vary significantly from one branch of the tradition to another. In Egypt, where the tradition seems to have begun, the standard practice was to build temples on low ground, close to the water table—the standard ritual for founding a temple included digging a trench in the ground until water began to seep into it. Many Egyptian temples are thus close to the Nile, with the red cliffs of the desert looming above them in the distance.

Hindu temples also tend to be on low ground near rivers, lakes, and other bodies of water. As noted in an earlier chapter, the traditional rules for siting and laying out a Hindu temple have been carefully preserved and are still used today. Much of what is in these documents, known collectively as Shilpa Shastras, belongs to later chapters of this book, but each set of rules includes precise instructions for locating an appropriate site, including a simple but effective form of soil testing: seeds of various plants are sown on a proposed temple site and their growth observed through the following season.

The Temple of Jerusalem, as we have seen, was built according to a completely different principle: located on high ground, so far above the water table that complex underground structures had to be built to get water to the temple for ritual and practical needs. Temples in ancient Greece, similarly, were placed on high ground far more often than not. Ancient writings on the subject suggest that the reason was to make the temple visible from the countryside around it, partly as an encouragement to piety, partly for the sake of the sheer visual spectacle—even today the ruins of a colonnaded Greek temple against the Mediterranean sky are a stunning sight, and when the temples were in their prime and the white marble had not yet darkened with age,[115] it must have been even more so. Still, there are good reasons to think that the choice may have been motivated by reasons unrelated to aesthetics.

The later forms of the tradition tended to combine these two approaches to location in various ways. Japan and Northern Europe, both of which inherited the temple tradition not much more than a millennium ago, are cases in point. It's common in Shinto temples and medieval Christian churches alike to find both high ground and low ground used in a single religious complex. At the Fushimi Inari shrine on the southern outskirts of Kyoto, for example, the main shrine complex is at the foot of a sacred mountain, while the peak of the mountain—a thirty-minute hike along a path marked by hundreds of torii gates—is equally sacred and marked by a cairn of stones.[116] Similarly, on the other side of Eurasia, the old pilgrimage center at Glastonbury in England features the ruins of the great abbey church on low ground not far from the foot of Glastonbury Tor, the highest hill for many miles around, while the peak of the Tor is occupied by the ruins of a chapel of St. Michael.

In the light of the hypothesis proposed in the previous chapter, all these variations make perfect sense. Ancient and medieval peoples, trying to make use of the effect at the heart of the temple tradition, had to contend with a galaxy of variables they had no way to measure. The electrical conductivity of the soil and stone underlying any given temple site was among these, and such variables as chemical composition and water content of the differ-

---

115   Spawforth 2006, 48–49.
116   Nelson 1996, 25–27.

ent layers beneath the surface play a role in determining this. Depending on local conditions and the fine details of temple design and practice, heights, low-lying places, or a mix of the two might get better results in any given region.

There may also be an unexpected meaning to the claim mentioned above that many especially sacred sites were revealed by deities or the like. Michael Persinger's research, as noted in chapter 6, shows that magnetic fields can put some people into states of unordinary consciousness, with visionary experiences a common result. A place that had an unusually strong geomagnetic field would tend to produce similar effects in people who were sensitive to it, and the results filtered through the religious traditions and folk beliefs of the time would readily take the form of miracle stories. The role of such miracle stories in the traditional location of many temples and churches suggests that geomagnetism may well be one of the forces involved in the temple technology.

Orientation

One of the most consistent elements of the temple tradition is the orientation of the structure toward a specific direction, most commonly a point on the eastern skyline where the sun rises at least once over the course of the year. The word "orientation," in fact, is a relic of this custom, as it literally means facing eastward: *orient*-ation. It can be traced all the way back to the fifth millennium BCE when the first long barrows of megalithic Britain were built; most of these have their entrances facing the rising sun.[117]

The same principle governs the majority of temples in the tradition, but not all. Most ancient Greek temples, for example, were oriented with their doors toward the sunrise, and the exact date of the sunrise in question was of as much importance as it would be in the later Christian tradition. Even within a single temple complex, different temples might be oriented toward the sunrise corresponding to a variety of festival dates. The temples and other structures atop the Acropolis in Athens, for example, have different

---

117   North 1996, 23 and 28–29.

orientations; the Erechtheum faces due east, but the Parthenon faces around ten degrees north of east, so that the sunrise shone through the Parthenon doors on the image of Athena at the time of the Panathenaic festival, which was around the middle of August in our calendar.[118] Greek temples that faced some direction other than east generally had some way to let the light of the rising sun into the sanctuary. The temple of Apollo at Bassai, for example, has its door facing north, but an opening in the eastern wall allows sunlight to enter the temple's innermost chamber at dawn.[119]

A similar blend of common themes with individual variations can be found in India and wherever else Hindu temples have been built. Most Hindu mandira are aligned on an east-west axis with the main entrance facing due east, just like the Temple of Solomon, so that the light of the rising sun at or near the equinoxes can shine through the entrance arches and doorways toward the garbhagrha, the innermost shrine of the deity.[120] Most of the Shilpa Shastras, the documents which give rules for the construction of Hindu temples, include methods to determine the cardinal directions using the moving shadow of a vertical pole over the course of a day; from the intersection of the north-south and east-west axes, and using cords and stakes to trace lines on the ground, the rest of the temple design unfolds with mathematical exactness.

There are several exceptions to this habit of sunrise orientation. The temple complex of Angkor Wat in Cambodia, as already noted, followed the Hindu version of the temple tradition closely, but its main entrance faces west, not east. The underground temples of Mithras, the god of one of the mystery cults celebrated in Roman times, also had their altars in the east and their doors in the west. The most important exception, though, is found in Christianity.

Christian churches from earliest times were oriented with the doors to the west and the altar in the east. One of the earliest Christian churches to

---

118   Connelly 2014, 231.
119   Spawforth 2006, 51–52.
120   Huyler 1999, 131.

be discovered, for example, is a house in the city of Dura Europos in Syria, which was refitted in 232 CE for use as a church. The centerline of the room for worship, which is a long and relatively narrow space much like later churches, is canted about 10 degrees north of due east, and the altar is on a dais in the eastern end of the room.[121] The variation away from due east, as we'll see, corresponds to a significant tradition that the early Christian church appears to have borrowed from their Pagan neighbors.

Once Christian congregations were able to build churches on a less hole-and-corner scale than the Dura Europos house-church, the same rule nearly always applied: the worship space was considerably longer than it was wide, the sanctuary with the altar was in the east, and the main doors were in the west. The one important variation from this before modern times took place in the immediate aftermath of the Edict of Milan, which legalized the practice of Christianity in the Roman Empire. A handful of important churches built under the Emperor Constantine's personal patronage in Rome between 313 and 327 CE—in particular, the church of St. John Lateran and the original church of St. Peter in what is now the Vatican—were built with their doors facing east and the altar in the west, like Pagan temples.[122] When St. John Lateran and St. Peter's were rebuilt in the Renaissance, the old orientation was kept. No one seems to know why.

Some other fourth-century churches in Italy and North Africa did the same thing, following the standard Pagan temple alignment in place of what was elsewhere becoming the standard Christian orientation. So did a church in Silchester, in the far-off province of Britannia, which was built around the same time.[123] The reasons for this variation are unknown. Whatever the purpose might have been, it did not catch on, and churches built after Constantine's time were consistently built with altars in the east and doors in the west. That habit remained standard all across the Christian world until after the Reformation.

---

121   Jones et al. 1992, 531.
122   McClendon 2005, 5–7.
123   Scullard 1979, 167–69.

As with Greek temples, though, Christian churches might or might not be aligned due east to due west. In western Europe in the Middle Ages, certainly, it was customary to set out the centerline of the church by marking the point of sunrise on the feast day of the saint to which the church was to be dedicated. The master builder hired to build a church dedicated to St. Michael would thus start laying out the structure on Michaelmas, September 29; if it was dedicated to the Virgin Mary, the laying out might begin on the Annunciation, March 25, or one of the many other days assigned to the Virgin in the Christian calendar, and so on.

The method that was used to trace out the centerline of the new church was simple and effective and has left traces in today's Freemasonry. Before sunrise on the chosen day, the master builder and two assistants—deacons, in modern Masonic practice—went to the building site, which had previously been cleared of vegetation and rubbish down to bare soil. Both deacons carried tall straight staffs. One deacon would go to the eastern edge of the site and stand where the sanctuary of the church would be located, holding the staff upright and well away from his body. The other would go some distance to the west and wait with his staff held in the same way while the master builder went farther to the west and waited.

When the sun rose, the master builder would direct the deacon standing in the west to move one way or the other until the two staffs were lined up on the sunrise like the two ends of a gunsight; both staffs were then pushed into the soil to mark the spots; stakes were driven into the spots marked by the staffs, a cord was stretched between them to mark the centerline, and the rest of the laying-out process followed, using stakes and cords on the bare soil. To this day, the two deacons in a Masonic lodge carry tall staffs as they go about their ritual duties. The senior deacon, whose seat is in the east, has a staff tipped with the image of the sun. The junior deacon, who sits in the west, has a staff tipped with the image of the crescent moon—a classic bit of medieval symbolism, since the crescent moon follows the sun across the sky, matching its movements to the movement of the sun the way the junior deacon on a medieval building site moved his staff to follow the location of the sunrise.

The traditional Masonic diagram of a point in a circle, flanked by two parallel lines, is another reflection of this custom. As noted back in chapter 1, the two parallel lines are held to represent St. John the Baptist and St. John the Evangelist; there's been an immense amount of speculation about why these two saints were chosen, but the reason is instantly clear once it's remembered that the feast day of St. John the Baptist is June 24 and the feast day of St. John the Evangelist is December 27, and these are therefore stand-ins for the two solstices. At the Northern Hemisphere's summer solstice, the sun rises and sets farther north on the horizon than any other day; at the Northern Hemisphere's winter solstice, it rises and sets farthest south; in between these days, it cycles back and forth from one extreme to the other.

A medieval master builder who wanted to instruct apprentices and fellow crafts in the movements of the sun could do far worse than to sit them down in front of the diagram of the point in the circle and use it as a teaching aid. That's very likely why, as Masonic tradition has it, that diagram may be found in every regular and well-governed lodge: it was essential for the proper training of apprentices in the days of the operative Craft.

Surroundings

The surroundings of the temple were also part of the old technology. Whenever possible, a temple was surrounded by an open space marked off by a wall or some other simple barrier. The size of the open space varied dramatically depending on local custom and land use. In some countries, a temple in a crowded urban setting might have only a narrow walkway around it, while in others, room was found somehow for a larger space. In all cases, access to the sacred precinct was restricted, and certain people, objects, and activities were forbidden within the barrier that surrounded the temple.

The habit of setting apart an open area for religious purposes, as already mentioned, dates back from long before the emergence of the temple tradition itself. Temple builders adopted the same custom to their uses, but there seems to be more going on here than the simple persistence of a habit. The area around most traditional temples is not simply empty space; far more often than not it has a specific relationship to the natural ecosystem of the region.

The standard practice, in fact, was to fill the space around a temple with greenery of one kind or another. In desert areas, this obviously had to be a planted and irrigated garden; the great temple complexes of Egypt, for example, were commonly surrounded with orchards of fruit trees.[124] Elsewhere, the greenery surrounding temples might be cultivated or wild. Temples of Athena in rural Greece were commonly surrounded by olive orchards, since the olive was sacred to that goddess, and temples of Zeus often had oak groves around them because the oak was Zeus's sacred tree, but many other Greek temples stood within groves of whatever trees happened to grow there. The laws of most Greek city-states protected such groves, whether cultivated or wild, by making harvesting wood from them an act of sacrilege, and ordaining that any animal who was allowed to graze in the temple's temenos became the property of the deity and was delivered promptly to its new owner by way of sacrifice.

The same variation between cultivated and wild vegetation is found in Shinto practice today. Urban shrines are very often surrounded by elaborate gardens in which trees play a major role. Out in the countryside, though, it's more common to see largely untouched woodland around a shrine, and the areas are larger. The sacred precincts of some very old and famous rural shrines include entire mountains which have been set aside for the kami and can be put to no secular use, while even the smallest neighborhood shrines, the sort that have no resident priest and are opened for ceremonial use once a year for a local festival, generally have a tiny greenbelt around them.

The transformation of the temple tradition by Christianity adopted the same principle but, in keeping with the logic of the great religious revolution, put it to a use that the Pagans must have found deeply disturbing. Old churches, like temples, routinely have a wall setting them apart from the sur-

---

124   Hamblin and Seely 2007, 12.

rounding area, and a sacred space—the churchyard—given over to greenery and sacred activities. The Christian churchyard, though, is primarily a place for the dead. As we've already seen, in most of the old temple traditions, bringing a corpse into a temple precinct was considered an act of profound impiety in the older religions; in Christianity, it became standard practice.

Nonetheless, the same broad principles still applied. The churchyards of medieval churches across western Europe routinely have trees planted in them, like the trees that surrounded Greek temples and still frame Shinto shrines. Yew was the standard tree in old English churchyards, for example, while other countries had their own preferences. Like the sacred precincts of temples, churchyards were off limits for certain persons, objects, and activities—in the Middle Ages, grazing animals on a churchyard was as unthinkable as doing the same thing in the temenos of a Greek temple a thousand years earlier, though the convenient habit of sacrificing animals that were allowed to stray there was misplaced during the religious revolution that replaced Apollo and Athena with Christ.

Linear Paths

The most controversial dimension of temple surroundings is also, curiously enough, one of the best documented. In most areas reached by the temple tradition, it was common practice to set out a series of ceremonial paths extending out from the temple in various directions. The most important of these paths usually extended from the main entrance of the temple for some distance—very often to a river, a seashore, or some other geographical boundary.

Most of these paths ran dead straight, though there were variations here as elsewhere between different cultures, and the way they were marked was equally varied. In ancient Greece, for example, the paths were originally marked by cairns—that is, heaps of stones to which each passerby added an additional rock for good fortune—and later by herms, stone pillars shaped like erect penises or the bearded face of the god Hermes and an erect penis carved on them.[125] In medieval Europe, the network of paths that extend-ed out from churches were known as church roads, corpse roads, or death roads—the latter two named because the bodies of the dead were tradition-ally carried along them to the churchyard—and were marked by stone cross-es at intervals.[126]

In Japan, as discussed earlier, the *seichu* or straight line leading away from the front entrance of a Shinto shrine is a sacred space marked at intervals by torii, open wooden gateways of traditional design, and may extend for some miles to the nearest river or the seashore. In prehistoric Europe, finally, paths of the same type seem to have been marked out by standing stones and oth-er megalithic remains—and in that last detail lies the reason why this subject has been mired in controversy for most of a century.

In 1922 a Herefordshire businessman and amateur antiquarian named Alfred Watkins proposed a theory to account for the distribution of ancient trackways, standing stones, and earthworks across much of England.[127] He had noticed and documented at great length that many ancient sites lie on straight lines extending across country, connected in some cases by footpaths or roads of great antiquity on the same alignments. His thesis was that these were the remains of a network of trackways—leys, he called them, having encountered that name-element over and over again in place names along the old straight tracks—that had been laid out in Britain long before the arrival of the Romans, and that travelers on these trackways had used the standing stones and earthworks as landmarks to find their way through what was then densely forested country.

It was a reasonable suggestion. Tribal peoples around the world find their way across the countryside by similar means. The Australian aborigines, to cite only one example, guide their journeys through the forbidding landscape of the Outback using traditional chants orienting them to visual landmarks

---

125   Burkert 1985, 156.

126   Devereux 2003, 25–36.

127   Watkins 1925 is a more complete statement of the theory.

that stand out against the horizon.[128] For that matter, the same approach to land navigation sees plenty of use today—"See that steeple?" says the country dweller; "just you keep on going toward it 'til you come to the bridge, and there you are." Despite the plausibility of the theory and the extensive body of data Watkins and, later, his friends and supporters amassed, though, British archeologists rejected the idea out of hand, and they still do, generally without taking the time to learn the first thing about what it is they're denouncing.

To understand this reaction, it's necessary to know a little about the intellectual climate of the time when Watkins's theory first appeared. During the years between the two World Wars, scientific archeology in Britain was still clawing its way to respectability. The idea of archeology as an academic discipline was new; universities had only just begun to set up programs in the subject, and professors of long-established disciplines such as history and philology were fond of looking down their noses at archeologists who spent their time grubbing in the mud. The resulting pressure toward respectability led archeologists to distance themselves as far as possible from the amateur antiquarianism from which their discipline had emerged not so long before. A theory about the past from a bona fide amateur antiquarian of the old school was thus guaranteed a hostile reception from archeologists, especially if it challenged the then-fashionable insistence that the people of pre-Roman Britain must have been howling, skin-clad savages barely out of the caves.

Once Watkins's theory had been angrily dismissed as nonsense by leading archeologists at the time, in turn, a phenomenon well known to sociologists guaranteed that it would receive no second hearing. Communities define themselves by what they reject, and once something has been assigned that outcast role, a tremendous weight of collective inertia has to be overcome to get the community to reassess it. Scholarly disciplines function as communities, with all the usual community dynamics. This is why, for example, once a theory is embraced by a scientific discipline, no matter how much evidence piles up against it, it rarely gets discarded completely until all its

---

128   Devereux 2003, 21–24.

original supporters are dead.[129] Rejection of Watkins's theory thus became something close to a badge of membership among the fraternity of British archeologists. While they didn't actually place their hands on a copy of the latest issue of *Archaeology* and swear never to admit a believer in leys to their sacred lodge, they might as well have done so.

To be fair to the archeologists, Watkins's theory attracted more than its share of strange ideas and wild speculations over the years, and from the 1960s to the present, it's been as much these latter as the original theory that has drawn their ire. It's only been in recent decades that enough research has been done to sort through the confusion and figure out what exactly stands behind the controversy and the florid mythmaking.[130]

Two points stand out from the confusion. The first is that there is unquestionably a system of old straight tracks oriented toward sacred places across much of Britain, and it dates from the Middle Ages. The church roads, corpse roads, or death roads already mentioned were found in most rural English parishes; precise equivalents also existed in the Netherlands, where they were called *doodwegen* (death roads), and in large parts of Germany, where *kirchwegen* (church roads) is the usual term.[131] The network survives only in fragments, but enough of it and of records concerning it have survived to make it clear that these straight tracks once crisscrossed much of northwestern Europe, and some of the alignments Watkins and his followers found likely came from this source.

The second point is that there are just enough traces of a similar arrangement dating from much earlier times to make Watkins's theory worth a second look. It was standard practice in many parts of Europe for Christian churches to be built on the sites of old Pagan sanctuaries, and so it's entirely plausible that some straight tracks may have passed in the same way from the old religion straight to the new. In areas where this didn't happen, though, the alignments of old tracks, standing stones, and earthworks Watkins

---

129   Kuhn 1970, 151.

130   See Devereux 1993 and Pennick and Devereux 1989 for good surveys of this research.

131   Devereux 2003 is the standard book on these.

discovered very often center on sites of prehistoric sanctity—Stonehenge, for example, is a point on which several well-documented leys converge.

All this is relevant to the thesis of this book because some lines of evidence suggest that the straight tracks and alignments extending out from temples and churches may have had some function distinct from their role as ways for people, or corpses, to move to and from the sacred center. A remarkable body of traditional folklore clusters around the church roads and their equivalents. In Ireland, nearly identical folk traditions focus on the paths of the *sidhe*—the ancient inhabitants of the island, now associated with burial mounds and other prehistoric sites; the stone crosses, stone cairns, and standing stones that trace out such routes in different parts of the world are, as we've seen, associated in tradition with fertility and good fortune. It's possible that straight routes extending outward from a temple using the secret temple technology serve some role in communicating the fertilizing effect to the surrounding fields. A great deal of further research, though, will be needed to find out if there's anything to this suggestion.

CHAPTER EIGHT

Sacred Geometry

The claim that ancient and medieval sacred structures have some special connection to geometry, something that relates to factors considerably more important than the mere practical requirements of the builder's trade, goes back a very long way. The term "sacred geometry" has come to be used for the ideas underlying these claims. As we'll see for at least two sets of sacred structures—the Gothic churches and cathedrals of medieval Europe and the Hindu temples of India—the concept of a special sacred geometry rests on solid documentation, and for several others—the temples of ancient Egypt and Greece among them—there is at least some evidence to support the claim.

Unfortunately, like so much of the spiritual legacy of the past, the entire subject of sacred geometry has become mired in a swamp of vague assertions, unprovable claims, and fragments of alternative pop culture tossed into the mix more or less at random. These days, if you pick a book at random that has the words "sacred geometry" in the title, you're as likely as not to end up reading a nearly random assortment of over-the-top conspiracy theories, speculations about lost continents, and wild claims about the profound spiritual powers of this or that fairly ordinary geometrical construction. There are some excellent books on sacred geometry in print as well,[132] to be sure, but the modern literature on the subject is a decidedly mixed bag.

Even among the better books on the subject, consensus on the geometrical patterns that underlie any given sacred structure of the past is often lacking. The Parthenon in Athens, to cite the most blatant example, has been analyzed by sacred geometers repeatedly for well over a century. No two of the resulting analyses have found the same underlying geometrical pattern.[133] The human mind's habit of pattern recognition is strong enough that it's possible to overlay almost any geometrical pattern over the Parthenon, or any other sacred structure you care to name, and get something that looks like a match. Skeptics have accordingly rejected the entire notion of a sacred geometry underlying the great churches and temples of the past.

A great deal of the difficulty here comes from the fact that geometry can have at least four roles in a religious structure. To begin with, of course, a structure of any size or complexity will need to be built with an eye toward at least the most basic forms of geometry to ensure that walls run straight, doors fit on their hinges, and ceilings stay up. Additionally, the human eye finds geometrical regularity pleasing, and so geometrical designs very often get used to make structures that are esthetically appealing. We can call these two functions "practical geometry" and "esthetic geometry," respectively, and assign them to the traditional Masonic principles of strength and beauty.

A third aspect of geometry in architecture, which we can call "symbolic geometry," comes into play when certain forms or patterns are assigned symbolic meaning within a given cultural and religious context. In Europe during the Middle Ages, for example, most churches were built in the shape of a cross, to reflect the symbolism that made the sacrament of the Mass a reenactment of the self-sacrifice of Christ; threefold patterns symbolized the Trinity, fourfold patterns the four apostles, and so on through an entire

---

132   Among the better examples are Critchlow 1970, Ghyka 1977, Lawlor 1982, Lundy 2002, and Michell 2009.

133   See Padovan 1999, 80–98.

vocabulary of geometrical symbolism. This dimension of the old operative Masonry may be assigned to the traditional Masonic principle of wisdom.

Finally, the central thesis of this book suggests that there is also a fourth, concealed dimension of geometry that relates to the biological effects on which practitioners of the temple tradition focused their efforts. For reasons that will be explained later in this chapter, we can call this aspect "resonant geometry." Before we can tease this fourth geometrical function out of the tangle, though, a more basic question needs to be asked and answered. Is there any evidence that geometry played any role in the sacred structures that belong to the temple tradition?

Sacred Geometry in the Hindu Tradition

In point of fact, there's a great deal of such evidence. The Hindu tradition is particularly rich in geometrical symbolism, for example. Throughout India and wherever else Hindu religious teachings spread, geometry plays an obvious and central role in temple design. The vast temple complex of Angkor Wat in Cambodia is among the best documented examples here. As already noted, its geometries and proportions were worked out so precisely that a modern scholar, Eleanor Mannikka, has been able to decode the symbolism of the entire structure from its measurements.[134]

There is also documentary evidence along the same lines contained in the Shilpa Shastras, the traditional Hindu manuals for temple construction. These give detailed geometrical procedures for laying out the ground plan of a Hindu mandira and developing the rest of the structure from the ground plan—the same broad procedure as was used by the master masons of medieval Europe, though the details differ. The following procedure from the *Manasara Shilpa Shastra*, one of the few Shilpa Shastras that has been discussed in detail in any Western language, provides a clear look at the geometrical basis underlying one very important manifestation of the temple tradition.[135]

---

134   Mannikka 1996.

135   I have based the following on the discussion in Critchlow 1982, 29–32.

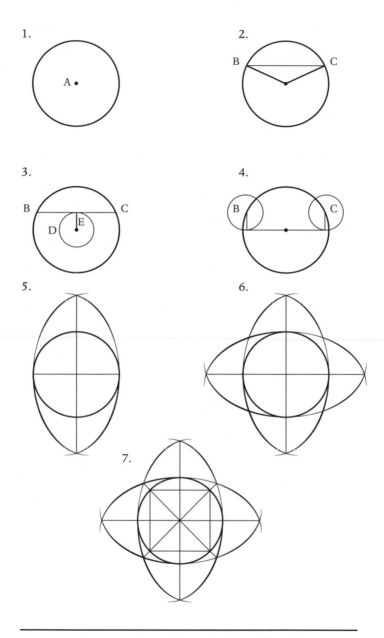

SHILPA SHASTRA GEOMETRIES

To lay out a mandira following the instructions of the Manasara Shilpa Shastra, once the site has been chosen and leveled, a vertical pole is erected in the center of the site, point A, and a circle is drawn around the pole with a radius twice the pole's height, using a rope looped around the central pole as compass; see figure 1. Over the course of a day, the master builder observes the shadow cast by the pole as it moves from west to east and marks the two points, B and C, where the end of the shadow touches the surrounding circle: a line connecting these two points will run exactly east and west; see figure 2. The builder then uses a rope looped around the pole to draw a smaller circle, measuring the distance from the pole to the east-west line BC; see figure 3. Using circles with the same radius around points B and C, the circle is divided into equal northern and southern halves by a second east-west line; see figure 4.

Next, with a rope equal in length to the circle's diameter, two arcs are drawn, one from each of the ends of the second east-west line. A straight line connecting the points where the two arcs cross divides the circle in half with a north-south line; see figure 5. The same operation is then done again, using the points where the north-south line crosses the original circle as centers for the two arcs; see figure 6. When this is finished, there are eight points where arcs intersect each other, and lines connecting them divide the circle exactly into eight; see figure 7. The intersection of the dividing lines and the circles define the corners of a square and the midpoints of the square's sides, providing the floorplan of the garbhagrha, the Holy of Holies at the heart of a Hindu temple. From there, further arcs and lines expand outward to define the other parts of the temple, and proportions derived from the geometries already laid out are then applied to all other parts of the temple.

The Manasara Shilpa Shastra is a crucial piece of evidence for two reasons. The first is that it demonstrates how at least one major architectural tradition with ties to the temple technology explored in this book did in fact use geometry as a core element of design. The other is that despite the huge cultural differences between classical India and medieval Europe, the geometrical principles that guide temple construction according to the

Manasara Shilpa Shastra are identical to one of the two main systems used by the master builders of the Gothic era in the European Middle Ages.

Sacred Geometry in the Gothic Tradition

There is a great deal of surviving information about the role of geometry in another major branch of the temple tradition—the Gothic churches and cathedrals of the high Middle Ages. We know that geometry had a central role in Gothic architecture because the builders and designers of the Gothic era say so repeatedly in their treatises on the subject.[136] Examples abound: the thirteenth-century French master builder Villard de Honnecourt filled his surviving sketchbooks with elaborate geometrical analyses of churches and building details; Matthias Roriczer, the fifteenth-century master mason who built Regensburg Cathedral, set out the geometrical way of designing buildings "according to true measure," and there are also the well-documented conferences held between master builders working on the Cathedral of Milan in 1391 where everyone present treated geometry as the foundation of architecture.

The same link between geometry and architecture remains central to the rituals and traditional teachings of Freemasonry, which equate the craft of building with the art of geometry. The traditional secrecy of the modern Masonic craft, for that matter, was once used to conceal the geometrical methods of building design. Thus the Regensburg ordinances of 1459—a set of rules established by an assembly of German master builders—barred any master from passing on certain geometrical secrets to anyone but a qualified candidate for mastership.[137]

The medieval master builder used geometry to make all the different parts of a church fit together according to a common scheme of proportions. There were two basic schemes used in Gothic architecture. One called *ad quadratum* ("by the square") took the ratio between a square and its diagonal as its basic module, as shown in the diagram of Gothic geometries on

---

136   The following examples are from Simson 1962, 13–20.
137   Hiscock 2000, 186–195.

page 142—the same geometry that appears in the *Manasara Shilpa Shastra*. In arithmetic terms, the side and diagonal of a square are related by the ratio of one to the square root of two, which is written 1:$\sqrt{2}$, and works out to 1:1.41427 . . . . Like π, the ratio between a circle's diameter and its circumference, $\sqrt{2}$ in decimal terms has an infinite number of digits. If the height or width of a square is equal to 1, the square's diagonal is equal to $\sqrt{2}$, and this relationship was used over and over again to provide a building with its proportions.

How would this work out in practice? Once the orientation was determined by the process described in an earlier chapter, a medieval European master builder working in the ad quadratum system would start by laying out a series of squares on the bare ground of the building site using ropes and wooden stakes. One square, for example, might be the floorplan of the sanctuary of the church; another of the same size might mark the floor of the crossing; two short rectangles, one on each side of the crossing, might be the same length as the original square but $1/\sqrt{2}$ as wide, setting out the north and south transepts; and then the floorplan of the church west of the crossing would likely be a rectangle as wide as the original square but $\sqrt{2}$ times as long. Meanwhile the heights of the walls would also be based on the original square, multiplied or divided one or more times by $\sqrt{2}$, so that every measure from the largest to the smallest was related to all the other measures by some multiple of the square root of two.

The other proportional scheme used by medieval master builders, the *ad triangulum* ("by the triangle") system, did the same thing with a different ratio: one to the square root of three, 1:$\sqrt{3}$, which works out to 1:1.73205 ... and so on for an infinite number of digits. Where the ad quadratum system unfolds from the square, the ad triangulum system unfolds from the circle: more specifically from two circles drawn so that the center of each one is on the circumference of the other, forming the figure traditionally known as the *vesica piscis* ("vessel of the fish"). If the distance between the centers of the two circles is equal to 1, as shown in the diagram on page 142, the distance between the places where the two circles intersect—the "points"

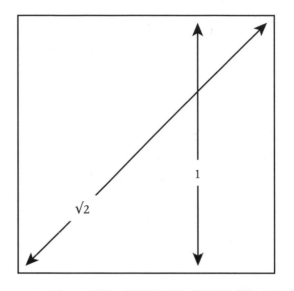

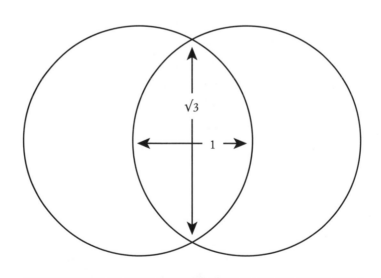

GOTHIC GEOMETRIES

of the vesica—is equal to √3. Connect the centers of the two circles and one point of the vesica with straight lines, and you have a perfect equilateral triangle, thus the name of the system.

In laying out a church using the ad triangulum system, a medieval master builder would start by laying out a series of overlapping circles on the bare ground of the worksite, again using ropes and stakes. Just as with the ad quadratum church, the various parts of the structure would be proportioned to one another using one or more multiples of the governing ratio—in this case, 1:√3—so that every measurement from the smallest to the largest was tied together in a single proportional scheme. Much of the beauty of Gothic architecture comes from the subtle visual harmony this practice creates in a building.

Both the ad quadratum and ad triangulum systems have an additional feature that makes them very well suited to architecture in an age that cared about proportions and harmony. Starting from either system, it's easy to pass by way of a series of simple geometrical constructions to the famous Golden Section, which geometers denote with the Greek letter Phi, Φ. In numerical terms, Φ equals 1:1.61803 ... and so on, once again, for an infinite number of digits. Psychologists have found in repeated experiments that shapes based on the Golden Section look more pleasing and balanced to the human eye than those based on any other ratio. Medieval architects may not have had access to modern psychological journals, but they knew all about the Golden Section and wove it into their architecture.

Chartres Cathedral, generally considered the greatest example of early Gothic architecture, is a case in point. The original groundplan of Chartres, which was derived from an earlier cathedral on the same site, follows the ad quadratum system. On that solid traditional basis, however, the master builder of Chartres—like so many of the great architects of the Middle Ages, his name has been lost to history—raised a structure that is permeated with Golden Section proportions.[138] The proportions of the entire structure combines √2 and Φ relationships in a bravura display of geometrical mastery

---

138   See Greene 1989 for a reconstruction, based on archeological data, of this process.

that contributes mightily to the pervasive sense of harmony and unity that strikes so many visitors to Chartres.

Despite their similarities, the division between the ad quadratum and ad triangulum systems ran deep. Masons' guilds in the Middle Ages used one or the other—never both. The conferences between master builders at the building of Milan Cathedral mentioned above took place because that construction project was large enough to attract masons from southern Germany as well as northern Italy, including partisans of both systems. Scholars today have traced out some of the extensive body of symbolism, philosophy, and traditional lore that went with each system, but there may have been more to it than that; we simply don't know.

One thing that is well known, though, is that the Scottish masons' guilds that gave rise to modern speculative Freemasonry were firmly on the ad quadratum side of the great divide. Thus the master of a modern Masonic lodge wears a stonemason's square around his neck, rather than a compass, and squares and right angles of various kinds play important roles in Masonic symbolism. The 47th proposition of Euclid, another bit of geometry that has a significant role in the symbolism of today's Freemasonry, also comes out of the ad quadratum system; this proposition is better known as the Pythagorean theorem, and medieval master builders who followed the ad quadratum method used it constantly as a way of tracing right angles on the bare ground of the building site. If you know the Pythagorean theorem, you can use a knotted cord or any other measuring device to get square corners on any scale you need.

Geometries of Resonance

That the Gothic churches of the Middle Ages were designed on a geometrical framework, then, is not in doubt. One of the major questions that has to be faced in tracing the temple tradition through history is just how far back the standard Gothic geometries went. The Temple of Solomon, as we've seen, had a much simpler geometry: the *debir* (Holy of Holies) was a cube thirty feet on a side, and the *heikal* (main hall) outside it was formed of two such cubes set end to end. Though any number of attempts have been made to find complicated schemes of the ad quadratum or ad triangulum sort in ancient temples, few of these are convincing; most other ancient temples seem to have had proportional schemes that were just as simple as the one that governed Solomon's famous structure.

What's more, the great Gothic cathedrals didn't always follow out their own geometry exactly. Chartres Cathedral, arguably the greatest of the early Gothic structures, is a case in point. Its design, as noted above, displays an extraordinary mastery of medieval sacred geometry—and yet the three bays (spaces between pillars) on the west end of the nave are squeezed together by a total of some eight feet.[139] Why? None of the theories discussing Chartres's geometry have managed to explain this.

If, as this book proposes, the design of buildings in the temple tradition had a practical as well as a symbolic significance, the question is easy to answer. As noted in chapter 6, at least one of the functions of ancient temples and medieval churches seems to have been related to some form of electromagnetic energy, and as we'll see, that function may have been triggered into activity by sound waves. All waves—electromagnetic, sonic, or any other kind—are affected by the phenomenon known as resonance, and the effects of resonance provide a straightforward explanation to the role of geometry, and of the curious variations from geometry just mentioned, in the temple tradition.

One easy way to experience resonance in action is to have two tuning forks that sound the same note. If you strike one of them on a hard surface so that it chimes, and then hold the other one to your ear, you'll find that the unstruck tuning fork is chiming as well. Why? Each note represents a particular wavelength of sound, and a tuning fork is designed so that it vibrates at exactly that note; as the sound waves from the struck tuning fork beat against the unstruck one, they set it vibrating at the same rate, and so it gives off its note.

---

139   Simson 1962, 207.

Electromagnetic waves have exactly the same effect, though you need something a little more elaborate than a tuning fork to demonstrate it. When you tune a radio receiver to the wavelength of a station you want to listen to, what you're doing is changing the "note" at which electricity goes back and forth in a circuit inside the receiver, and the radio waves coming in from the antenna have exactly the same effect on the tuned circuit that sound waves from one tuning fork have on another of the same note. The tuned circuit resonates with radio waves of the wavelength you want, and the signal carried by those waves is then picked up by other circuits, amplified, and sent to your loudspeaker or headphones for you to hear.

Among amateur-radio hobbyists, working with resonance becomes a fine art. If you want to talk with someone on the other side of the world using an amateur radio rig, you need to make sure that the antenna over which you're broadcasting your signal is in resonance with the radio-frequency alternating current you're pumping into it, so that as much as possible of the energy in the transmitter output goes zooming out into the atmosphere. The goal is what's called a standing wave: that is, each pulse of electricity reaches the base of the antenna, zips to the far end, and comes back to the base, taking just long enough for the whole trip that it arrives at the base at the exact moment that the next pulse hits. An antenna trimmed just right, so that you get what's called a standing wave ratio of 1:1—that is, a perfect standing wave—can take a relatively weak signal and take it astonishing distances; the further from 1:1 your standing wave ratio is, the less efficiently your antenna broadcasts your signal.

All this may seem unrelated to the architecture of Chartres Cathedral or the temple tradition in general, but there may be a direct connection. Making an antenna get as close as possible to a 1:1 standing wave ratio can't be done entirely by formula because radio waves are affected by a galaxy of subtle factors, not all of which can be worked out in advance. Amateur radio operators who make their own antennas thus measure them out by formula, leaving some extra at the far end, and then test the result, cutting off a fraction of an inch at a time until the standing-wave meter hits 1:1.

My thesis is that this is exactly what led the builders of Chartres to lop off, in effect, eight feet from the west end of the nave of the cathedral. Like all the Gothic cathedrals, Chartres was built in sections, and the west end of the nave was the last part to be completed; long before it was done, the master builder in charge would have been able to work out—quite possibly using direct methods of the kind mentioned in chapter 6—the point at which the nave should end so as to establish a standing wave, or something like one, in the nave of the cathedral.

As a way of building a resonance chamber, Gothic architecture is extremely complex, and the great Gothic cathedrals—with their pillars, pointed arches, and side chapels—add further layers of complexity. The Temple of Solomon, by contrast, was a simple cubical structure, and so its builders would have had no difficulty calculating the resonance and making the structure fit a straightforward system of measurements. Most ancient temples followed this simpler and more functional approach. The complexities of the Gothic churches were profoundly shaped by the theological and symbolic ideas of the age that created them, which marked a crucial point in the process where those ideas obscured and then replaced the traditional rules of thumb that made the effect at the heart of the temple tradition work.

The Twilight of Sacred Geometry

Modern people routinely have a difficult time of it when they try to understand the ideas of the Middle Ages. A core reason for the trouble is the way that medieval thinkers so constantly fused things that most people today see as naturally separate. The first three kinds of geometry discussed at the beginning of this chapter provide a good example of this habit of fusion. In the writings of the master builders and Catholic theologians of the Gothic era, the practical, esthetic, and symbolic sides of geometry weren't three different things. In the medieval way of thinking, it was the fact that geometry symbolized divine realities that caused a geometrically designed church to be beautiful and sturdy.

This didn't always work in practice. The history of the high Middle Ages is punctuated with accounts of beautifully designed Gothic churches that collapsed and had to be rebuilt to a more solid design because the geometries that made them beautiful didn't necessarily make them stay up. Over the course of the Gothic era, the increasing technical mastery of the builders made such disasters less common, but the entire medieval way of thought made it harder to tease out the competing requirements of wisdom, beauty, and strength from a geometrical construction—or from its architectural expression.

The same thing will have been even more true of the fourth function, the resonant geometry needed to generate the effects at the heart of the temple tradition. That tradition was a secret teaching known to certain people—primarily, as we'll see, members of monastic orders and the guilds of operative masons who worked closely with them in the construction of monastery churches. Those who knew the secret knew that it worked, but they had no way of knowing how or why it worked—just that churches built in certain places, oriented in certain directions, using certain geometries, built out of certain materials, and in which certain ceremonial actions were done reliably got certain effects on local agriculture that to medieval minds must have looked like miracles performed by the saints or by God Himself. To see the resonant geometry that helped produce those effects as something distinct from the practical, esthetic, and symbolic aspects of geometry was a leap considerably greater than most medieval thinkers were capable of making.

Several pieces of evidence suggest, in fact, that the medieval monks and master builders who knew about the temple tradition followed it strictly by rote, without any understanding of the principles behind it. The most important of these is the way that so many famous churches of the Middle Ages, when they were destroyed by fire—a constant risk when candles and incense played important roles in religious services and flammable materials had a significant part in every kind of building—were rebuilt on exactly the same ground plan as before, no matter what oddities of design this required.

One classic example was Glastonbury Abbey, one of the great monastic centers of medieval England. Glastonbury's great fire took place in 1184, and when the monks got to work rebuilding the abbey church, the growth of the abbey required a much bigger church than the one that had burned. The monks duly laid out a great church, but they built it to the east of the site of the old church and then built a Lady Chapel on the original site to exactly the same proportions as the little Anglo-Saxon church that had served the first monks of Glastonbury. The result was a Lady Chapel sitting incongruously off by itself to the west of the main abbey church until a later generation of monks connected the two with a porch. All this suggests that the monks of Glastonbury were in no way confident of their ability to design a new structure that would have the same effect as the old one, and so they had to copy the structure they knew as exactly as possible in order to get the desired result.

A set of rules of thumb recalled by rote can last for many centuries, but it has its vulnerabilities, and one of the worst of these comes with the arrival of a new generation that thinks, incorrectly, that it understands the underlying principles. That eventually played an important role in obscuring and then erasing the geometries of the temple tradition. With the coming of the Renaissance, the old customs that left building design to the master builders of the guilds of operative masons came to an end over much of Europe. Instead, architects trained in the new secular, humanistic ideas of the era took over the design of churches.

For such men, the practical and esthetic sides of geometry were the ones that mattered, with a little symbolism thrown in here and there if the client wanted it. Impatient of the old rule-of-thumb traditions and unaware that anything but superstition might be behind them, they built churches that are among the masterpieces of European architecture but lack the effects of the older tradition. At the same time, the elimination or transformation of the old monastic traditions as a result of drastic changes in European society closed off the other route by which the temple tradition and its distinctive geometries could have come down intact to the modern world. Obscure references to the powers of geometry in a variety of ancient and medieval writings, and the curious scraps of geometry in modern Freemasonry, were the only fragments left of the geometrical side of the tradition.

CHAPTER NINE

Structure and Substance

The temple tradition was never a static thing. The architectural forms and material substances that gave the tradition its embodiments, in particular, changed over time. This was partly due to shifts in ideology and cultural fashions, but it also depended in part on the varying results of differences in design. During the centuries when temples were expected to have an effect on the harvest, when a newly built or renovated temple helped bring about more than the usual increase in agricultural fertility, its distinctive features were more likely to be copied. Where innovations failed to bring the usual results, on the other hand, they were unlikely to be repeated.

Evolutionary biologists have a concept called "convergent evolution." This is the process by which creatures from very different ancestral lineages end up looking and acting similar to one another because pressures from their environment favor development along similar lines. Porpoises are a good example. The ancestors of porpoises fifty or sixty million years ago were furry, hooved mammals related to pigs and deer. Once their descendants took to the water, though, the requirements for survival and success favored each mutation that made them a little more like fish. Generation by generation, those with slightly smoother skin and slightly flatter paws tended to do better than their shaggier and blunter-pawed rivals, until after millions of years the descendants of this process resemble fish so closely that many people have trouble telling the difference.

Cultures don't evolve in exactly the same way that species do, but a form of convergent evolution shows up in the history of cultures as well. Medieval Europe and medieval Japan, for example, had no contact with one another, but the two societies developed feudal systems that were remarkably similar to one another. European nobles and Japanese daimyo, European knights and Japanese samurai, the European code of chivalry and the Japanese code of bushido: these had functions that parallel each other the way the flippers of porpoises parallel the fins of fish. Behind these remarkable similarities stood profound parallels in the technological and historical background. Just as living in the ocean makes fins and flippers more useful than legs, living in the wake of political and economic collapse in a society with the metalworking capacity to produce effective armor makes feudalism more useful than other options.

In exactly the same way, variants of the temple tradition in distant societies followed remarkably similar trajectories of development. India and Europe, for example, received the secret technology at nearly the same time; the first stone temples in India were built in the fifth century CE,[140] only a short time after Christian missionaries began establishing churches across western Europe. Early Indian temples and early Christian churches also followed similar plans derived from the Greek version of the temple tradition: a rectangular hall for worship, with the focus of ritual and ceremony at one end.

From that starting point, in turn, both traditions evolved in remarkably parallel ways. Both moved the core ritual activities into a secluded space—in a Hindu temple, the garbhagrha; in a medieval Christian church, the sanctuary—while the worshippers remained in an equivalent of the original rectangular hall—the mandapa in India, the nave in Europe. Both established secondary worship spaces around the outside of the central holy space. Most

---

140   Wangu 2009, 96.

striking of all, both traditions transformed the shape of their sacred places by raising a massive vertical structure with a sharp point at its zenith. The shikhara in India and the steeple in Europe have no obvious relevance to the religious dimension of temple or church; they play only the most minor roles in ritual and belief; considered from the ordinary perspective of the theologian or the architectural historian, the parallel evolution of structures so similar in such radically different religious traditions can only be a puzzle.

Bring the temple tradition into the equation, by contrast, and the puzzle is easily solved. The steeple and shikhara can be seen, in fact, as late equivalents of that very ancient element of the tradition, the standing stone. The influence that concentrates in a single tall mass of the right kind of stone seems to concentrate just as effectively in a more artificial construction of the same general shape and orientation, built of the proper materials. Just as fins and flippers make sense in the context of ocean life, tall stone masses make sense in the context of trying to exploit the effect at the heart of the temple technology, and different cultures using the technology were likely to discover this independently if they had the means to do so.

It's clear, to continue the example already mentioned, that steeples and shikharas had completely different origins. In India, the shikhara seems to have emerged as a straightforward elaboration of the temple roof. In Christian Europe, by contrast, bell towers in the Mediterranean region and the mysterious round towers that flanked monastic churches in early medieval Ireland, which will be discussed in more detail in chapter 11, seem to have been the original form of what later became the steeple. It was only after the original rectangular floor plan of churches gave way to the classic medieval cross-shaped design did it occur to anyone to put a steeple over the church itself, and even then the process didn't happen overnight; instead, master builders experimented with a raised roof over the crossing, then with a low tower, then with a taller one, until finally the familiar steeple took its standard place over the crossing.

By the time the Middle Ages reached their zenith, tall steeples rising to dramatic points were a common feature of church design: "the spear borne before the chalice" of the Grail romances. Since the relation of the design to the mysteries of the temple tradition was a trade secret of masons' guilds and, as we'll see in a later chapter, also seems to have had certain connections with heretical religious ideas, the steeple passed for an ordinary design feature—and it survived as an ordinary design feature, relocated more or less randomly in the church building, long after the hidden technology underlying the temple tradition was lost.

The Evolution of Temple Design

As shown in previous chapters, temples working with the temple tradition have taken a galaxy of different forms. The core architectural requirements of the temple technology seem to be relatively simple; any enclosed space of certain proportions that is made of the right materials will apparently have some effect if located in an appropriate place and aligned more or less to the compass directions. All the changes rung on the temple form through the millennia are essentially refinements on that basic recipe.

Certain refinements, though, tend to appear repeatedly in different branches of the temple tradition, in ways that converge on one another. The European steeple and Hindu shikhara are examples of this process, but they're by no means the only ones. Another even more striking example is the emergence of a square or rectangular inner sanctuary at one end of the main structure of the building in most of the cultural forms taken by the temple tradition. Egyptian temples of the New Kingdom and later periods nearly all had this feature; so, of course, did the Temple of Solomon and its successors; so did Christian churches in medieval Europe; so do Hindu temples; and so do Shinto shrines.

What makes this convergence especially fascinating is that only one of these traditions started out with any kind of inner sanctuary. The Jews are the exception. The oldest form of worship space recorded in their tradition, the Tabernacle of the nomadic Israelite tribes, had a sanctuary in the same position of the Holy of Holies of the later temple. According to their own traditions, though, the Israelites lived for many generations in Egypt, and as shown in an earlier chapter, the basic design of the Tabernacle and Temple of Solomon alike was very close to the standard Egyptian temple design during the New Kingdom, the period during which the Exodus traditionally took place.

By contrast, Egyptian temples, Christian churches, Hindu temples, and Shinto shrines didn't start out with a sanctuary. Instead, each form of temple gradually evolved one over a period of centuries. The history of the sanctuary in Christian churches is particularly instructive, since churches started out in Roman times as very simple rectangular buildings with the altar for the celebration of the Mass on the eastern end. From there, as the temple tradition worked its way into church architecture, the interior of the church was gradually divided more and more strictly into spaces for clergy and laity.

In the Catholic West, the main body of medieval churches was divided into three parts—the nave, where the congregation sat; the choir, where the clergy sat; and the sanctuary, where the high altar was located and the actual ceremony of the Mass took place. Over time, the division between the nave and the choir became more and more marked. By the twelfth century, as already noted, a barrier called the rood screen made it impossible for the congregation to see any part of the ritual at the high altar. Many cathedrals of the Gothic era have the choir and sanctuary walled off on all four sides, an enclosed church within a church. Historians of liturgy like to suggest that this was driven by an exaggerated sense of the terrifying nature of the sacrifice of the Mass,[141] but as noted in chapter 4, no such terror seemed to interfere with the regular performance of the Mass in full view of the congregation in the many chapels found in every medieval church of any size.

In the Orthodox East, a process of convergent evolution reached the same endpoint, though it took longer to get there. By the early medieval period, the sanctuaries of Orthodox churches were separated from the rest of the church by a low screen, but it was not until the sixteenth century that an equivalent of the rood screen, the iconostasis, came into use in Orthodox churches. Like the rood screen, the iconostasis makes it impossible for the

---

141   See, for example, Jones et al. 1992, 64.

congregation to see the ritual of the Mass. Despite the obvious inconveniences of this practice, it remains in place in most Orthodox churches to this day.

The rood screen did not have a similar longevity. As we'll see in a subsequent chapter, the temple tradition seems to have been thrown out of Christian churches in the Western world at the time of the Reformation. In Protestant and Catholic countries alike, rood screens were torn down, sanctuaries were opened to the sight of the congregation, and rituals were drastically revised and standardized. Protestant churches either cut back the ritual dimension of worship or got rid of it altogether, refocusing church services on preaching, scripture readings, and the singing of hymns.

In many denominations, the entire legacy of Christian church architecture was thrown out wholesale by the reformers, resulting in church interiors that were reduced to rows of seats facing a pulpit and exteriors that were plain peak-roofed boxes with a steeple tacked on somewhere for show. The changes were accelerated by the transformation of architecture from a craft practiced by master builders following traditional patterns to a fine art practiced by architects who were celebrated for their originality rather than their understanding of the lore handed down from the past.

Catholic church architecture also changed dramatically, though not so completely as in the Protestant denominations. Catholic churches built after the Reformation era did away with the rood screen and the enclosure around the choir and sanctuary, moved the pulpit into a much more central position, and reshaped church interiors as well as the rituals performed there to make preaching more central than it had been. Here again, as professional architects replaced master builders, what had once been the components of an ancient technology got redefined as design elements and rearranged to suit the whims of architects and patrons. That process reached its logical conclusion in the twentieth century with the creation of churches that resemble high school gymnasiums, shopping malls, opera houses, and the like, rather than sacred spaces of any description.[142]

---

142   Rose 2001 is a useful discussion.

Paramagnetism and Diamagnetism

The lore of the old master builders was not limited to issues of design, however, and among the things that got misplaced with the coming of professional architects was a knowledge of building materials that went beyond the purely practical. The old builders' guilds, it bears remembering, took care of everything that happened on or around a building site. The master builder in charge of a medieval building project, like his equivalent in many other temple-building societies, started out his career hauling stones and mortar, sharpening tools, and doing other menial labor of the kind assigned to apprentices; as his knowledge and technical skill developed, he was assigned increasingly complex tasks, and so every detail of the building process was known to him from personal experience.

The proper selection of materials was among the things master builders learned on their way up the ranks. A competent mason, in particular, had to know the difference between freestone—the kind of fine-grained stone that can be used for carvings—and the various other types of stone that might be used in a building project, from the rubble in foundations to the slate that went on the roof. The term "Freemason" itself is a contraction of the phrase "freestone mason," a stonemason sufficiently skilled to be trusted to work in freestone, while "cowan"—an old term used by Freemasons for those who are not members of the Craft—originally meant the sort of untrained day laborer who could only handle less demanding kinds of stonework.

All this is relevant to the temple tradition because structures built to make use of the old temple technology are made, almost without exception, from materials that have a little-known physical property in common: the property of paramagnetism. While a great deal of research needs to be done here, as elsewhere, it's possible that paramagnetism represents one of the keys to the entire temple tradition.

Most people these days, if they remember anything at all from the science classes they took in school, know that some materials are attracted to magnets and others aren't. Iron is the most famous magnetic material—if you take a magnet of any strength and hold it over a small iron object, the iron will defy gravity and leap upward to attach itself to the magnet. Try the same thing with a nonmagnetic material such as lead, and nothing happens.

Most science classes never get around to mentioning paramagnetism and its opposite, diamagnetism, which is unfortunate. A paramagnetic material is slightly attracted to a magnet—not enough to leap into the air but enough to register on sensitive measuring equipment and concentrate magnetic lines of force in itself. A diamagnetic material, on the other hand, is repelled by a magnet—again, not enough to jump away from a magnet but enough to register on measuring equipment and bend lines of magnetic force away from itself.

Most solid materials are paramagnetic, at least to some degree, unless they contain plenty of water. Water is strongly diamagnetic, and anything that has a lot of water in it shares in that property. Your body, for example, is diamagnetic, because it's 70 percent water. A living tree is diamagnetic, and so is a tree trunk that's just been cut down. When it's been stripped of its bark, sawed into lumber, and dried, on the other hand, its wood is paramagnetic.

The materials used in temples and churches tend to be very strongly paramagnetic. The same thing is true, curiously enough, of the old standing stones of Britain and northwestern Europe—for example, the stones of Stonehenge—and of stones at a great many other ancient sacred sites. Investigators for the Dragon Project discussed in chapter 6 noticed that many standing stones in Britain will reliably deflect compass needles.[143] While the investigators apparently had not encountered the concept of paramagnetism, and so did not reference it in their reports, this is exactly what would be expected from strongly paramagnetic stone.

What makes this intriguing from the standpoint of this book's inquiry is that the presence of paramagnetic materials has a remarkable effect on plant growth. Those effects have been replicated repeatedly by investigators of this phenomenon, but as with the Dragon Project discussed in chapter 6—or, for that matter, the network of leys mentioned in chapter 7—these findings have been roundly ignored by scientists, even in those fields that might be

---

143   Devereux 1990, 96–99.

expected to have an interest in them. Research into the biological effects of paramagnetism has thus been published almost entirely in periodicals and books in the alternative science field, where they routinely rub elbows with strange speculations of various kinds.[144]

Readers who wish to test the effects of paramagnetism themselves are encouraged to perform the simple experiment described on the sidebar on page 161.[145] Remarkably, seeds grown on the north side of something that's strongly paramagnetic—for example, a cylinder like the one in the experiment—tend to grow more rapidly and vigorously than those on the south side. Why? Nobody knows; as with so many other factors related to the temple tradition, the experiments that would be necessary to figure out the cause haven't been done.

Whatever the precise mechanism, strongly paramagnetic substances seem to have an important role in the temple technology, as well as some of the more ancient methods of increasing fertility that appear to have fed into the temple tradition. The powerful paramagnetism of ancient standing stones has already been mentioned, but an even older form of construction combined paramagnetic and diamagnetic materials in a specific, carefully arranged way.

A Megalithic Technology?

The structures in question are the long barrows of Neolithic northwestern Europe, the oldest surviving monumental structures in the world. The oldest known long barrows were built around 4300 BCE, and they continued to be built until 3000 BCE or so—around the time that the first ditches and earthen banks were excavated at Stonehenge.[146] While archeologists today identify them as burial sites, the number of human bones found in long barrows is tiny compared to the total number of people who died in the vicinity during their active lifespans, and it's at least possible that the role of the

---

144   See, for example, Callahan 2001 and Davis and Rawls 1980.
145   This experiment is adapted from Callahan 2001, 26–37.
146   Souden 1997, 18–19.

skeletal remains in long barrows had more in common with the relics of the saints treasured in medieval churches than with the churchyards outside.

In constructing a barrow, diamagnetic and paramagnetic substances were arranged in one or more layers. In the simplest barrows, a central chamber was made either of large stones or of massive wooden posts, and this was surrounded by heaped flints, blocks of chalk, or other strongly paramagnetic materials. Atop this went a thick layer of turf, which absorbs and holds water in damp climates and is thus strongly diamagnetic.[147]

In more elaborate barrows, several layers of stone and turf were stacked atop one another. The famous mound at Newgrange in Ireland is a classic example. It was made out of neatly stacked layers of stone, turf, and soil, some 300 feet in diameter and 36 feet high. The presence of water in the turf and soil is clearly shown by the design of the inner chamber; the stones forming the corbel vault of the chamber all tilt slightly outward, so that water drains off sideways rather than dripping into the central chamber.[148] The exact reasons for the layering await rediscovery by careful experimentation, but similar patterns can be found in many other earth mounds of the megalithic era, including the famous Silbury Hill in England, near the great Avebury stone circle.

Silbury Hill, the largest ancient artificial mound in Europe, is worth careful attention in its own right. As far as anyone knows, it was never used for burials or associated with the cult of the dead, but it remains a huge testimony to the importance that it must have had to the people of its time. It stands 130 feet above the surrounding landscape, and contains an impressive 12.5 million cubic feet of chalk, clay, soil, and gravel. When it was complete, an artificial lake was constructed around its base by damming a local stream. It must have been a stunning site when it was new. The white chalk sides would have been blindingly bright against the green Wessex countryside and reflected in the still water of the surrounding lake.

---

147   North 1996, 18.
148   O'Brien and Harbison 1996, 15–16.

For all its impressive scale, Silbury Hill is by no means unique in design. A similar flat-topped mound without a burial rises thirty-six feet above the hill of Knocknarea in Sligo,[149] and mounds of the same basic form with no burials inside them are scattered over much of northwestern Europe. Their purpose likely involved the effects of terrestrial electricity described in chapter 6. In their research into those effects, John Burke and Kaj Halberg carried out experiments at Silbury Hill and found strong electric charges there of a kind well suited to the electron seed treatment method they explored.[150] Similar experiments carried out atop other mounds in Britain got even more dramatic bursts of electricity—in one case sufficient to fry the internal circuitry of an electrostatic voltmeter.[151]

These traces of a megalithic technology are relevant to the temple tradition in more than one sense. On the one hand, they demonstrate that ancient peoples working with the synthetic sciences of their own culture seem to have been able to harness an assortment of natural energies to enhance the fertility of their fields—the same thesis that lies at the heart of the argument of this book. The electrical and paramagnetic technologies of the megalithic age have a more direct relationship to the temple tradition, though. The areas of northwestern Europe in which megaliths and barrows are found also played a crucial role in the rediscovery of the temple technology in early medieval Europe—and an equally important role in transmitting the last fragments of the ancient knowledge to the guilds that became modern Freemasonry. These points will be explored in a later chapter.

---

149   O'Brien and Harbison 1996, 12–13.
150   Burke and Halberg 2005, 123–127.
151   Ibid., 122.

An Experiment with Paramagnetism

Materials needed:

- an index card
- transparent tape
- spray adhesive
- powdered limestone, powdered flowerpot clay, or good potting soil (these are all strongly paramagnetic substances)
- a flowerpot full of potting soil
- seeds of any plant
- a low wattage grow-lamp
- a magnetic compass, or any other means of identifying north

Start by bending the index card into a cylinder and taping the ends together. Prepare the limestone, flowerpot clay, or potting soil—it should be as fine a powder as you can get—then coat the cylinder with the spray adhesive and roll it in the paramagnetic powder. It may take up to three coats of spray adhesive to get all of the cylinder coated with powder. Let each layer of powder dry before spraying on more adhesive, and when the cylinder is entirely coated, let the whole assembly dry for at least twenty-four hours.

While it dries, take the flowerpot full of potting soil, moisten the soil well, and plant a ring of seeds close to the outside of the pot. Once the cylinder is dry, put it upright in the center of the flowerpot, as shown in the diagram. Push it down a short distance into the soil so that it stays in place.

Once this is done, wait for the seeds to sprout, watering the soil in the pot whenever it begins to dry out. Don't splash water on the cylinder, as potting soil only has a strong paramagnetic effect when it's dry! Once the first seedling has appeared, place the flowerpot directly under the grow-lamp, and leave the lamp on for twelve hours each day—this is to make sure that all the seedlings get the same amount of light. Note the compass directions, and see if the seedlings on one side of the paramagnetic cylinder grow more vigorously than those on the other.

index card bent and taped into
cylinder, sprayed with adhesive,
and coated with paramagnetic
substance

seeds in soil

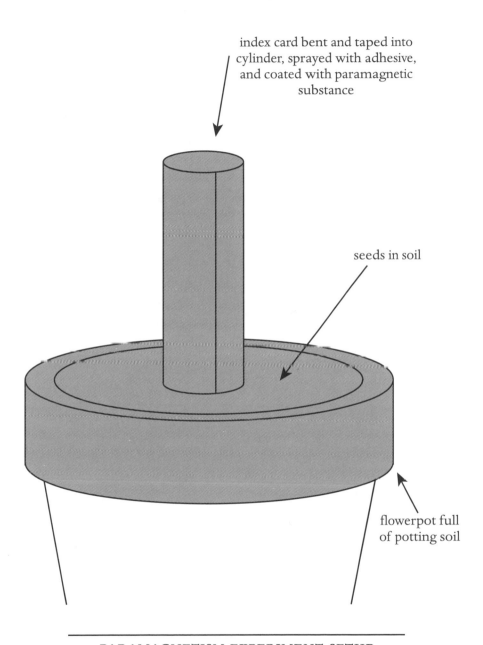

flowerpot full
of potting soil

PARAMAGNETISM EXPERIMENT SETUP

CHAPTER TEN

Rite and Ceremony

There are plenty of challenges that have to be faced in attempting to reconstruct the lost technology at the center of the temple tradition, but among the most difficult of them center on what was done inside and around the temples after they were built. Architecture, after all, is durable. Researchers today can visit a Shinto shrine or Hindu temple, a church that was built during the Middle Ages, or the remains of a Greek or Egyptian sacred building and look at the physical structure in detail. In many cases, the researchers can go on to study documents on the design and construction of these buildings and learn a great deal about why they have the location, orientation, structure, and surroundings that they do.

The activities that go on inside a temple are another matter because many of them leave no enduring physical traces, and even when there are such traces, it's rarely possible to work back from them to the ideas and actions behind them. A team of archeologists thousands of years from now who happened to dig up the ruins of a long-abandoned Masonic lodge building, for example, might be able to figure out the design and layout of the lodge in quite some detail. If the closets of ritual gear happened to be preserved intact, the archeologists might also end up with a good idea of the material culture of a Masonic lodge. The words and actions of the rituals that were enacted in the lodge, though, would be lost forever unless some written disclosure happened to survive intact—and even then, depending on the cultural changes that took place in the interval, the meanings that give those words and actions their value to millions of Freemasons today might be impossible to reconstruct.

With the temple tradition, things are at least as challenging. It's not hard to compare temple designs from the various temple-building cultures with one another, extract the elements that clearly had to do with local religious ideas, and work out the common factors that probably played a central role in making the secret technology work. It's a good deal harder to do the same thing with rituals and other activities performed within temples because in many cases the details have been partly or completely lost. Of the rituals performed in ancient Egyptian temples, we know the general outline of the daily temple service, as well as some of the hymns and prayers, and we have some information about some of the many other ceremonies that took place; everything else is gone forever.[152] We know even less about the rituals performed in ancient Greek temples and almost nothing about the ceremonies of the Greek Mysteries.

Even in those traditions that embraced the temple tradition and have survived to the present, such as Hinduism and Shinto, there have been huge losses. No religion is changeless, and societies hammered by drastic social change routinely have to discard many things in the struggle to maintain those parts of their heritage that matter most. India and Japan have both been through wrenching change in recent centuries, and the indigenous religions of both countries have had to struggle for survival more than once. It's entirely possible that oral traditions or old documents in various corners of one or both nations include information that would answer the questions posed by this book, but nothing of this kind has yet been published—and of course that raises another important issue. It's far from certain that the

---

152   Ritner 1993 is a good survey of the surviving information.

keepers of such knowledge would be interested in letting it get into the hands of the profane.

Beyond this, another difficulty rises, and it's one that has bedeviled the whole project of this book at each step of the way. Temples are primarily places where people who belong to a given religion go for the purpose of worship. Anything else that a temple does, any other activity that may help shape the patterns of design and ceremony there, is secondary to that overriding concern. If the core hypothesis of this book is true, and a secret technology for enhancing agricultural fertility helped shape the temple traditions of a number of Old World civilizations, that doesn't reduce temples to fertility generators. It means that temples had this role among many others—and it was a secondary role to the use of the temple as a place of worship.

Thus it's foolish to assume that anything done in a temple must have been done as part of the activation of the secret technology. Much of what was done in every temple of every kind was done in order to worship the sacred powers whose presence was sought and sensed there. Many other things were done to fulfill the various roles that religious institutions have in the communities that support them. A small number of things—perhaps a very small number—were done in order to awaken the effect at the heart of the temple tradition and direct its benefits outward to the fields, and these things will have been understood as religious acts, part of the priestly work of bringing down divine blessings on the human community. Teasing those few threads out of the complex fabric of temple ritual is no easy task.

One detail of the history of the temple tradition, though, offers at least some small hint of guidance. Over the millennia that the tradition existed, it was adapted for use in a remarkably diverse array of cultures with their own distinctive religious traditions and institutions. The theologies and religious outlook of ancient Egypt have very little in common with those of medieval western Europe, say, and even between more closely related traditions such as those of ancient Greece and medieval and modern India, for example, the differences are still substantial. When common practices appear across those boundaries, especially when the practices can be shown to have arrived at the same time as the temple tradition, it's worth exploring the possibility that those practices may be part of the secret technology this book attempts to explore.

Incense

One simple but important example is the use of incense in religious ritual. The idea of burning sweet-scented vegetable gums as an offering to deities may seem obvious, but there are many cultures around the world that don't do this, and some major religions—Islam is an example—where the use of incense in religious ceremony is strictly forbidden. The early Christian church was just as hostile toward the use of incense because of its role in Pagan worship. Around the same time that Christian churches started incorporating the same linear architectural structure found in ancient Egyptian temples, though, incense came into use, and clouds of carefully formulated incense still have an important role in Christian worship in the more traditional denominations.

Incense is important here because, as suggested in chapter 6, volatile aromatic compounds may be a core ingredient of the technology at the heart of the temple tradition. Under the right circumstances, such compounds emit electromagnetic waves on the border between microwave and infrared radiation, in a part of the spectrum to which plants and insects are both highly sensitive. If, as the evidence already surveyed suggests, temples functioned among other things as resonance chambers for some physical effect capable of making aromatic compounds fluoresce in those frequencies, burning the right sort of incense would be an effective way to get the aromatic compounds in the air so the effect could take place.

Shinto is the outlier here, but its use of an alternate means to the same end offers some confirmation of support to this thesis. As already mentioned, Japanese culture assigns some things to Shinto and others to Buddhism, and incense is one of the things that goes on the Buddhist side of the division; incense of various kinds is burnt in large quantities in Buddhist ceremonies but it is not found in Shinto practice. In a traditional Shinto shrine, however, it's not necessary to burn vegetable gums to fill the air with resinous odors. The *hinoki* or Japanese cypress, the tree that provides most of the lumber for a shrine built in the traditional style, is a powerfully fragrant tree; for at least a century after the building of a shrine, the air within the inner rooms is saturated with the scent of hinoki.[153] The ancient custom of rebuilding Shinto shrines after a fixed number of years was partly a matter of ensuring adequate purity for the dwelling places of the kami, but it may also have had the side effect of keeping the air inside the jinja sufficiently loaded with evaporated resin for one of the effects at the heart of the temple tradition to function. It's not impossible that the cedar wood that featured so substantially in the structure of the Temple of Solomon had a similar role.

Chanting

Another possible element of the temple technology is the use of chanting with prolonged vowel tones. Religious traditions around the world use various forms of speech and song to offer praise to their deities, and chants with vowels stretched out at length are found in faiths that show no sign of contact with the temple tradition, but it may not be accidental that this specific form of chanting is found wherever the classic temple tradition seems to have flourished.

According to the ancient Greek author Demetrius, Egyptian priests chanted hymns to their gods that consisted solely of a sequence of vowels.[154] Scraps of surviving information suggest that the same practice found its way into Greek religion as well,[155] and certainly there's ample documentary evidence that vowel tones in various sequences were chanted as part of Gnostic rituals in the first centuries of the Common Era.[156]

Also relevant is a curious set of divine names and holy syllables found over much of the ancient Mediterranean world, which are composed of vowels

---

153   Nelson 1996, 94.

154   Quoted in Godwin 1991, 22.

155   Godwin 1991, 41–47.

156   See, for example, Layton 1987, 118.

only. According to contemporary scholarship, the holy unspeakable name of the God of Israel, represented by the Hebrew letters יהוה (YHVH), was pronounced "Yahweh." The supreme god of the Romans was Jupiter or Jove; this latter name was pronounced "Yoweh" in classical Latin. "Iao" is a divine name routinely used among the Gnostics, and "Io" was a cry of praise in the ancient Greek worship of Pan and Dionysos. None of these resemblances are definitive, but they suggest the existence of a common body of religious lore involving vowel chants in ancient times.

Further east, the Hindu tradition includes a vast body of lore concerning chanting in religious contexts, and vowels play a crucial role in much of this lore. The holiest of Hindu mantras, the sacred syllable Om, is only the most widely known example.

Though it's not as well known as its Hindu equivalent, an equally rich tradition of vocal lore and symbolism survives in Japan and plays an important role in Shinto tradition. Its name is *kotodama* (literally, "word-spirit"), and it gives symbolic meanings to every syllable used in the Japanese language, with the five Japanese vowels playing a role of special importance.[157] Each of the *norito*—traditional Shinto prayers in a very ancient form of Japanese—is held to have a special meaning and importance deriving from kotodama, alongside its literal meaning, and there are also sacred syllables that have no obvious meaning at all, but that play important roles in Shinto spiritual practice.[158]

From the perspective of this book, the most intriguing of these is the *kei-hitsu*, the vowel-tone used to call the kami into manifestation or send them back to the High Plain of Heaven. The vowel used is O, and it rises and falls several times as the priest intones it, as though searching for the right note. The effect is remarkably eerie.[159] It may be that this, or the similar action of a Hindu priest chanting the sacred syllable of the deity in the innermost sanctuary of a mandira, are the closest modern analogues to what went on in the

---

157   Gleason 1995, 54–72.

158   Evans 2001, 41.

159   Nelson 1996, 94.

Holy of Holies of the Temple of Jerusalem when the High Priest, once each year, intoned the holy Name of God.

Finally, of course, the role of chant in medieval Christian ritual is well known and just as well documented. There are various traditions of chant in traditional Christian practice, but all involve prolonged vowel tones. In the Middle Ages, what is now usually called Gregorian chant was the most common form of chant across western and central Europe and played important roles not only in the ceremony of the Mass but also in the Divine Office, the sequence of prayers, psalms, and scriptural readings that priests, monks, and nuns were expected to recite over the course of each day.

From the late Middle Ages on, the chants used in the Mass and Divine Office became subjects of musical compositions and occasions for musical performance, and the older traditions of plainchant dropped out of use for the most part. The Gregorian chants still performed by some Catholic monasteries today are mostly based on the nineteenth-century revival of the art at the Solesmes monastery in France; how close these reconstructions are to medieval practice remains an open question.

Bread Offerings

Another practice that appears with remarkable regularity in the temple tradition, despite huge differences in theology and worship, is the custom of leaving foodstuffs—especially bread and other grain-based foods—in the temple space for a time, and then distributing them to be consumed either by the priesthood or by worshippers in general. Whether or not this practice relates to the temple technology is a difficult question to resolve. Wherever it appears, the foodstuffs in question are surrounded by a rich body of theological tradition, but the sheer consistency of the practice suggests that the possibility is worth exploring.

The Temple of Solomon, the starting place of our exploration, made much use of this custom. As long as the Temple of Jerusalem stood, the Table of Shewbread, a gilded wooden table, stood inside the heikal or Holy Place and held twelve loaves of bread, which were kept there for a week at a time and then taken away to be eaten by the priests. Along similar lines, barley cakes were placed on bronze tables in Greek temples as offerings for the gods and goddesses. Ancient Egyptian temples took the same process to a more elaborate level, serving up feasts to their deities, which were taken away once the gods and goddesses had partaken of their spiritual share and eaten by the priests and priestesses of the temple.

To this day in Hindu temples, foodstuffs of various kinds, called *prasad*, are placed before the deities and then eaten reverently by worshippers. In Shinto shrines, similarly, foodstuffs are set before the kami for their enjoyment and then taken away, and the priests, priestesses, and honored members of the congregation enjoy the foods at the *naorai*, a reception and meal held after the rite. Bread has no place in traditional Japanese cuisine, but rice, the grain food par excellence in Japanese tradition, has an equivalent role in Shinto practice; uncooked rice in particular is inevitably present at any Shinto offering—right down to the daily rites performed at the kamidana or household shrine in most Japanese homes, and the rice thus offered is cooked and eaten by the family once it has been blessed by the kami. Mochi, cakes made of pounded glutinous rice, also have an important traditional role as offerings to the kami later consumed by worshippers.

In the more traditional denominations of Christianity, of course, bread plays an even more important role as the material substance transformed, according to Christian teaching, into the body of Christ in the sacrament of the Mass. The elaborate ritual that surrounds the offering of bread, its storage and handling in the church, and its distribution to the clergy and congregation alike is as rich with theological meaning as any of the other ritual uses of bread just mentioned. Setting aside the theological and spiritual side of these ceremonies, though, the customs that surround the consecrated bread in traditional Christianity have remarkable similarities to those that frame bread offerings in other traditions.

In a Catholic church built along traditional lines, for example, the consecrated bread is kept in the tabernacle, which is at the center of the sanctuary, behind the high altar along the main axis of the building. Catholic architectural critic Michael S. Rose has written movingly about the importance of that placement in the experience of his faith—understandably so, since to a devout Catholic, the consecrated bread embodies the literal, physical presence of Jesus Christ.[160] This book does not presume to pass judgment on that belief. Still, just as the preparation of the bread involves farming and cooking practices that are distinct from religion, though they may be interpreted in religious terms, it is at least possible that the storage and distribution of the consecrated Host may also have once involved certain practices that were not, strictly speaking, religious in nature. The effect at the center of the temple tradition would have lent itself to such use, especially in a time and place where the boundary between the sacred and the secular was far less precisely drawn than it is today.

A final, speculative note about another class of offerings may be worth including here. Alcoholic beverages of certain kinds also have a very long and rich history in relation to the temple tradition. Ancient Egyptian priests and priestesses offered beer to their deities, just as ancient Greeks offered wine to theirs. In contemporary Shinto, no visit to a shrine ceremony is complete without a sip of *miki*, rice wine (*sake*) that has been previously offered to the kami. In the Christian sacrament of the Mass, in turn, the place of wine is equal to that of bread. The usual practice seems to be, as with bread offerings, to place the beverage in or in front of the inner sanctuary for the duration of the ritual, and then to distribute it to those qualified to partake of it. Whether or not this has a place in the temple technology parallel to bread is a question that will require much more research to settle.

Blood Taboos

One additional practice that is found with remarkable regularity wherever the temple tradition appears is a strict prohibition against bringing blood inside the temple itself. This is all the more remarkable because some of the religions that adopted the temple tradition had animal sacrifice among their central religious rites. To any devout Greek or Roman Pagan, for example, the only proper way to worship the gods and goddesses on any formal

---

160   Rose 2001, 184–189.

religious occasion was to sacrifice a bullock or some other edible animal, burn certain ritually prescribed portions on the altar, and cook the rest as a feast for the human participants. Much the same principle applied to Judaism from ancient times until the final destruction of the Temple of Jerusalem. Though faithful Jews had many other religious obligations, the requirement to sacrifice to the God of Israel at the Temple was central among them.

However central it was to the religious life of the people, though, animal sacrifice—and any other activity that involved spilling blood—belonged outside the temple, not within. The Temple of Jerusalem and the temples of Greece and Rome all featured sacrificial altars well outside the temple building itself, and going into the temple with the blood of a sacrifice on one's hands was utterly forbidden. Only the two oldest Greek religious centers, Olympia and Delphi, kept an older custom by which portions of a sacrificed animal were burnt inside the temple.[161] Elsewhere in the Greek and Greek influenced world, the offerings that went into the temple were strictly defined to exclude blood: incense, burnt in great silver or gilt censers; barley cakes and other bloodless food, which were placed on tables before the main statue of the deity; votive gifts of various kinds; and an assortment of decorations for the divine statue, including garments, wreaths, and woolen ribbons. These latter were bestowed with such enthusiasm that Pausanias writing in the second century CE noted wryly that the mass of ribbons made it impossible to get a clear view of some divine images at all.[162]

Other religions that adopted the temple tradition did not practice animal sacrifice at all. The feasts presented to the deities by ancient Egyptians, the food offered to the kami in a Shinto shrine, the prasad placed reverently before Hindu deities, and the bread and wine central to the sacrament of the Christian Mass involve no literal shedding of blood in any sacred space.[163] In these traditions, though, the blood taboo was just as deeply rooted as it was in cultures that practiced animal sacrifice.

161　Spawforth 2006, 21.

162　Ibid., 80.

163　Even so, the symbolic shedding of blood in the Christian Mass must have seemed astonishingly edgy to converts from Greek and Roman Paganism.

Blood of any kind—human blood spilled in warfare or homicide, animal blood shed in the butchering process, menstrual blood or the bloody lochia that follows the delivery of a child—was considered a dangerous impurity wherever the temple tradition took root and had to be cleansed by some combination of ceremony and ritual bathing before the person touched with blood could safely be admitted into the sacred precinct. The tradition of the mikveh, or ritual bath in Orthodox Judaism, is a survival of this practice, and so is the old Christian practice of "churching" a woman after she gives birth and before she returns to attendance at regular services.

On a more robust level is the Shinto tradition of *misogi shuho*, or ceremonial purification in running water or the ocean.[164] This is practiced regularly by many Shinto clergy and lay worshippers, and it is mandatory when certain kinds of impurity have been encountered and when laypeople are to take on certain roles that bring them close to the kami, such as carrying the portable shrines that feature in many Shinto festivals. The same practice, oddly enough, was part of ancient Greek Pagan religion from very ancient times—when Agamemnon and his men cleanse themselves of their offense against the god Apollo in the first book of the *Iliad*, for example, they do it by purifying themselves in the sea.

It's anyone's guess, frankly, whether the traditional taboo against blood had to do with the temple tradition explored in this book or whether it derives from some more strictly religious source. Curiously, though, it's not found with any consistency in the older fertility workings that used ziggurats and the equivalent: Mesoamerican religious rites routinely spilled great quantities of blood in and around temples, for example, and what scraps are still remembered of Chinese religion from before the revolt against the gods suggest that animal sacrifice once took place on or near the miniature ziggurats still used as altars to the Chinese earth gods. The traditional taboo may therefore be worth keeping in place in any modern attempt to explore the temple tradition in practice.

---

164   Nelson 1996, 140–142; see also Evans 2001, 126–132.

PART THREE

The Legacy

CHAPTER ELEVEN

The Ancient Secret

The first ten chapters of this book have summarized the evidence that certain traditions of religious architecture in the ancient and medieval world embodied a technology that used simple but subtle means to yield significant benefits to local agricultural fertility—a technology that has not yet been recovered by modern science, though there's no reason to assume that the forces that it used are unknown to today's physicists. That hypothesis raises many questions, of course, and a great deal of further investigation will be needed to provide answers to most of those. Two of the most important, though, can be answered readily enough from the information already surveyed. The first of them is how the temple tradition came into existence in the first place. The other is how it came to be lost.

The first is not hard to understand once it's remembered that people who lived before the scientific revolution, while they had different ways of understanding the world than their descendants do today, were just as capable as we are of noticing changes in their environments and drawing conclusions from their experiences. Anthropologists noticed a long time ago that tribal peoples who explain the natural world in terms of elaborate mythologies about the doings of gods and spirits are perfectly capable of using that knowledge base to anticipate the movements of game animals, treat diseases effectively with the local medicinal herbs, and find their way safely across trackless deserts or long stretches of open sea. The same process of learning through experience, extended over millennia, was doubtless the source of the temple tradition as well.

It's easy to imagine how such a thing might have happened. All it would have taken was one temple that happened to be built of the right materials in the right place and therefore got some trace of the effect at the center of the technology. Local farmers, noticing that fields close to the new temple were suddenly producing better yields than fields a few miles farther up or down the river valley, would have brought this to the attention of the temple priests or priestesses, if only by the enthusiasm with which they offered prayers of thanksgiving. The priests or priestesses of other temples that didn't have the same effect would have had a potent incentive to figure out what accounted for the difference, and though most of their guesses were doubtless very wide of the mark, all it would have taken was one successful replication of the effect to kickstart the process that brought the temple tradition into being.

As mentioned back in chapter 9, the ways in which cultural forms develop over time have certain similarities to the evolutionary process by which living things develop over much vaster periods of time. One of those similarities is that in both cases diversity is crucial. Just as the genetic diversity of a population of living things provides the variation among individuals that natural selection works with, the cultural and religious diversity of the ancient world gave the emerging temple tradition an ample supply of variations, and those that turned out to be more successful than others became the basis on which the future built. All the variables discussed in the last four chapters—location, orientation, geometry, structure, substance, and the details of ritual—were sorted out over thousands of years of trial and error by people who had no idea of the forces at work but were perfectly capable of noticing when a new temple in this place yielded sudden improvements in crop yields, while a change in the rituals performed in that shrine caused the effect to diminish in the fields nearby.

There's no reason to think that the resulting lore was ever codified into anything like a coherent theory. It may have never even been written down. One common feature of ancient religious traditions is that they rarely wrote much about sacred things. Even in highly literate societies such as Egypt and Babylonia, religious writings tended to consist of myths about the gods and goddesses, hymns, prayers, and not much more. The sort of detailed accounts of theology and practice that fill the shelves of religious bookstores these days were for all practical purposes absent in ancient religions. If you wanted to learn such things, you normally did that by becoming a priest or priestess or by participating in special, secret religious activities such as the ancient Greek Mysteries.

These Mysteries in particular may have had a very close connection to the temple tradition. One of the curious things about the Greek Mysteries, in fact, is that so many of them centered on agriculture. The most famous of them all, the Eleusinian Mysteries, were sacred to Demeter, the grain goddess. One of the few ancient testimonies about the ceremonies of initiation at Eleusis claims that at the high point of the ceremony, a ripe ear of grain was reaped in silence and shown to the new initiates.[165] A tradition with that theme would be a logical place to look for elements of an archaic technology focusing on agricultural fertility. Whether or not those elements were actually part of the Mysteries of Eleusis will never be known, though, since the lore of those Mysteries was lost forever more than fifteen centuries ago—but a body of initiates whose teachings focused on agriculture would be a logical place to find the inheritors of the process outlined above.

In the heyday of the ancient world, if the thesis at the core of this book is correct, a band of urban societies extending across Eurasia from Britain to northern Pakistan had learned how to build temples that had a beneficial effect on crop yields. In all probability, this effect was understood in purely religious terms: if the temple is built in this way and this sort of ceremonies

---

165   Burkert 1985, 285.

are performed in it, the logic ran, the gods and goddesses will be well pleased, and their blessings will make the grain flourish. If the philosophers who were beginning to explore the possibility of a science of nature in those same centuries ever noticed that something not quite so theological was involved, their writings have not come down to us.

In order to understand what happened thereafter, it's crucial to keep in mind that the temple tradition was part of the fabric of ordinary life in ancient societies. If you had lived in those days, it would never have occurred to you that anything strange was involved. To the Jews who flocked to the Temple in Jerusalem to offer prayers and sacrifices to the God of Israel, for example, the fact that some influence from the temple made the countryside around it more fertile was simply the sort of thing you can expect when you please the Lord. Eight hundred miles or so northwest of Jerusalem, the Greeks of the same era would have said exactly the same thing about what happens when you make the proper offerings to Demeter, and any other religious center in the ancient world that made use of the temple tradition, no matter what god or goddess was worshipped there, would have had something similar to say.

Ancient religions, as noted in chapter 4, had a very different relation to the facts of life than the prophetic religions that mostly replaced them. The deities of the old Pagan faiths were expected to do things in this world for their worshippers, and their worship was entirely integrated with the fabric of everyday life. The temple tradition shared this same immersion in the ordinary—and this turned out to be the most important factor in the tradition's eventual disappearance. When the fabric of everyday life was shredded by traumatic change, many of the threads that had been woven into it vanished forever.

Two Shapes of Time

It's very difficult for most people today to understand the crisis of confidence that swept the ancient world beginning in the second century BCE and the long trajectory of decline and fall that followed it. Our industrial civilization has an incurably optimistic attitude toward history, and most people in the modern world tend to think that history always moves in the direction of progress. It's almost unthinkable that a society could reach a relatively high level of civilization, stall out, and then gradually revert to barbarism—even though this has happened over and over again in the course of human history.

People in the ancient world didn't share the modern faith in perpetual progress. There were two common ideas about the shape of history in ancient civilizations, one of which has a certain similarity to modern ideas about progress, while the other flatly contradicts it. The first of these ideas held that the universe began in chaos, but was gradually reduced to order by the mighty deeds of the gods and would stay that way forever. According to this view, in other words, something like progress had happened in the past, but once the proper order was established, that process came to an end. The future would be like the present, changing only in detail, and human affairs could be counted on to prosper so long as individuals and societies obeyed the laws handed down by the gods.

The other idea offered a bleak counterpoint to this confident vision. The Greek poet Hesiod, who lived toward the end of the eighth century BCE, was far from the only exponent of this view, but he was the most famous in the western half of Eurasia, and his account has now been in circulation in the western world for some twenty-seven centuries.[166] In Hesiod's harrowing vision, history began with a golden age in the distant past. In point of fact, the widespread fame of his great poem *Works and Days*, where his account appears, is the reason why people nowadays use the phrase "golden age" in the first place.

Each age that followed the golden age—the silver age, the bronze age, the age of heroes, and the iron age in which we live today—was worse than the age before it. Nor can things be expected to improve in the future. In due time, Hesiod warns, infants will be born with their hair already white from old age, the last traces of virtue and happiness will trickle away from

---

166   Hesiod 1973, 62–65.

humanity; shortly thereafter the human race will die out, and that will be the end of the story. Where the modern belief in progress imagines history as a road leading ever upward from the caves to the stars, and the vision of time mentioned earlier imagines it as a road leading out of chaos into a permanent steady state of stability and peace, Hesiod's—and the visions of his equivalents elsewhere in the ancient world—imagined it as a road leading down from golden heights into darkness and silence forever.

One way to talk about what happened in the last centuries of the ancient world is that Hesiod's view of history, which had been the opinion of a minority before that time, gradually became the view of the majority. There were valid reasons for the shift. For many centuries beforehand, in large parts of the ancient world, economic expansion had been the rule rather than the exception, and while civil rights and political liberty were still restricted to a minority, that minority became much larger than it had once been. More influential still in shaping the earlier optimism of the ancient world was the birth of philosophy. It's a remarkable detail of history that China, India, and Greece all invented philosophy about the same time in the sixth century BCE. The extraordinary adventure of ancient philosophy led the intellectuals of that age to imagine a utopian future in which human affairs might be guided by reason and justice—and in which, of course, intellectuals would have a far more privileged position than they were used to.

Unfortunately for them, the philosophers of the ancient world, like so many intellectuals before and after them, proceeded to find out that it's one thing to tell people how to manage their affairs in accordance with reason and quite another to get them to do it. Plato, the most famous of the Greek philosophers, was among those who learned that lesson the hard way. When he tried to encourage the dictator of the city-state of Syracuse to reform his government, he ended up being sold into slavery for his pains and had to be rescued by an admirer. Meanwhile the ancient world's long age of economic growth came to an end as further expansion ran headlong into environmental limits, and increasingly bitter and destructive wars followed. When relative peace finally came, just before the beginning of the Common Era, it arrived at the point of a sword as the armies of three great empires—in the west, the Roman Empire; in India, the Maurya Empire; in China, the kingdom of Ch'in—swallowed one exhausted and bankrupt kingdom after another.

The ideologies of these empires drew heavily on the first of the two visions of history sketched out earlier. According to Rome's propaganda, for example, just as Jupiter, the king of the gods, had beaten the unruly Titans into submission and established peace and good order in the universe, so Rome had done the same thing to the equally unruly peoples of the ancient world. In both cases, at least according to the propaganda, the resulting peace and good order would last forever.

That way of thinking about history was doubtless as comforting as it was convenient for the wealthy elites that prospered from the rule of the new empires. It was considerably less satisfactory for the rest of the population and especially for those toward the bottom of the social hierarchy who received few of the benefits of the imperial system and had to pay most of the costs. As each of these three great empires began the long slide downhill toward the dark age that followed, and the lot of the common people became increasingly unbearable, religious ideologies that rejected the imperial systems and everything they stood for began to spread through the crawlspaces of the ancient world.

The Revolt Against the Gods

It was at this point that the religious shift discussed in chapter 4—the change from worshipping the old gods of nature to revering dead human beings—became a massive political fact. The way that this played out, though, took one path in the Roman west and the Chinese east and a very different path in India. In the Roman and Chinese worlds, the state religion was based on the worship of the old gods of nature, and the religions that became the focus of popular dissent—Christianity in the west and religious Taoism in the east—rejected the old gods. In India, by contrast, one of the new religions, Buddhism, had become the official faith of the Maurya empire, and so the popular revolt took the form of a return to the worship of the old Hindu gods and goddesses.

In all three cases, the resulting revolution had immense political as well as religious implications. The religious side of it was profound enough, to be sure. In China, the replacement of the old religion was so complete that archeologists studying the physical remains of the old faith—for example, painted silk banners from Han dynasty tombs, covered with the images of unknown gods and spirits—have been reduced to guesswork in an attempt to figure out what these relics might once have meant. In India, Buddhism was all but eliminated, and only the fact that missionaries had already established secure bases in countries outside India preserved Buddhist teachings and scriptures for the future.

The Roman west took a different path. There the imperial government began early on to try to co-opt the religious revolution by offering the disaffected an assortment of human beings to worship. The Roman emperors themselves were among the first beneficiaries of this strategy, and temples dedicated to various emperors duly sprang up across the Roman world. As the revolt against the gods gathered strength, though, the temple tradition in the classical world retained its old loyalties. Historians have noted that when the worship of Roman emperors as gods spread to Greece and the Greek-speaking nations of the eastern Mediterranean, temples built on the traditional colonnaded naos plan were used for emperor worship only when the emperor was paired with one of the Olympian gods, usually Zeus. When the emperor was worshipped by himself, or paired with Roma (the deified city of Rome) or some other human or abstract focus of worship, the temple was built to a different, nontraditional plan that lacks the core elements of the temple technology.[167]

Then, over the course of the fourth century CE, a series of Roman emperors desperate to shore up their power in the face of spiralling collapse first came to terms with Christianity, the strongest of the rising religions of the dispossessed, then made it the state religion of the empire, and finally out-

---

167   Spawforth 2006, 99.

lawed all other religions. That political maneuver had an immense impact on the new faith, as a great deal of material from the older worship of the gods of nature found its way into Christian thought and practice. The intellectual borrowings mentioned in chapter 4, and in particular, the wholesale adoption of Neoplatonism as the philosophical basis for Christianity, were one result of this era of adoption, but there were also more pragmatic borrowings as well.

Many Christian churches built in the last century or so of the failing Empire, for example, made lavish use of *spolia*—literally "spoils" or "booty" stripped from demolished Pagan temples. Columns and the ornate capitals that topped them were especially common pieces of spolia.[168] The enthusiastic use of architectural plunder may have played at least as important a role as the philosophical borrowings in getting some elements of the old temple tradition across the divide between Pagan and Christian faiths.

Incense was a more significant borrowing, not least since it seems to play an important role in the secret technology at the heart of the temple tradition. In the first three centuries of the Christian church, as already mentioned, incense was not used in Christian practice because of its powerful contemporary associations with the Jewish temple ritual, Pagan temple practices, and Roman emperor-worship.[169] Once the new faith was legalized and brought under imperial protection, that changed rapidly. The writings of the Christian Neoplatonist author Dionysius the Areopagite, which date from around 500 CE, assume as a matter of course that churches were filled with incense smoke before the ceremony of the Eucharist.

While these transformations were taking place, the collapse of the Roman world shifted into overdrive. By the time Dionysius wrote his treatises, the empire had been divided into western and eastern halves, the western half had been overwhelmed by barbarian invaders, and the eastern half was scrambling for survival. Christianity in the eastern Empire had been wholly incorporated into the imperial system and was accordingly rejected by a

---

168   McClendon 2005, 6.
169   Jones et al. 1992, 486.

growing fraction of the poor and dispossessed, who went looking for other religious options. A galaxy of alternative versions of Christianity, including the Nestorian church that transmitted the temple technology to Japan, were among the popular options, but the option that finally came out on top was Islam, which came surging out of the Arabian peninsula in the middle of the seventh century CE and conquered most of the eastern Empire in little more than fifty years.

Islam was far more uncompromising in its attitude toward the legacies of Paganism than the state Christianity of Constantine's heirs had been. Across the Dar al-Islam—the portion of the world in which Islam became the dominant faith—Christianity and Judaism were permitted to survive, but the bulk of the population promptly converted to Islam, and mosques took the place of churches and temples in the religious life of communities. A mosque, as any devout Muslim can tell you, is not a temple. It's a place where the Muslim community assembles to hear the Quran and pray to Allah, and the practices and design elements of the old temple tradition are not welcome there. Wherever Islam became established, accordingly, the ancient secret of the temple tradition seems to have died out completely.

It is a curious coincidence, if that's all it is, that every part of the ancient world where Islam established itself became a desert over the centuries that followed. Many people today think of North Africa and the Middle East as deserts by definition, but as recently as Roman times, this wasn't the case. The North African provinces that are now the nations of Libya and Tunisia, for example, were the most important grain growing areas in the Roman world and shipped millions of tons of wheat annually to other parts of the empire. In the same way, the great river valleys of Mesopotamia, in the modern nations of Syria and Iraq, were green and fertile not that many centuries ago.

Scholars of ecological history have tried to explain that transformation in many ways. The fourteenth-century Muslim scholar ibn Khaldun was one of the first to discuss the matter, pointing to the destruction of canal systems by nomadic tribes as the cause.[170] Later theorists have talked about the impact of goat herding on fragile arid soils, soil salinization caused by irrigation practices, deforestation of highland areas, and many other factors. These things doubtless played a part, but all of them also took place along the Mediterranean coasts of Europe, and yet the same results did not happen there. It's at least possible that the abandonment of the temple tradition and the secret technology at its core turned out to be one blow too many to an already fragile and damaged agricultural ecosystem, while the preservation of the same technology outside the Dar al-Islam allowed local agriculture to maintain itself despite other ecological problems.

The Celtic Connection

The western half of the Roman Empire, meanwhile, went its own way once the empire shattered and the barbarians swept in. To the conquerors of the west, Christianity wasn't the official faith of a hated and despised ruling elite; it was part of the booty they had won at sword's point, and literate Christian clergy proved to be useful to the warlords of the invading tribes once they settled down to rule the domains they had seized. The Christian church, for its part, was ready to meet the new rulers of the western world more than halfway, and the marriage of convenience between the church and barbarian kings generally ripened into close alliance once the kings and their families converted to the new religion.

Over the centuries that followed, Christianity in what had been the western half of the Roman Empire gradually drifted away from the version practiced in Byzantium and in those formerly Roman lands that had fallen under Muslim rule. The Catholic Church—as the western branch of the faith came to be called—was in its early days much more diverse and decentralized than the Orthodox Church of the east. So long as local congregations and their clergy kept within very broad doctrinal boundaries and acknowledged the primacy of the Bishop of Rome, they could get away with quite a bit of innovation. Among the transformations that slipped into the church as a

---

170   ibn Khaldun 1958.

result of this openness to innovation were the changes that brought the temple tradition into medieval churches across Europe.

The Celtic lands of far northwestern Europe were among the least regulated and most innovative areas of the Christian west, and Ireland was unruly and innovative even by the standards of the other Celtic nations. This is not surprising, since Ireland was also one of the very few corners of the post-Roman world that received Christianity and classical culture without getting overrun by barbarians shortly thereafter. Protected by their isolation, Irish monasteries thrived straight through the fall of Rome and the years of chaos that followed, and when the era of barbarian invasions drew to a close, it was Irish monks who spread Latin culture through most of western Europe.[171]

They may have spread a heritage considerably older as well. As discussed in chapter 9, the builders of the mounds and standing stones of the megalithic era in northwestern Europe appear to have had some knowledge of the way that terrestrial electricity and magnetism can be used to improve agricultural yields. As one of the few parts of northwestern Europe that was never conquered by Rome and subjected to Roman culture, Ireland is known to have retained religious customs dating back to the Stone Age. The conversion of Ireland to Christianity, while it involved a certain amount of turmoil and violence, was considerably less traumatic than the equivalent transitions from Pagan to Christian religion elsewhere in the Roman world, and it has been suggested by reputable scholars that significant amounts of the Pagan priestly traditions of the Irish Druids found their way into the hands of Irish monks in the century or so after the conversion took place.

Celtic traditions in Ireland and elsewhere included something else that has already appeared in a different context in this book: the idea that something of great importance might be buried in an underground vault, awaiting the right moment for its recovery. Irish legends to this day portray some of the most famous mountains and hills in Ireland as "hollow hills," inside which magical treasures are hidden away, and dozens of locations in Britain are

---

171   Cahill 1995.

pointed out as the place where King Arthur sleeps an enchanted sleep, waiting for the hour of his return.

Even more relevant is an extraordinary and little-noticed passage from
The History of the Kings of Britain by the medieval Welsh author Geoffrey of
Monmouth, written sometime before 1150.[172] Geoffrey's legendary history
drew heavily on ancient Welsh lore about Arthur, Merlin, and a great many
other figures of Celtic antiquity, and so it is more than a little startling to
find what looks very much like a Masonic legend tucked away in his chron-
icle. According to Geoffrey, when King Lear of Shakespearean fame died,
his daughter Cordelia buried him in an underground vault beneath the river
Soar, a few miles downstream from the town of Leicester—and in that vault,
the craftsmen of the town performed ritual activities once a year thereafter.
The echo of Masonic legends about hidden vaults and secret ceremonies is
fascinating, and it suggests that Masonic tradition may include scraps of lore
from very old Celtic traditions.

In any case, the Irish church—and especially Irish monasteries—seem to
have taken the lead in adapting the temple tradition to Christian use. Early churches in Ireland were basically large huts made of wood, wattle and
daub (mud plaster over woven twigs), or stacked sod. By the seventh century,
though, more impressive structures were being built. The *Hisperica Famina*,
an Irish text of that period, describes a wooden church supported by heavy
timbers with a central altar, a porch on the western side, and no fewer than
four steeples.[173] Stone churches followed soon thereafter, along with high
stone crosses, the Christian equivalent of the standing stones of the megalithic era. By the tenth century, these were joined by the most distinctive and
enigmatic of medieval Irish structures, the famous round towers.

There are sixty-eight of these remaining, some complete or nearly so,
some reduced to stumps; there were probably many more in the past. Those
that are intact stand between 70 and 100 feet tall, tapering gently as they rise,
and most are topped by a conical roof. All but one has a door 10 feet or so

---

172   Geoffrey of Monmouth 1966, 86.
173   O'Brien and Harbison 1996, 60–61.

above ground level. The interiors were made of wood, supported on stone offsets or corbels, and a stair zigzagged up the inside to the very top, where four windows looked out over the surrounding landscape.

The received wisdom about the round towers is that they were built as refuges against the Vikings. The problem with this often-repeated claim is that the round towers were useless as defensive structures: a few fire arrows in the wooden door, or shot through one of the windows into the wooden floors within, and the whole thing would go up like a rocket—as did in fact happen from time to time, according to Irish chronicles.[174] They were not fortifications, then, and they weren't bell towers, either—the technology of bell casting didn't reach Ireland until long after most of the round towers were built. What was their purpose?

The answer has already been discussed in chapter 9: they served as a medium for the phenomenon at the heart of the temple tradition. The experiment with paramagnetism presented in that chapter actually came from investigations into agricultural effects observed around some of the surviving round towers, which shows what a hollow paramagnetic cylinder will do for plant growth. A standing stone generates the same effect, and it's tempting to speculate that the first of the towers might have risen because some abbot in a corner of Ireland devoid of large stones, and familiar with fragments of Druid tradition, decided to use mortared stone to build an artificial standing stone on the grand scale.

Whatever the process that brought them into being, the round towers can best be seen as prototypes, the first very rough draft of what later became the lance carried before the Holy Grail, the soaring spires of the Gothic churches and cathedrals. Little enough remains of Irish monastic churches from the Dark Ages that it's difficult to tell what other experiments may have been made in the monasteries of the Emerald Isle during those same years. As Irish scholarship, and a great many Irish monks as well, spread out over western Europe, those experiments that proved to be successful will have found their way to many other lands.

---

174   O'Brien and Harbison 1996, 100.

These discoveries, enriched by whatever lore might have survived in Ireland from Druid times and combined with scraps of the tradition recovered from Roman Pagan temples, played at least some role in bringing the ancient temple technology into use in medieval Christianity. What came from Ireland through monastic channels, though, appears to have been fragmentary, and another source of information was needed to complete the transfer of the ancient secret to the Christian west. The circumstances of its arrival include some of the most dramatic events in the history of the temple tradition.

CHAPTER TWELVE

The Knights of the Temple

A case could probably be made that monasticism was the most important cultural and religious innovation to come out of the revolt against the old gods of nature. Across much of Eurasia, certainly, the history of cultures and ideas alike was profoundly shaped by the rise of monasteries and nunneries as important religious institutions. In Christianity, Buddhism, Taoism, and a great many smaller religious movements that arose in the wake of the great religious revolution, monks and nuns living in self-supporting rural enclaves became the custodians of any number of texts and traditions that would otherwise have been lost forever. The Christian monks who painstakingly copied surviving works of Greek and Roman literature by hand had exact equivalents wherever monasticism spread.

Monasteries in the Christian west and elsewhere also tended toward a decentralized style of governance that provided ample room for diversity in thought and practice. In western Europe in the Middle Ages, for example, there were many different orders of monks and nuns, each living under its own distinctive monastic rule and celebrating the rites of the church in its own idiosyncratic ways. Most monastic orders maintained a prickly independence from the authority of local bishops, and even the Pope could not always expect obedience from powerful abbots. That independence made it possible for a great many new and old traditions to spread through monastic channels.

Agriculture was a particular focus of monastic innovation, as most monasteries raised at least part of the food that the monks ate. Even in the later Middle Ages when monks in most Christian orders rarely worked in the fields, monastic landholdings were still working farms staffed by lay brothers drawn from the local peasantry. It's not accidental that Benedictine and Cistercian monasteries played important roles in introducing such innovations as crop rotation to medieval agriculture, nor is it likely accidental that many of the variations in church architecture that brought it into line with the temple tradition elsewhere appeared in churches connected to monasteries before they found their way into cathedrals and churches meant for the general public—the Irish round towers were among the first examples of this, but they were far from the last. Furthermore, certain lines of evidence suggest that a form of the temple technology endured in at least one English monastery until the end of the Middle Ages.

The Glastonbury Secret

"The Abbey will one day be repaired and rebuilt for the like worship which has now ceased, and then peace and plenty will for a long time abound."[175] These were the final words of Austin Ringwode, the last survivor of the monks who were driven out of Glastonbury Abbey when it was seized and sold off by the English government in 1539. What exactly was the "worship that has now ceased" is a hard question to answer at first glance because the daily offices and other liturgies of the English church in Henry VIII's time were still being celebrated at cathedrals and large churches all over England long after Glastonbury and England's other monasteries were seized and desecrated.

Whether or not the first church at Glastonbury was actually founded by Joseph of Arimathea, as a persistent legend claims, a Christian presence there

---

175   Quoted in Michell 1969, 145.

goes back far into the Dark Ages. The first well-documented structure there, a stone church of Saints. Peter and Paul built about the year 725 by Ine, the Saxon king of Wessex, replaced an earlier wooden structure of unknown date. Traditions from the early Middle Ages connected the abbey with the legends of King Arthur and the Holy Grail.

Those connections included the kind of evidence medieval minds favored most, the relics of the blessed dead. In 1191, during excavations following a disastrous fire, the monks of Glastonbury claimed to have found the grave of Arthur himself, and while this may have been partly a stunt to attract pilgrims and their donations to pay for the rebuilding, many contemporary scholars have argued that the details mentioned in accounts in monastic chronicles only make sense if the monks actually did discover an ancient grave where and when they claimed. A link between the historical Arthur and Glastonbury has been defended on grounds convincing to modern scholarship by Geoffrey Ashe among others.[176]

The most important link between Glastonbury and the temple tradition, though, is found in its links with the Grail legend. Those are extensive enough that entire books have been written on the subject, and the earliest of them is actually a Grail romance—the *Perlesvaus* or *High Book of the Grail*, one of the first Grail stories to be written in prose rather than verse, which was written in the early decades of the thirteenth century.[177] The unknown author of *Perlesvaus* was intimately familiar with Glastonbury and the surrounding landscape, and places much of the Grail story in that setting.

Plenty of medieval folklore made the same geographical connection, not least in Glastonbury itself. It's probably not accidental, for instance, that one old thoroughfare in Glastonbury is named Chilkwell Street, the rounded-off modern form of its medieval name Chalice Well Street, after the well where the Grail was traditionally hidden. In the same way, the bridge leading to the nearby town of Street still has the name Pomparles Bridge; "Pomparles" is another rounding off, this time from the medieval Latin *Pons Perilis*, the

---

176   See, for instance, Ashe 1957.

177   Bryant 1978 is a capable modern translation.

Bridge of Peril, across which Arthur's knights were said to have ridden on their way to seek the Grail. If the Grail legends were a medieval way of talking about the temple tradition, as suggested in chapter 5, this is at least suggestive.

Something more significant than a royal corpse or an enigmatic story may once have been present at Glastonbury, though. This is the purport of a brief but intriguing passage in *The Antiquities of the Church of Glastonbury* by William of Malmesbury, a monk who spent several years at the abbey studying its records in the early twelfth century. Speaking of the church of St. Mary, the oldest surviving structure in the abbey, he writes:

> One can observe there upon the paving, in the forms of triangles and squares, stones carefully interlaced and sealed with lead. If I believe that some sacred mystery is concealed under them, I do no harm to religion.[178]

Modern researchers have speculated that the "stones carefully interlaced and sealed with lead" may have traced out some pattern of sacred geometry. This is certainly possible, but a more prosaic possibility is that the stones and lead may have sealed the entrance to an underground vault. If there was such a vault, it was removed at the beginning of the sixteenth century, only a few decades before the destruction of the abbey. At that time, the floor of what had originally been the church of St. Mary, and had become the Lady Chapel of the abbey church, was torn up and a new crypt excavated beneath it.

Buried vaults play such a large role in the mythology surrounding the temple tradition that it's not surprising to find such claims at Glastonbury as well. Rumors of an underground vault somewhere on the abbey grounds containing the abbey's most secret treasures have been circulating since the sixteenth century. These rumors may have been more than wishful thinking—that, at least, is suggested by the fate of the last abbot of Glastonbury.

When the abbey was seized and desecrated by the agents of Henry VIII in 1539, Abbot Richard Whiting and his two chief subordinates were accused of hiding the abbey's most important treasures, dragged up to the top of

---

178   Quoted in Michell 1997, 145.

Glastonbury Tor, and hanged, drawn and quartered for their supposed crime. There were more than eight hundred monasteries, nunneries, and friaries in Britain when the dissolutions began in 1536, and only a few of their leaders suffered any punishment at all—much less one as barbarous as Whiting's. When the floor of the church of St. Mary was removed and a new crypt excavated beneath it, was whatever lay hidden under those stones sealed with lead moved to a new and more secret location? The possibility deserves more attention than it has received from mainstream scholarship.

None of this proves that Glastonbury Abbey was still in possession of the secret temple technology until its destruction. With Glastonbury, as with so many other things that may have been connected to the temple tradition, all that remains is an assortment of riddles, hints, and enigmatic remains. The traditional connection between the abbey and the Arthurian legend has focused more attention on Glastonbury than on most other monastic establishments and brought out certain puzzling details; it may be that the same sort of attention directed to other ancient monasteries might turn up similar examples elsewhere.

Of all the monastic orders of medieval Europe, though, one seems to have played a role in the transmission and development of the temple tradition that was more important than any other. The order in question was not noted for its scholarship, or for that matter its sanctity. For the last seven centuries, in fact, its name has been surrounded by a cloud of speculation and scandal. From its mysterious origins to its terrible fate, it followed a trajectory all its own, and in the process, became the link connecting the Temple of Solomon with the lost secrets of Freemasonry. That order was, of course, the Knights Templar.

The Knights of the Temple

The Order of the Poor Knights of Christ and the Temple of Solomon, to give the Templars the dignity of their official title, has been the focus of an immense amount of scholarship and an even larger mass of speculation over the last three centuries. The scholarship is justified by the great importance of the Templars as shock troops of the Crusades, a major force in medieval politics, an equally important factor in the transmission of Arabic knowledge to Europe, and the founders of the first European system of banking, among many other things. The speculation, though, is equally justified. From the mysteries surrounding the Order's foundation to the unanswered questions surrounding its gory end, the Templars are wrapped in enigmas.

Despite the uncertainties, missing pieces, and conflicting information from sources, an account of the order's history that is more or less accepted by modern scholars can be assembled, and it runs more or less as follows.[179] In 1096, infuriated by the refusal of Muslim authorities in the Middle East to allow Christian pilgrims to visit shrines in Jerusalem and Bethlehem, an army of European knights and soldiers set out for the Holy Land on the First Crusade under the leadership of the French nobleman Godfrey de Bouillon. After a great deal of fighting, they conquered Jerusalem in 1099 and established a series of Christian kingdoms in parts of what are now the nations of Israel, Lebanon, and Syria. It was in the aftermath of the First Crusade and in response to continued fighting between the Crusaders and their Muslim enemies that the Order of the Temple was born.

In 1118 nine French knights who had remained in the Holy Land presented themselves before Warmund de Picquigny, Patriarch of Jerusalem, seeking to become monks of a kind that the Western world had never before seen: warriors bound by a monastic rule, combining the discipline of the monastery with that of the battlefield. Their request was granted, and they were assigned quarters on the site of the Temple of Solomon. Their official mission was to protect pilgrims against Muslim raiders on the dangerous trip from the ports on the Mediterranean coast to Jerusalem and back.

For the first nine years of Templar history, the order consisted only of these nine knights, and how much help so small a number might have been to pilgrims on the Judean roads is an open question. Funds were so short that at times two Templars had to ride a single horse. A number of modern researchers, however, have suggested that the nine knights spent these

---

179   I have used Ralls 2003 for the following historical summary.

years digging tunnels into the Temple Mount, and in the year 1126 made an important discovery of some sort. Certain traditions of the high degrees of Masonry, cited in chapter 1 of this book, doubtless underlie these claims. As we'll see in the next chapter, though, there is at least one very good reason to think that a remarkable reality might lie behind these rumors.

In 1127 the leader of the little group, Hugh de Payens, sailed home to France and made contact with Bernard of Clairvaux, the nephew of one of the other nine original Templars, who was well on his way to becoming the most famous monastic reformer of the age. With Bernard's energetic assistance, a church council was held at Troyes in 1128, granting the Templars official recognition and a monastic rule specially designed for their needs.

Immediately afterward, noble families from across western Europe vied with each other to donate lands and other assets to the order, and scores of new members sought admission. What had been a small and poorly funded community that deserved its title of "poor knights" became, with astonishing speed, one of the largest and wealthiest religious orders in Christendom. No other monastic order in history has ever grown so fast or acquired wealth and influence so quickly—a detail that has driven plenty of speculation about just what it was that the Templars might have discovered deep within the Temple Mount.

The order's future secured, Hugh returned to the Holy Land, and the Templars began an extraordinarily ambitious construction campaign, building six massive castles at strategic points to defend the Kingdom of Jerusalem and staffing them with newly initiated knights and men-at-arms. Along with the castles, the Templar order obtained substantial tracts of real estate in the Holy Land, large enough that the order had to hire a great many native people to help run, cultivate, and guard their estates; the order had an officer called the Turcopolier whose job was to manage these native auxiliaries. All this required the Templar order to expand its membership to include not only knights but foot soldiers, light cavalry, engineers, masons, and practitioners of many other necessary crafts.

From that point until the final downfall of the Kingdom of Jerusalem, the Templars were among the most important military forces defending the European bridgehead in the Middle East. Meanwhile, back in Europe, the Templar order turned the immense gifts donated to it into a thriving network of landholdings that served to funnel a steady stream of wealth to the Holy Land. Arabic building methods learned by Templar builders in the Holy Land and brought back home helped spark a revolution in European architecture, leading to the rise of the Gothic style of the high Middle Ages.

The example of the Templars quickly inspired imitation. The Order of the Hospital of St. John of Jerusalem, originally founded as an ordinary monastic order providing shelter and medical care to Christian pilgrims, reformulated itself shortly after 1128 along Templar lines as the Knights Hospitaller and provided another body of trained, dedicated fighting men to the defense of the Crusader states. Later, in 1190, a third order—the Teutonic Knights of the Hospital of St. Mary at Jerusalem, founded by German knights uncomfortable with the Francocentric culture of the existing knightly orders—joined the Templars and Hospitallers in the defense of the Crusader states.

The Templars, however, were always the most important of the military orders. They had the largest and wealthiest support infrastructure of estates and priories back in Europe, and the arrangements they made to funnel income to the fighting in the east and provide safe storage of assets for Crusaders made them the first international banking system Europe had ever known. Every time you sign, cash, or deposit a check, you're using a technique for money transfer that the Knights Templar invented.

All their efforts, however, could not keep the Kingdom of Jerusalem secure in the face of a steady stream of Muslim counterattacks. In 1187, just eighty-eight years after it was captured by the Crusaders, Jerusalem was retaken by the armies of the great Arab commander Saladin. The Crusaders regrouped and fought on, but it was a losing struggle. When the last Crusader enclave in the Holy Land fell to the Muslims in 1291, the Templars kept fighting, striking from naval bases in Cyprus while calling on the kingdoms of Europe to join them in launching another Crusade. What happened instead was the stuff of legend.

At dawn on Friday, October 13, 1307, officers of the French government carried out coordinated raids across France and arrested every Knight Templar they could find, including the Order's Grand Master, Jacques de Molay. The charge was heresy. Later that month, Pope Clement II ordered every king in the Christian world to arrest the Templars in their dominions. Not all obeyed, but by the end of the year most Templar knights were in custody.

Trials followed. More than a hundred Templar knights, after savage torture, confessed to the charges. Those who recanted their confessions after the torture ended were promptly burnt at the stake as relapsed heretics. Jurisdictional squabbles between King Philip IV of France and the Pope dragged out the proceedings. In 1311, at the Council of Vienne, Clement formally dissolved the Order, and in 1314, Jacques de Molay was burnt at the stake in Paris.

It's a common misconception that all the Templars were put to death for their supposed crimes. In fact, most of the Templars who had been in France, and essentially all those in other countries, survived the trials and were allowed to join other knightly or monastic orders. The king of Portugal created a new order, the Knights of Christ, for the Templars in his dominions, while Templars east of the Rhine were welcomed into the Teutonic Knights. All across Europe, ordinary monastic orders also accepted a great many former Templars into their monasteries. To all appearances, that was the end of the Knights Templar.

The Templar Secret

The consensus of modern historians is that the destruction of the Templars was motivated purely by the greed and ambition of Philip IV, king of France, and that the accusations of heresy were a cynical exercise in royal propaganda—in the words of historian Malcolm Lambert, "a farrago of nonsense"[180] meant to provide a legal excuse for the theft of the Order's

---

180   Lambert 1992, 180.

immense wealth. Certainly there's good reason to think that the Templars' wealth had a very large role in motivating Philip's actions, and he and his courtiers had used accusations of heresy more than once to target enemies for destruction. Still, the fact that an accusation has dubious motives does not by itself show that the charges are wholly unfounded.

The charges brought against the Order amounted to no fewer than 104 articles. Many of the accusations were lifted wholesale from old books on heresies of the past, a common practice in heresy trials then and thereafter. Thus the Templars were accused of denying Christ, spitting on the Cross, meeting secretly at night, practicing homosexuality, worshipping a cat, and being required to kiss the anus of the presiding officer during the ceremony of initiation; these were all standard canards directed toward heretics by Catholic propagandists of that era.

These overfamiliar charges did not stand alone, though. The Templars were also accused of worshipping an idol named Baphomet, which was shaped like a bearded human head, and of believing that worshipping this idol caused flowers and trees to grow. Each Templar was said to wear a cord around his waist that had been wrapped around the idol. Templar priests, according to the charges, spoke something other than the usual words of consecration during the Mass; Templars were only allowed to confess their sins to members of the Order, and Templar officials who had not taken priestly vows claimed to be able to absolve Templars from sins they had committed, a power the Church only granted to ordained priests.

These accusations don't merely copy the standard propaganda of the time. Rather, they reflect the actual practice of dissident sects of Christianity in medieval Europe, many of which had their own clergy that claimed the same rights as Rome's, understood and celebrated the sacraments in unorthodox ways, and had sacred images and relics of their own, which orthodox thinkers inevitably dismissed as idols.

The name of the Order's supposed idol, Baphomet, offers an intriguing clue to the nature of the beliefs the Templars may have brought back to Europe from the Holy Land. Historian of religions Hugh Schonfield has pointed out that a simple mode of secret writing in common use in the Middle Ages makes unexpected sense of the idol's name.[181] This is the so-called Atbash cipher, which replaces the first letter of the Hebrew alphabet, Aleph, with the last, Tau; the second, Beth, with the next to last, Shin, and so on. The name of the cipher comes from these same letters—שבתא (Aleph, Tau, Beth, Shin) spells Atbash in Hebrew.

In the Hebrew alphabet, Baphomet is spelled בפומת (Beth, Peh, Vau, Mem, Tau). Treat that series of letters as a message in the Atbash cipher, and it becomes שופיא (Shin, Vau, Peh, Yod, Aleph). This is the Hebrew spelling of Sophia, Wisdom, the name of the central figure in many versions of Gnostic Christianity.

The Gnostics were a complex and poorly understood movement that emerged in the Roman Empire and combined elements of Christian and Pagan tradition to pursue a diverse series of spiritual quests united only by a common faith in personal experience—in Greek, *gnōsis*—of spiritual realities. It's a mistake, though one that has very often been made, to see Gnosticism as an anti-Christian religion, or for that matter as a single religion at all. All through its history, Gnosticism has been a diffuse movement consisting of many diverse traditions. Far from rejecting Christianity, furthermore, most historically attested Gnostic teachings claim to be the true Christian religion, and many Gnostics have seen the Christian orthodoxy of their time as a corrupt and blasphemous counterfeit of true Christianity—roughly, that is, the way that the defenders of Christian orthodoxy have generally viewed Gnosticism.

The raw diversity of the Gnostic movement has too rarely been recognized by scholars who lack familiarity with surviving Gnostic scriptures and texts. The sole theme common to them all, the characteristic that gave the movement its name, was the belief that personal experience of the spiritual realm, rather than faith in doctrinal formulas, was the key to salvation. Thus it simply isn't true, for example, that all Gnostic teachings reject the physical body and the material universe as the evil creations of a wicked antigod.

---

181   Schonfield 1984, 164.

That was the theme of one broad current of Gnostic speculation, and the fact that texts from that end of the Gnostic spectrum were very well represented in the Nag Hammadi collection of Gnostic scriptures from Egypt has misled quite a few people, including scholars who should have known better, into thinking that all Gnosticism shares that emphasis.

On the other end of the Gnostic spectrum was a current of thought that affirmed the living presence of the divine in nature, to the extent of making use of Pagan fertility myths and rituals in their teachings. In ancient times, this aspect of the Gnostic movement was exemplified by a sect known as the Naassenes.[182] Most of the little that is known about this sect comes from the writings of Hippolytus, one of the most tireless and vitriolic heresy-hunters among the fathers of the Catholic Church, who cites most of a Naassene document in the course of his denunciations.

Among the things that set the Naassene sect apart from many other branches of the Gnostic movement was its enthusiastic adoption of the language and symbolism of the ancient Greek Mysteries and the participation of its members in the Pagan celebrations of those Mysteries. There are, according to the document quoted by Hippolytus, two aspects to the Pagan Mysteries, a lesser aspect and a greater one; the lesser aspect is that of "fleshly generation," that is, agricultural fertility and human reproduction, while the greater aspect is that of the heavenly mysteries of spiritual initiation. Beyond these two gates of the Mysteries, said the Naassenes, stands a third gate, which is the Gnosis of Christ: "And of all men we alone are Christians, accomplishing the mystery at the Third Gate."[183]

The possibility that the Templars may have embraced one of the Gnostic alternatives to mainstream Christianity has been suggested repeatedly over the last few centuries and just as repeatedly rejected.[184] It has not often been realized, though, that if the Templars revered a sacred image in the Pagan fashion, believing that the spiritual power the image represented made the

---

182   See the discussion in Weston 1983, 149–163.

183   Cited in Weston 1983, 157.

184   Partner 1981 discusses some of these claims in their historical context.

flowers and trees grow, they were following a well-established Gnostic precedent.

What is more, the fusion of alternative religious views and magical practices with agriculture was well established in the Holy Land and elsewhere long before the nine founders of the Order of the Temple arrived in Jerusalem. It's an interesting fact that manuals of magic and heretical religion in circulation in the Middle East in the early Middle Ages were crammed with agricultural advice, some of it remarkably practical.[185] While nothing directly connected to the temple tradition appears in the few surviving examples of this literature, the connection between alternative spirituality and agriculture was certainly present in the minds of people in the Middle East before, during, and after the years when the Templars ruled there.

Then as now, a galaxy of small religious communities of various kinds lived in various corners of the Middle East, and their members—many of them unsympathetic to the Muslim cause after centuries of persecution— would have been prized recruits for the Templars' native auxiliary corps. Among the surviving minority faiths of the Middle East today are several, such as the Mandeans of southern Iraq, that can trace their descent to the ancient Gnostics, and other such groups such as the Sabaeans are known to have become extinct since the time of the Templars. It is thus at least possible, given the evidence surveyed above, that it was through contact with such a group in the Holy Land that the Templars came to embrace a Gnostic Christianity of something like the Naassene type as the true teaching of Christ.

We may, however, have another source of information about the tradition that the Templars adopted, though it comes by a roundabout route. This is a body of legends about a sacred item as mysterious as the Templar's supposed idol Baphomet, which shared with that rumored object the same connections with knighthood and secrecy and the same power of causing flowers and trees to grow. Those legends are, of course, the medieval narratives about the Holy Grail.

---

185   See, for example, Greer and Warnock 2011.

The Quest of the Grail

Exactly why a set of folktales about a long-dead warlord in post-Roman Britain happened to turn into one of the main symbolic channels for the temple tradition is a complicated question, and very possibly one that will never be settled with any kind of certainty. Historians chasing the origins of the medieval legends of King Arthur have traced them to itinerant story-tellers from Brittany, who took their traditional tales to France and other corners of Europe and found eager audiences there. Brittany also produced some of the toughest mercenary soldiers in Europe; the army William the Conqueror led to the conquest of England in 1066 included many Breton knights and men-at-arms, and a very large Breton contingent also joined the First Crusade on its long journey to Jerusalem.

These Breton Crusaders brought their stories with them. The Porta della Pescheria of the cathedral of Modena in Italy was built in the early years of the twelfth century, and its archivolt features a carving of "Artus de Bretani" and his knights "Che" and "Galvagnus"—in modern terms, King Arthur, Kay, and Gawain—storming a castle; they wear knee-length coats of mail and conical helmets, like the Norman knights in the Bayeux Tapestry.[186] Modena is close to Bari, one of the main staging areas for the First Crusade, where contingents of Breton warriors spent the winter of 1096–7 preparing for the invasion of the Holy Land.

An interesting detail helps link the Grail legends to the Crusades—the word "grail" itself. As noted earlier, it's a medieval French word for an expensive dish or platter, but it was not much used in the northern French regions where Chrétien de Troyes's patron Count Philip of Flanders had his home, and not much more common in central France, where Chrétien was born and raised. Before Chrétien's poem made the word famous, it was mostly used in Provence, on France's Mediterranean coast, and across the Pyrenees in Catalonia and Aragon. Still, there was one other place where the word

---

186   Miller 1969, 19–20.

was common, and it remained a common term there even after it dropped from common use elsewhere: the Crusader kingdoms of the Holy Land.[187]

The connection with the Crusades is of considerable importance because similar points of contact run all through the aspect of Arthurian legend that bears most directly on the theme of this book: the legend of the Holy Grail. As already mentioned, most modern scholars tend to support one of two theories for the origin of the Grail legend—the theory of Celtic origins on the one hand and the theory of Christian origins on the other—while a minority has pointed out that medieval storytellers were perfectly capable of combining material from both these sources, and others as well, into a single narrative.

According to Chrétien de Troyes, however, the raw material for the *Conte del Graal* came from a book given to him by Count Philip of Flanders.[188] Scholars have argued at length about whether the book existed or not, and proposed any number of speculations about the contents of the book, but the man from whom Chrétien claimed to have received it has received a good deal less attention.[189]

This is all the more curious because Count Philip of Flanders was not a minor figure in twelfth-century Europe. His life and activities are well known, and they point in directions that will be familiar already to readers of this book. His father Thierry was a famous Crusader who went to fight in the Holy Land four times; his mother Sibylla was the daughter of Fulk of Anjou, King of Jerusalem; Philip himself followed the family tradition, went on Crusade three times, and died in the Holy Land in 1191 during the last of these adventures. Like all the leaders of the Crusades, Philip was in constant contact with the Knights Templar in the Holy Land and also at home in Flanders and northern France—the Templars had extensive holdings in

---

187   Carey 2007, 12.

188   Chétien de Troyes 1991, 382.

189   John Carey is a welcome exception; see Carey 2007, 9–10.

and around Philip's domain and close connections with most of the noble families in the region.[190]

Philip's crusading tendencies also tended in another direction: against the Cathar movement. This was a medieval Gnostic sect that emerged in southern France and northern Italy in the twelfth century. By their opponents, they were also called Albigensians—literally "the people from Albi"—because the town of Albi in southern France was one of their first important centers. They drew their doctrines from the end of the Gnostic spectrum that considered the natural world to be the creations of an evil god, and they rejected the Catholic Church and its sacraments as creations of the powers of evil. The Catholic Church heartily returned the favor, and turned out to have more swords on its side; in a series of violent persecutions that lasted most of the thirteenth century, the Cathars were annihilated by the Pope's armies and inquisitors, and only scraps remain of their teachings and traditions.

What makes this history relevant to the theme of this book is that Philip of Flanders was a bitter enemy of the Cathars even before the Catholic Church formally denounced the movement in 1190. This has usually been taken as proof that Philip was strictly orthodox in his beliefs. It could mean that, to be sure, but those of my readers who have watched controversies between small religious sects or old-fashioned Marxist political parties know that the fiercest opponents of one alternative belief system usually come from another alternative belief system, not from the mainstream.

As already noted, the Cathars rejected the natural world and the validity of the Catholic sacraments. The teaching that the Templars seem to have embraced came from the other Naassene end of the spectrum, and the teachings affirmed the validity of the Catholic sacraments as useful first steps on the way to gnosis. Hostility between two such diverse belief systems would be hard to avoid, and only the bad habit of assuming that all Gnostic teachings must amount to the same thing and be on the same side of every conflict has obscured that factor.

---

190   Schenk 2010 documents this at length; see particularly 127.

It's in this light that Wolfram von Eschenbach's riddling name for the Grail can best be understood. *Lapsit exillis*, as we've seen, works out to "he, she, or it fell from among them." In the vast majority of Gnostic teachings, that sentence applies precisely to one and only one figure: Sophia, the spirit of wisdom, who fell from among the Aeons—the timeless, perfect powers of the Gnostic world of light—into our world of generation and decay. The fall and redemption of Sophia plays a central role in most Gnostic mythology, and it's remarkable, to use no stronger word, that Wolfram's term for the Grail and the name of the Templar's supposed idol work out to the same name for the same core Gnostic figure.

Chrétien's *Conte del Graal* was composed, according to most scholars, in or around the year 1190. Those were tumultuous years in western Europe and the Crusader states alike. In 1187 Saladin crushed the Crusader armies at the battle of the Horns of Hattin and conquered Jerusalem. In 1189, in response, the Third Crusade got under way. In 1190 Pope Alexander II declared the Albigensians anathema, setting the stage for the beginning of the Albigensian Crusade nineteen years later. In 1191 the Knights Templar established a new headquarters in the Holy Land at Acre, on the shores of the Mediterranean, and began the occupation of the island of Cyprus as a potential base of operations if Acre fell. In that same year, 1191, the monks of Glastonbury Abbey announced their discovery of the lost grave of King Arthur.

If the long-rumored Templar discoveries in the Holy Land included, among other things, a body of information relating to the temple tradition, 1190 was a good time for that information to be put in circulation in western Europe in a new, covert form. The fall of Jerusalem must have made it clear to everyone involved that divine providence could not be counted on to defend the Crusader states from their Muslim enemies, and the reorientation of Templar activities to Cyprus shows that the Knights of the Temple, at least, were preparing for the possibility that the Holy Land might be lost completely. At the same time, the hardening of attitudes toward the Cathars must have provided a stark warning to the custodians of the secret temple technology that practices and teachings that strayed too close to the borders of heresy might have lethal consequences for anyone caught participating in them.

The invention of the Grail legends was a masterly response to that predicament. Drawing on the already rich medieval heritage of allegory and typological thinking, it allowed the core of the tradition to be transmitted in a form that looked perfectly innocent, except to those who happened to have the key to its interpretation. The legends could even say in so many words that there was a profound and terrible secret associated with the Grail, and those who weren't in on the secret would just treat that as a narrative device and nothing more.

It's entirely possible that the idea of weaving the temple tradition into a legendary tale—and into the specific set of tales about King Arthur, for that matter—had deeper roots as well. The Bretons in the First Crusade whose propensities for telling stories left lasting traces in the carvings of Modena Cathedral could well have brought scraps of the temple tradition in its Celtic Christian form with them; all it would have taken is one Breton monk or priest who knew enough of the traditional lore to grasp the connection that linked those teachings with the Templar discoveries. Whether anyone in the early twelfth century recognized the remnants of older versions of the same tradition in Celtic folklore is another question, and it is almost impossible to settle with the information we now have, but the possibility is there.

Not all of those who spread the story of the Grail were necessarily aware of the message it concealed. Jessie Weston, who arguably came closer to the Grail's secret than anyone else in recent times, was convinced that Chrétien de Troyes had no notion of the inner meaning of the story he was embroidering, but simply thought of it as a lively romance of the sort he had already reworked successfully in the past.[191] Others, in particular the anonymous author of *The Elucidation*, seem to have been much better informed. There were still others, finally, such as the equally anonymous authors of the *Perlesvaus* and the *Prose Lancelot*, who were apparently aware of the existence

---

191   Weston 1983, 161–62.

of the Grail secret, and even of its nature, and deliberately rewrote the story to replace the fertility symbolism with orthodox Christian theology. These last were harbingers of the final phase in the history of the temple tradition in the Western world: the process by which it was abandoned and forgotten.

CHAPTER THIRTEEN

The Coming of the Waste Land

It's controversial enough in scholarly circles today to suggest that the Knights Templar may have been something other than a body of ordinarily devout Catholic warrior-monks. It's even more controversial to suggest that the Templars may have possessed a body of secret knowledge that was passed down to successors after the destruction of the Order. The consensus view among historians of the Middle Ages holds that the odd reputation of the Templars was purely a product of slanders against them that were concocted by the French monarchy, and that there's no evidence that any fragment of Templar tradition survived in any form.[192]

Standing apart from that consensus is a minority of researchers who argue that some elements of the Templar tradition can be shown to have survived after 1311. While this view is unpopular in scholarly circles these days, there is much to recommend it. As already noted, most of the Templars survived the end of their order and were permitted to join other knightly or monastic orders, and presumably took with them whatever teachings they had learned from the defunct Templar order. This might explain some of the evidence for the temple tradition at Glastonbury, among other things, and

---

192   See Partner 1981 for a crisp exposition of the consensus view.

this suggests that it would be worth studying monastic culture, agriculture, and architecture across Europe after the downfall of the Templars, to see if more traces of the survival of the temple tradition might be found there.

Whatever did or did not find its way into monastic communities by this means, there is another route by which Templar teachings seem to have survived the order, and this involves the long-rumored Templar foothold in Scotland. It has been pointed out that during the years of the Order's dismemberment, from 1307 to 1314, the kingdom of Scotland was subject to a papal interdict. While an interdict was in force, no Christian sacraments could be administered and the Church suspended all its activities. In a strict sense, the dissolution of the Order of the Temple at the Council of Vienne in 1311 thus had no legal effect in Scotland.

There are a great many tombstones in Scotland with Templar symbols on them, some dating from well after the Order's dissolution, and Templar symbols abound in certain important works of Scottish medieval architecture, including Rosslyn Chapel, which will be discussed later in this chapter. It has therefore been suggested that the Templars who were in Scotland in 1307, along with some who fled there from elsewhere, continued to function as an organization for some time after 1311, and preserved many of the traditions of their Order; that some of these surviving Templars, given the Order's known expertise in building castles and churches, would have found ready employment in the construction trades; that they passed on Templar teachings to Scottish stonemasons' guilds; and that these teachings, in jumbled, fragmentary, and incoherent forms, can now be found among the symbols and practices of Freemasonry.

It's by no means an impossible suggestion. Stranger things have happened often enough in history, and serious historians such as John Robinson have lent their considerable support to the claim.[193] What renders the theory all the more intriguing is that some such connection is required to account for one of the most important themes of the higher degrees of Freemasonry—the tradition, discussed in chapter 1, that a secret chamber lies directly

193   Robinson 1989.

beneath the Holy of Holies of the Temple of Solomon and can be reached by a hidden tunnel.

What makes this tradition of critical importance is that the tunnel actually exists.[194] It was discovered in 1968 by a team of archeologists headed by Meir Ben-Dov; it starts at an undisclosed location outside the Temple Mount, passes under the Triple Gate and Stables of Solomon, and proceeds directly beneath the Dome of the Rock on the site of the Temple. Ben-Dov's team identified it as dating from the time of the Crusader Kingdom of Jerusalem. The explosive religious politics surrounding the Temple Mount in1968, one year after the Israeli conquest of east Jerusalem, forced Ben-Dov to dig only as far as the Muslim authorities permitted, and the latter were adamant in refusing to allow any excavation beneath the Temple Mount itself. To this day, what might be at the far end of the tunnel remains unknown.

From 1118 until the Crusaders lost Jerusalem in 1187, most of the Temple Mount, and in particular the Stables of Solomon, were in the hands of the Knights Templar. A tunnel excavated by Crusaders in that place was almost certainly the work of the Templars and would certainly have been known to them even if it had been dug by other Crusaders before the Templars took over the Temple Mount. A great deal of speculation has fastened on that fact and spun various narratives about what the Templars may or may not have dug up. It's less often noticed that the existence of the tunnel provides remarkably strong evidence for a direct lineal connection between the Knights Templar and modern Freemasonry.

Until the archeologists uncovered the tunnel in 1968, to be precise, there was no way that anyone could have known that it existed unless that information had descended to them from the original excavators of the tunnel. Nor could they have known by any other means that the tunnel ran from underneath a royal palace—the palace of the Kings of Jerusalem was on the southern end of the Temple Mount, directly over the Triple Gate and the Stables of Solomon—more or less horizontally toward the location of the Holy of Holies of Solomon's Temple.

---

194   Ben-Dov 1985 describes the tunnel's discovery.

The Masonic degree of Perfect Elu, which describes the horizontal tunnel in detail, can be found in manuscripts dating from no later than 1771[195]—that is, nearly two centuries before the 1968 excavations, and also well before earlier archeological digs in 1867 and 1911, which found some evidence of tunnels and chambers under the Temple Mount.[196] The relevant question here is as simple as it is challenging: how did Freemasons in the eighteenth century know about the existence, location, and direction of a tunnel that was not discovered for more than two centuries, unless they inherited that knowledge from the people who dug the tunnel in the first place?

The vertical descent of the workmen to the secret vault, the legendary incident at the heart of the Royal Arch degree, also makes considerable sense in the light of the Temple Mount's archeological realities. The very few archeological surveys that have been done of the Mount itself show, as already noted, that the entire hill is riddled with abandoned tunnels, cisterns, storerooms and drains. Workmen clearing away rubble on the Temple Mount, whether their labors took place in the time of Zerubbabel or of Hugh de Payens, would very likely have encountered the sort of opening in the ground described in the Royal Arch degree. Whether that opening gave indirect access to a secret vault under the Holy of Holies is another question, one that will probably never be settled until and unless archeologists are permitted to excavate the Temple Mount—but the possibility can't be dismissed out of hand.

What the Templars found in their excavations beneath the Temple Mount, if they found anything at all, remains a mystery, and it's impossible to say for certain whether that mystery has anything at all to do with the temple tradition that has been explored in this book. The relevance of the tunnel to the theme of this book is simply the evidence it offers that at least some elements of Templar knowledge must have been passed on to operative masons' guilds in Scotland after the abolition of the Templar order in

---

195   These are the Francken Manuscripts, the foundational manuscripts of the Scottish Rite. See de Hoyos 2015.

196   See Ralls 2003, 145–50, for a summary of these earlier expeditions.

1311, and therefore fragments of the same knowledge may have reached the speculative Masonic lodges that emerged out of the operative guilds some four hundred years later.

The exact process by which that knowledge made its way from the Templars to the Freemasons has not yet been traced, and may never be known. One important piece of the puzzle, though, may be found in an enigmatic building in Scotland, the famous Rosslyn Chapel.

The Rosslyn Secret

The Collegiate Chapel of St. Matthew, to give this remarkable structure its proper name, stands on the hill above Roslin Glen, eight and a half miles from Edinburgh—close enough to attract a steady stream of day-trip buses and private cars in tourist season. Rosslyn Chapel is among the most beautiful surviving works of medieval Scottish architecture, but that fact accounts for only a modest fraction of the visitors. The rest are there because of the legend that has come to surround the chapel—a legend that touches on most of the themes discussed in this book and focuses with particular force on the Knights Templar, the origins of Freemasonry, and the rumored secret that connects them.

Rosslyn Chapel was a creation of the fifteenth century and thus falls precisely into the gap separating the last known Templars from the first known Freemasons. The span of years during which it was built, curiously enough, also frames the period in which Fütrer and Malory revived the legends of the Holy Grail. Its cornerstone was laid on St. Matthew's day, September 21, 1446, and it was finished in 1486. It was originally built by William Sinclair, Earl of Caithness, as a place of worship for his family close to their home at Roslin Castle—this was a common custom of the medieval aristocracy, in Scotland as elsewhere.

Even in its present, half-ruined state, the chapel is a masterpiece of late Gothic design, and it also shows most of the telltale marks of the temple tradition discussed in part 2. Readers of this book will already know, for example, that it stands atop a hill, is built of strongly paramagnetic stone, and has

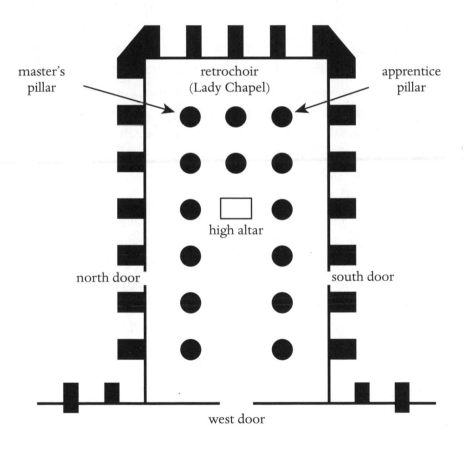

master's
pillar

retrochoir
(Lady Chapel)

apprentice
pillar

high altar

north door

south door

west door

ROSSLYN CHAPEL

an axis running due east and west, aligned precisely on the rising sun at the spring and autumn equinox. In point of fact, all the elements of the temple technology that were able to survive the ravages of time and the violence of the Reformation are present and accounted for in Rosslyn Chapel.

Various researchers on Rosslyn Chapel have claimed that the structure is modeled on the Temple of Solomon.[197] A more precise description is that it borrows certain design elements of the Temple of Solomon and combines them with those of Gothic church architecture. For example, the usual orientation of Christian churches, with the altar in the east, has been modified to make room for a representation of the temple's design, with the doors in the east: the Lady Chapel in the retrochoir beyond the high altar stands in for the porch of the Temple of Solomon, with the famous Apprentice Pillar and Master's Pillar filling in for the great pillars Jachin and Boaz, respectively. On the other hand, many other aspects of the design of Solomon's Temple have no equivalent in Rosslyn Chapel; to note the obvious example, there is no Holy of Holies, just a standard high altar in the middle of the eastern half of the building.

As in most medieval churches and chapels, there is also a crypt—that is, an underground space used for burials and certain other traditional purposes. Rosslyn's crypt is east of the main structure and can be reached by a stair on the south side of the Lady Chapel. This is closed off to the general public, and what exactly might be found there by careful excavation is an interesting question. Many Rosslyn Chapel researchers have argued, for various reasons, that there may be an additional crypt concealed somewhere near the chapel, perhaps reached via a sealed door in the known crypt, perhaps not.[198] For reasons we'll be discussing shortly, this hypothesis seems worth following up; it would be especially interesting to see, if any secret crypt is discovered, whether it has anything in common with the secret vaults that play so important a role in the rituals of the higher degrees of Freemasonry.

---

197   Ralls 2003, 181.
198   Butler and Ritchie 2013, 183–184.

Other references to higher Masonic degrees are certainly present at Rosslyn. The only line of text anywhere in Rosslyn Chapel, for example, is found on an architrave in the Lady Chapel. It reads *Forte est vinum, fortior est rex, fortiores sunt mulieres, super omnia vincit veritas*—"wine is strong, the king is stronger, women are stronger still, but truth overcomes all things."[199] From most perspectives, this is an odd thing to read in a medieval chapel, not least as the only inscription in the structure. Seen in the proper context, though, it's extraordinarily revealing.

These words are part of a story found in the apocryphal book of Esdras and also the writings of the Hebrew historian Josephus. It is by saying these words, according to the story, that the Jewish prince Zerubbabel wins a competition at the court of the King of Persia and, as a reward for his wisdom, receives the king's permission to complete the rebuilding of the Second Temple. That same story plays a central role in the rituals of some of the oldest high degrees in Masonry—the three Knight Mason degrees and their equivalents in other Masonic rites, as described in chapter 1 of this book.

Most versions of the degree, including that preserved by the Knight Masons, quote the words carved into the stones of Rosslyn Chapel. It's remarkable, to use no stronger word, to find this connection to Masonic rituals about the rebuilding of the Temple of Solomon in a structure that may, in some sense, have been intended as a reconstruction of that temple. It is even possible—though much more research would be needed to settle the question one way or another—that in the Knight Mason and kindred degrees, today's Freemasons still have a version of rituals that were once secretly performed at or near Rosslyn Chapel.

It's also possible, if this is the case, that the old and otherwise puzzling tradition of referring to higher Masonic degrees as "Scottish," whether or not they have any obvious collection to Scotland, may ultimately derive from that connection. If a ritual originally practiced among stonemasons at Rosslyn Chapel ended up in the hands of speculative Masons in England, "Scots Master" would be a reasonable name for it.

---

199   Butler and Ritchie 2013, 216–218.

The case for a Templar link to Rosslyn Chapel need not rely on anything so indirect as Freemasonry, though. It's a matter of record that the elaborate carvings of the chapel are full of Templar symbols. These include the most distinctive emblem of the Order, the image of two riders on a single horse, as well as an assortment of emblems the Templars shared with other medieval monastic orders. It's also very much worth noting that four miles east of Rosslyn Chapel is the village of Temple.

The name is not an accident. Seven centuries ago, when it was called Balantrodoch, that same village was the headquarters of the Order of Knights Templar in Scotland.[200] Wherever else in Scotland Knights Templar may have been in 1307, there were certainly some in the vicinity of Rosslyn Chapel, and those will have included the officials in charge of the Order's Scottish presence, among others. If the legacy of the Knights Templar survived anywhere in Scotland, in other words, the vicinity of Rosslyn Chapel would be an excellent place to look for its traces.

The Dolorous Blow

The last link in the chain of connections I've attempted to trace here connects surviving Knights Templar in Scotland with the first lodges of Freemasons in the same country. That some connection must have existed is hard to dispute, as nothing else will explain the fact that Freemasons in the middle of the eighteenth century knew about a tunnel under the Temple Mount that was excavated at the time of the Crusader Kingdom of Jerusalem in the twelfth century and not rediscovered until 1968. That the connection will be difficult to document is just as certain, for nothing else will explain the failure of generations of researchers to turn up more than the most equivocal evidence for the connection.

There were very good reasons for the heirs of the Templar secrets, whatever those may have included, to keep a very low profile during the years between the dissolution of the Order in 1311 and the emergence of Freemasonry as a public phenomenon in 1717. That period of four centuries saw

---

200   Lord 2013, 186–191.

Christian Europe turn on itself in a cascade of violent persecutions and religious wars as brutal as any in history. During those four centuries, anyone suspected of unpopular religious opinions risked being accused of heresy, seized by the local religious authorities, tortured until he or she confessed, and put to death. Anyone suspected of unapproved religious practices ran an equal risk of being accused of witchcraft and treated the same way.

When the Reformation burst on the scene in the first half of the sixteenth century, and Europe cracked asunder into hostile Catholic and Protestant blocs, the situation became even worse. All through Protestant Europe—and Scotland, it bears remembering, was well over on the radical wing of the Protestant camp—anything too reminiscent of medieval Catholicism was the target of savage reprisals. Monasteries and the orders that ran them were among the first targets, and throughout Protestant Europe, the entire monastic system was destroyed before the sixteenth century was over.

The dissolution of the monasteries in England is among the better documented examples.[201] There the government of Henry VIII began closing down smaller monasteries in 1535, and the pace accelerated thereafter; by the end of 1541, every monastery and nunnery in the kingdom had been seized by royal officers, its monks or nuns driven off, its libraries and relics hauled away as trash, its buildings left to crumble into ruin, and its lands sold off to local landowners—at prices well below market rates, curiously enough, even though Henry VIII's government was perpetually short of money. The same drama was played out everywhere in Protestant Europe over the course of the sixteenth century. In the process, in all probability, one of the main repositories of the temple tradition disappeared forever.

The situation in Catholic countries was less brutal but no less destructive to what remained of the temple technology. In response to the rise of Protestantism, the Catholic Church imposed a uniform set of rituals, the Tridentine Rite, on the entire church: the first time in the entire history of Christianity that anything like this had ever been done.[202] The rich diversity

---

201   See Youings 1971 for a good summary.
202   Jones et al. 1992, 285.

of medieval rites and ceremonies—in the words of one ecclesiastical scholar: "every country, every diocese, almost every church throughout the West had its own way of celebrating Mass"[203]—gave way to a strictly enforced uniformity.

For almost four hundred years thereafter, under the watchful eyes of a newly founded bureaucracy, the Sacred Congregation of Rites, Catholic priests throughout the world spoke exactly the same Latin words and performed exactly the same actions. Even so simple and apparently harmless a project as translating the text of the Mass out of Latin, so that members of the congregation could understand what was being said, was strictly forbidden—vernacular translations of the Mass were on the Catholic Church's Index of Forbidden Books until 1897. Monasteries were as subject to the new comformism as any other activity of the Catholic Church, and local traditions and customs were swept away in favor of a strict obedience to the dictates of officials from Rome.

The hypothesis at the core of this book would suggest that when such measures were put into place and the temple technology stopped being used across most of Europe, the result would be a significant decrease in agricultural productivity—and that's exactly what happened. Historians noted a long time ago that many regions of Europe were more fertile in the Middle Ages than they are today. In upland regions across Europe, it's not at all uncommon to find abandoned villages that were once thriving agricultural communities, where the only thing that grows today is sparse forage for sheep or goats.

Until recently it was thought that the European climate in the Middle Ages was much warmer than it is today. Recent research by climatologists, however, has shown that the supposed Early Medieval Warm Period never happened, and the European climate in the Middle Ages was not significantly warmer than it was in more recent centuries.[204] The fact remains that something made it possible during the Middle Ages for wheat and barley

---

203   Jones et al. 1992, 286.
204   See, for example, Lemonick 2014.

to be grown on bleak uplands in Yorkshire and for wine grapes to flourish across southern England. Whatever that "something" was, it went away as the Middle Ages ended, leaving Europe struggling to feed itself—a struggle that played a large role in driving mass emigration from Europe to the New World and Australasia over the three centuries thereafter.

Was the collapse of the ancient temple technology the Dolorous Blow that, just as in the legends of the Holy Grail, caused a Waste Land to spread where crops and villages once flourished? Considerably more research will be needed before that question can be answered conclusively, but the possibility can't be dismissed out of hand.

From Templars to Freemasons

With the monasteries gone or reduced to strict theological conformity, and a harsh spirit of religious repression and violence abroad throughout late medieval Europe, the remaining custodians of the temple tradition faced an uphill fight. Exactly how that struggle unfolded and how the tradition itself came to be lost will probably never be known for certain. Little evidence on the subject survives from the four centuries that separate the last known Templars from the first Masonic Grand Lodge and much of what has been discovered has too often been interpreted in unhelpful and implausible ways.

Some theorists who have explored the possibility of a link between the Knights Templar and the Freemasons, for example, have painted this connection in grandiose colors, imagining whole armies of Templar knights fleeing to Scotland with the Ark of the Covenant, the Holy Grail, and the mummified body of Jesus of Nazareth in their baggage. There's precisely no evidence for any such mass migration—to say nothing of the relics in question!—and there's also no need to posit anything so overblown. There were already Knights Templar in Scotland in 1307, some of them at the village of Balantradoch four miles from the hill where Rosslyn Chapel would one day rise, others in the many other properties owned by the Templar order across the Kingdom of Scotland.

The transmission of Templar traditions to Scottish lodges of operative stonemasons could have involved only a few Scottish Templars, or even just one. It's not at all difficult to imagine a Templar brother trained in the builder's art, say, whose experience helping to construct churches and chapter houses for the order in Scotland gave him the knowledge and skill to earn a place in an operative lodge, and who then passed on some of what he knew to his own apprentices and to other members of the guild. Even so slender a connection would account for the fact that Masons knew about the secret tunnel into the Temple Mount in Jerusalem two centuries before its rediscovery.

The question that remains is what else might have passed from surviving Knights Templar to the operative lodges. If, as I've suggested, the Templars may have learned some form of the ancient temple technology in the Holy Land, it would have been logical for them to have applied it to their vast landholdings across Europe, since the income from the agricultural production in those holdings helped pay the substantial costs of maintaining the Templar fortresses and armies in the Crusader Kingdom of Jerusalem. If, as suggested in an earlier chapter, the Templar version of the temple tradition was connected to heretical beliefs akin to those of the ancient Naassenes, that connection would have made the heirs of the Templars all the more likely to try to preserve the temple technology as a sacred knowledge connected to their most deeply held beliefs. The question is how they might have tried to do this.

One possibility—though it is only a possibility, and a great deal of further research will be needed to confirm or disprove it—is that the building of Rosslyn Chapel may have been an attempt to construct a working example of the old temple technology. By the time the cornerstone of the chapel was laid, 135 years had passed since the formal dissolution of the Templar order, and whatever scraps of knowledge might have been passed on from former Templars to their heirs would have had ample time to be assembled and understood by the operative Masons who inherited it. William Sinclair, Earl of Caithness, the builder of the chapel, was also the patron and titular grand master of stonemasons in Scotland, a title that remained in the Sinclair family for centuries thereafter. If anyone in fifteenth-century Scotland was going to try to revive the temple technology, Sinclair was the man.

If that was the purpose for which Rosslyn Chapel was built, though, it failed. Once the Reformation got under way in Scotland, Rosslyn Chapel was among the targets of Protestant rage. In 1592, officials of the Presbyterian Church ordered the altars of the chapel demolished and put an end to services there. In 1650, during the English Civil War, the chapel was used by Roundhead soldiers as a stable for their horses, and in 1688, a Protestant mob from Edinburgh diverted themselves after looting and burning Roslin Castle by doing more damage to the already battered chapel. After that it sat empty and abandoned, a windowless ruin. Whatever secrets might have gone into its construction, whatever traditional practices might have taken place there, were lost forever.

Not until 1736 did matters begin to change. In that year, the last Sinclair to hold the title of grand master of Scottish stonemasons, another William Sinclair, formally resigned it in favor of the first grand master of the Masonic Grand Lodge of Scotland. In the same year, John St. Clair, the owner of the dilapidated ruin of Rosslyn Chapel, repaired the damaged roof, put new flagstones on the floor, and filled the empty windows with new glass. He was urged to do this by Sir John Clerk of Penicuik. It's probably not a coincidence that 1736 was also the year in which the Masonic Grand Lodge of Scotland was founded, and Clerk was one of the most prominent Scottish Freemasons of his day.

By that time, though, whatever secrets might have been passed down from the Templars to the operative lodges had apparently been lost. Exactly how that happened will probably never be known. Secret teachings are fragile things; the fewer the people who know them, the more likely they are to become garbled or forgotten. In the tremendous political, religious, and social convulsions that swept over Scotland in the seventeenth century, it would have been all too easy for the thread of tradition to snap. A few stray bullets in the many battles of the time, a few of the many political executions in those years, or simply a climate of opinion that made passing on a heretical religious teaching too dangerous to risk would have been enough.

Even so, there's some reason to think that Masons in the early eighteenth century still retained a last flickering memory of the Templar secrets. This is suggested by a curious passage in the very first exposé of Masonic high degrees, *Les Plus Secrets Mystéres de la Hautes Grades de la Maçonnerie Dévoilés* (*The Most Secret Mysteries of the High Degrees of Masonry Unveiled*), published in 1766. In this passage, the origin of Masonry is traced back to Godfrey de Bouillon, the leader of the First Crusade, who supposedly invented the symbols of Masonry so that the Crusaders could conceal the fact that they were Christians from their enemies.[205] As literal history, this is nonsense, and the passage gets even stranger when it claims that Godfrey de Bouillon was the leader of the Crusaders "toward the end of the third century," which makes no straightforward sense no matter how it's interpreted.

If "Godfrey de Bouillon" is a cover for some other more secret name, though, the passage makes a great deal of sense. The Naassenes, as already mentioned, believed that "of all men we alone are Christians, accomplishing the mystery at the Third Gate." Once the Catholic Church gained ascendancy in the western world, Naassenes would have been in exactly the position of the imaginary Crusaders in the passage just cited, forced to conceal their religion from hostile believers in a different faith, and the camouflage of Masonry would have been a plausible way for them to do so. That this happened in the third century of the Common Era seems vanishingly unlikely, but then it's anyone's guess what date would have served as the starting point for the calendar of a medieval Gnostic heresy descended from, or related to, the Naassenes. "The third century" from that starting point could have been almost anywhere from the early Middle Ages to the early modern era.

There is at least one other piece of evidence, furthermore, that the lost secrets of Masonry had a connection to alternative religious beliefs—the frantic hostility the Catholic Church has directed toward the Craft, mentioned back in chapter 1, is one of the enduring oddities of Masonic history. Factor

---

205   de Hoyos and Morris 2011, xvii-xx.

in the history described in chapters 11 and 12, though, and the riddle becomes clear at once. If, as I've suggested, the Templars embraced the old temple tradition along with a heresy that was either the Naassene gnosis or something more or less parallel to it, Catholic authorities would have become aware of that once Templar properties were handed over to the church, if they had not been aware of it long before.

When Freemasonry turned up with symbols obviously derived from the same tradition, in turn, the logical response of Rome would have been exactly what in fact happened. This link to ancient heresy, I suggest, explains the unnamed and unexplained "just and reasonable motives known to us" mentioned in the papal bull *In Eminente* better than any alternative. That the Freemasons themselves had lost the teachings for which they were condemned so harshly is just one of history's many ironies.

What remained then, and what remains today in Masonry, is a collection of beautiful but enigmatic ceremonies and symbols, pervaded by a traditional sense that these things were once the keys to a tremendous secret. Then as now, the men who became Freemasons were taught that the words and signs they were given were substitutes for something else and encouraged to look forward to the day when the true secrets of a Master Mason would once more be revealed. It may well be that the brothers who founded the first Grand Lodge of England in 1717 and the Grand Lodge of Scotland in 1736 hoped to recover those lost secrets.

If so, those hopes were not fulfilled. Freemasonry evolved in different directions, away from the studies that might have revealed the temple technology, and toward its present role as a men's social club with ornate initiation ceremonies and a variety of praiseworthy charitable commitments. To this day, Masons continue to confer degrees that hint at a lost secret, preserve symbols that none of the Craft know how to interpret, and scatter grain and pour wine and oil on cornerstones—a fragmentary survival, perhaps, of ancient ceremonies that once linked certain buildings to a technology of agricultural fertility. Only these mute fragments of the lost operative knowledge remain, the last fading echo of an ancient mystery.

CHAPTER FOURTEEN

The Recovery of the Grail

If the hypothesis at the core of this book is correct, something like seven thousand years ago, people in several parts of the world began to notice that certain kinds of structures they built had beneficial effects on the crops that sustained their lives. As the generations passed, and people in different regions interacted and shared knowledge, a body of traditional lore slowly evolved, guiding the priests and priestesses of ancient tribes in activities that made use of those effects for the good of their communities. The result of this long, uncertain, and haphazard process of evolution was the emergence of what I've called the temple tradition, a set of architectural design features and apparently ceremonial practices that harness certain natural forces to improve harvests in the surrounding region.

The Temple of Solomon was only one of many ancient structures that drew on the temple tradition to benefit the people who worshipped there. Once Christianity became the established religion of post-Roman Europe, though, Solomon's building became the one ancient temple that could be linked symbolically to Christian churches without risking accusations of heresy, and so for many centuries, it served as the archetype of the temple in the imagination of the western world. This may have been one reason why the order that apparently spearheaded the recovery of the temple tradition in western Europe during the Middle Ages, the Knights Templar, placed the Temple of Solomon at the center of its collective identity. It may also have inspired the last custodians of the temple tradition in Europe, the Freemasons, to see themselves as the heirs of Solomon and the rebuilders of the Temple—and to retain that sense of identity even after the secrets they once preserved were lost.

Outside the western world, of course, different influences prevailed and different factors shaped the rise and fall of the temple tradition. It's entirely possible that even today, despite all the convulsions of recent centuries and the wholesale destruction and abandonment of ancient traditions, there are Hindu temples in India or Shinto shrines in Japan that preserve documents or oral teachings relevant to the temple technology. It's even possible that similar knowledge lingers in some corner of Europe, perhaps preserved in neglected documents in one of the European languages that few scholars can read.

Some chance discovery someday might provide the missing pieces of the temple technology and make it possible to go beyond the limited evidence and the speculative hypotheses I've been able to gather in this book. Until and unless that happens, though, all that remains of a forgotten technology millennia old—a secret that many people once considered sacred enough to justify risking their lives—is an assortment of enigmatic traditions and fragmentary lore, some of it preserved by rote within Masonic lodges, much more scattered far and wide in the history of architecture, the folklore of many lands, and the obscure and poorly researched areas of science where physics influences biology and ecology.

If the story of the temple tradition ended there, it would be a melancholy tale indeed. In today's troubled, overpopulated, environmentally unstable world, a set of principles and practices that could increase vegetative growth using simple, natural, readily available means would be an extraordinary asset. Improved harvests would be only one of the many possible benefits. The effects of the temple technology on the natural environment might be even more important, especially at a time when so many ecosystems are under strain from climate change. The old custom of surrounding a temple or a church with a grove of trees or other natural vegetation takes on a new importance when it's remembered just how much carbon dioxide healthy, thriving trees can take out of the atmosphere and bind in their tissues. Even so, if the story ends at the point to which I've traced it, if the temple tradition and the secret technology at its heart have passed beyond any hope of recovery, all those possibilities went whistling down the wind forever when the last heir of the Knights Templar who knew the secret took it with him to his grave.

But the story of the temple tradition need not end there. Though the thread of the tradition in the western world snapped more than three centuries ago and the knowledge that once made it work apparently survives only in hints and fragments, it may still be possible to reconstruct enough of the temple technology to revive it.

Seeking the Holy Grail

At first glance, any such project poses immense challenges. If the hypothesis at the heart of this book is correct, after all, the temple technology most likely produced a complex cascade of effects that influenced crop fertility in ways that contemporary science has yet to duplicate. While there's no reason to assume that the forces behind those effects are unknown to today's physicists, research into the ways that electric and magnetic fields and low-frequency infrared radiation affect living systems hasn't been a priority for scientific research. A great deal of original research would have to be done and some very large blank spaces would have to be filled in to make sense of the temple technology if, in fact, these are the forces that mediate it—and because of the fragmentary nature of the evidence, it's only a guess that these were the specific energies involved.

Given a great deal of grant money and the support of capable research teams, this could still probably be done. To begin with, the sort of research carried out on a shoestring by the Dragon Project researchers described in chapter 6 would have to be applied on a much larger and more comprehensive scale to surviving temples that are likely to retain important elements of the old tradition—structures in India and Japan sacred to agricultural deities, for example. If unexpected energy effects were detected, controlled trials could be used to see whether and how those energies influenced crop growth, while further research in and around temples might sort out some of the variables involved, place the temple tradition on a sound theoretical basis, and enable further work to proceed from there.

Possibility is one thing, of course, and probability is something else again. I would be astonished, to use no stronger word, if any research program of the sort just outlined got serious consideration, much less the funding and personnel that would be needed to do the thing properly. A galaxy of prejudices stand in the way of any such attempt. The modern conviction that people in ancient times couldn't possibly have known anything we don't know today remains strong. So does the distaste, very common among scientists, for religion and everything that might possibly be connected to it. In the historically Christian countries of Europe, the Americas, and Australasia, for that matter, most scientists who don't share that distaste for religion belong to mainstream faiths and have their own reasons for discomfort with a tradition historically connected to Pagan faiths and heretical religious ideas.

I would be delighted, in other words, if a major research laboratory were to set out to try to put the hypothesis at the center of this book to experimental test. For that matter, it would be cause for celebration if something as simple and relatively inexpensive as modern ground-penetrating radar were to be used on the grounds of Glastonbury Abbey and Rosslyn Chapel to find out once and for all if there's anything to the traditional claims of buried vaults in the vicinity. I don't expect either of those things to happen, not until and unless there's a profound shift in attitudes toward the past and a new openness to the possibility that ancient peoples might just possibly have stumbled across a discovery or two that we haven't made yet. Fortunately, the sort of research project just outlined isn't the only possibility that exists.

The thing that brings a revival of the temple technology within reach is precisely the same thing that made its rediscovery so difficult: it doesn't look anything like the kind of technology we use today. Its tools were those of ancient architecture and religion, not those of modern physics and biology, or for that matter modern agriculture. A technology that was based on the movement of natural energies through the landscape, amplified by structures of stone and wood laid out according to precise geometries and carefully positioned relative to the Earth's magnetic field, and stirred into activity by some combination of sound waves and volatile organic compounds in an enclosed airspace is so alien to modern expectations that it has been far too easy for people not to notice that it was a technology at all.

That disadvantage, though, is balanced by an even more important advantage. The old temple technology required no expensive laboratory equipment, no highly refined materials, and no energy supply beyond the one the Earth naturally receives every day from the sun. The people who discovered it in ancient times did so using their five unaided senses and simple methods of recordkeeping to track changes in the world around them. Those who reassembled it from scattered fragments in medieval Europe had no better tools to work with. In both cases, the tools they had were adequate to the task, and it's worth suggesting that the same tools could do the job once again, even in the difficult conditions of the present.

Asking the Right Questions

There are at least two directions a search for the lost technology of the temple tradition might take, and they're both equally valid—and equally necessary. The first is documentary research. This book has attempted to carry out a first reconnaissance of a forgotten landscape of ideas, drawing on the limited scholarly resources available to me in the handful of languages I can read. Meanwhile, all through those countries where the temple tradition once flourished, ancient religious texts, myths and legends, collections of folklore, and scholarly works of various kinds sit in libraries I have not had the opportunity to visit, and some of them could well contain pieces of information that could be of crucial importance in reconstructing the temple technology.

Like the quest for the Holy Grail, the search for scraps of lore concerning the temple tradition is very largely a matter of knowing enough to ask the right questions in the right places and times. When modern readers encounter passages in old texts talking about how this building or that ritual made the crops flourish, the normal reaction is to treat such statements as superstitious nonsense or, at best, a storyteller's whimsy. This is the way that the temple tradition as a whole has been approached for centuries now, and just as in the Grail legends, those who forgot to ask questions about what they encountered wound up right back in the Waste Land where they started.

The alternative is to take seriously the possibility that any given item of folklore or mythological reference dealing with agricultural fertility might have some basis in physics, botany, ecology, or the interactions among them. In some cases the basis is obvious. An old tradition among my wife's Welsh ancestors, for example, had it that a little bowl of milk should always be left outside the back door at night for the Tylwyth Teg, the faeries of traditional Welsh folklore, who would then bless the house and the fields around it with good luck. Factor in the earthy realities of rural Welsh life in which rats and mice were major agricultural pests and cats were among their main predators, and the benefits of a habit that would encourage cats to frequent one's property after dark are not exactly hard to work out.

The same logic applies on a much larger scale. In Shinto, for example, a great many items of lore make practical sense when the ecological context of traditional Japanese agriculture is kept in mind. The taboos that placed sacred groves and entire mountains off limits to logging and farming, for example, were not randomly applied; studies have shown that many of these sacred spaces were precisely located to control erosion and aid in the absorption of rainfall into groundwater.[206] Similar logic seems to have guided the

---

206   See Sonoda 2000.

location of sacred groves in many other societies, ancient Greece among them.[207]

The same logic applied to a different set of effects can govern inquiries into folklore, mythology, and religious teachings relevant to the temple tradition. All through the lands the temple tradition reached, customs, beliefs, practices, and stories can be found that relate temples and temple worship to agricultural fertility. The survey of the temple technology in the second part of this book gives a very rough, tentative, and preliminary sketch of what might be accomplished by work of this kind. More extensive explorations of the same general type could quite conceivably turn up a body of data substantial enough that the temple technology could be reconstructed—and there remains the tantalizing possibility that somewhere there might still survive a written account of the technology complete and detailed enough to allow a working temple to be built and tested on that basis alone.

Even without some such document, it may be possible to follow the example of the unknown discoverers of the temple technology and work out the requirements of the temple effect by sheer trial and error. Enough is known about some of the better documented structures that used the temple technology—Shinto shrines, Hindu temples, western European churches between the Crusades and the Reformation, and so on—that it's entirely possible today to locate, orient, design, and construct a building to the traditional design, perform appropriate services inside, and keep track of any noticeable effects on plant growth around it. Alternatively, where temples built according to traditional rules still exist and function in something like their original manner, detailed study of gardens and fields nearby in comparison with others not so sited could provide crucial data.

For obvious reasons, either of these latter projects would need either the acquiescence or, better still, the active participation of clergy and congregations in one or more of the temple- or church-building faiths. Whether that would be forthcoming is a question that can't be answered in advance, and

---

207   Birge 1982 is a good introduction to sacred groves in the Greek tradition.

will depend among many other things on how the theory proposed in this book is received by the various religious traditions in question.

Finding the Lost Word

One other institution, of course, is deeply concerned with the matters discussed in this book, and that is Freemasonry. If the hypothesis I've proposed is correct, the Lost Word—the original secret of the Craft, for which the current Master's Word and the secrets of the Master Mason's degree conferred today are substitutes—was a symbolic key that explained the secret technology at the heart of the temple tradition. Knowing the Lost Word, the master builders of the Middle Ages were able to site, orient, design, and build churches that made effective use of that technology for the benefit of their communities.

Exactly what form the Word might have taken in medieval operative lodges is anyone's guess today. It's possible that once the details of the medieval European form of the temple technology are better understood, some puzzling word or neglected symbol in medieval documents will suddenly make unexpected sense, and the Lost Word will be restored to the Craft. It's just as possible that whatever symbolic key the operative masons of the past used to communicate their secret will remain lost forever, even after the secret itself has been revealed.

What does all this imply for the present and future of Freemasonry? Certainly it takes away nothing from the reputation of the Craft if the secret that it once guarded was an ancient technology of immense benefit to all, which was woven into the structure of some of the greatest architectural creations of our species. Though the secret was lost, generations of Masons have devoted their best efforts to its recovery. While their quests for the Lost Word often went tolerably veering off in strange directions, a great deal of good has come out of their labors: from Masonic hospitals and benevolent institutions, through quieter and more personal acts of charity, to the simple efforts of millions of men who have been inspired by the moral teachings of Masonry to lead better lives. None of that is erased or rendered irrelevant if the original secret of the operative Craft was something that was beneficial to human life in a very different way.

Even if future discoveries prove beyond a doubt that the temple tradition as I've outlined it was the secret communicated by the old operative lodges, modern Freemasonry is not the operative Craft, and its commitments remain what they have been for the last three hundred years. To the Grand Lodges that govern contemporary Freemasonry, whose central task is the preservation of the currently accepted landmarks of the Craft, this book and any future discoveries it may inspire can be at most a matter of historical interest. Most Masons will very likely treat it the same way, and it's entirely appropriate that they should do so. All things considered, the ancient temple technology is no more necessarily relevant to modern Masons than the right way to build an arch or a pillar out of freestone.

That said, I don't think it's unreasonable to hope that some Freemasons who share an interest in the relics and traditions of the operative Craft will be inspired to join in the search for the Lost Word that once made the fields flourish. In the same spirit, I hope that at least a few believers and clergy in those religions that once made use of the temple tradition, and perhaps still preserve remnants of the old lore, will be inspired to search the scriptures, teachings, and practices of their faiths for traditions that might bear on the temple technology, and that at least a few people with the scientific back- ground needed to make sense of the data—whether or not they share either the Masonic or the religious commitments just mentioned—will contribute their talents to the search.

According to Sir Thomas Malory's version of the story, when the quest for the Holy Grail began, "every knight took the way that liked him best."[208] It remains good advice for seekers after the Grail that has partly been unveiled in this book, not least because no one knows which of the available routes is most likely to lead to the discoveries that could heal the Waste Lands of the modern industrial world. I can only hope that the fragmentary evidence I have been able to gather in this book will be helpful in that quest.

---

208   Malory 1994, 668.

GLOSSARY

ad quadratum: literally "by the square," one of the two standard systems of sacred geometry used in Gothic architecture.

ad triangulum: literally "by the triangle," one of the two standard systems of sacred geometry used in Gothic architecture.

adyton: literally "not to be entered," the spaces in ancient Greek temples that were not open to the general public.

Albigensians: see Cathars.

Cathars: members of a medieval Gnostic heresy.

churching: in medieval Christianity, a ceremony to bless a woman who had recently given birth, performed before she returned to regular attendance at services.

circumambulation: the rite of circling a sacred space, usually in a clockwise direction.

cowan: among Masons, a person who is not a Mason; originally an unskilled laborer who did not have the skills necessary to work with freestone.

diamagnetism: a physical property of certain materials that cause them to be slightly repelled by a magnetic field.

freestone: building stone suitable for fine carving.

garbhagrha: in a Hindu temple, the innermost holy shrine.

Gnosticism: a religious movement originating in ancient Roman times, which considered personal experience of spiritual realities more important than faith in doctrines.

goma: the fire-offering ritual of Japanese esoteric Buddhism.

hieron: in ancient Greece, an open-air holy place.

hinoki: the Japanese cypress tree, the usual source for lumber for Shinto shrines.

hypostyle hall: in ancient Egyptian temples, a large room with pillars supporting the roof.

jinja: the usual Japanese word for a Shinto sacred building, normally translated "shrine."

kami: the divine powers worshipped in Shinto.

keihitsu: in Shinto, a vowel tone used to bring the kami into manifestation.

kotodama: "word-spirit," the traditional Japanese science of vocal symbolism.

mandapa: in a Hindu temple, a pillared hall for worship.

mandira: the classic Hindu temple.

miki: in Shinto, rice wine (sake) consumed by worshippers at the conclusion of a ceremony.

mikveh: in Orthodox Judaism, a ritual bath used by women for purification.

misogi shuho: in Shinto, ceremonial purification in running water or the sea.

Naassenes: members of an ancient Gnostic heresy, which may have survived to influence the legends of the Holy Grail.

naorai: in Shinto, a reception and meal held after a ritual, at which food offered to the kami is eaten by priests and honored parishioners.

naos: the classic Greek colonnaded temple.

norito: in Shinto, a traditional prayer in archaic Japanese.

paramagnetism: a physical property of certain substances that causes them to be slightly attracted by a magnetic field.

peristyle court: in ancient Egyptian temples, an open courtyard surrounded by a portico supported by columns.

prasad: food offerings to Hindu deities, which are later reverently eaten by worshippers.

rekhyet: the common people of ancient Egypt.

seichu: in Shinto, the straight line extending from within the temple down the main entrance route; visitors are expected not to walk or stand upon it.

shide: in Shinto, zigzag strips of white paper hung from a rope to mark off sacred space.

shikhara: in a Hindu temple, the stone tower above the innermost holy shrine.

Shilpa Shastras: traditional manuals for the design and construction of Hindu temples.

Shingon: one of the two great denominations of Japanese esoteric Buddhism.

sŏnang: in Korea, the guardian deity of a village.

sŏnangdang: the shrine of a sŏnang, usually either a heap of stones, a tree with a rope tied around it, or a combination of the two.

spolia: in early Christian churches, architectural features such as columns salvaged from Pagan temples and used to beautify the buildings of the new faith.

temenos: in ancient Greece, an open-air holy place, or the sacred space surrounding a temple.

Tendai: one of the two great denominations of Japanese esoteric Buddhism.

torii: a ceremonial gateway outside a Shinto shrine.

yazata: in Zoroastrianism, a minor deity subordinate to the supreme god Ahura Mazda.

BIBLIOGRAPHY

Allen, Arthur H. *Electricity in Agriculture*. London: Isaac Pitman and Sons, 1922.

Ashe, Geoffrey. *King Arthur's Avalon: The Story of Glastonbury*. Glasgow: William Collins, 1957.

Aylsward, Thomas F. trans. *The Imperial Guide to Feng-Shui and Chinese Astrology*. London: Watkins, 2007.

Barber, Richard W. *The Holy Grail: Imagination and Belief*. Cambridge, MA: Harvard University Press, 2004.

Bell, Lanny. "The New Kingdom 'Divine' Temple: The Example of Luxor," in Shafer 1997, 127–184.

Ben-Dov, Meir. *In the Shadow of the Temple*, trans. Israel Freedman. New York: Harper & Row, 1985.

Birge, Darice E. "Sacred Groves in the Ancient Greek World," doctoral dissertation, University of California at Berkeley, 1982.

Boyce, Mary. *Zoroastrians: Their Religious Beliefs and Practices*. London: Routledge and Kegan Paul, 1979.

Breen, John, and Mark Teeuwen. *Shinto in History: Ways of the Kami*. Honolulu: University of Hawai'i Press, 2000.

Bryant, Nigel, trans. *The High Book of the Grail*. Cambridge, MA: Cambridge University Press, 1978.

Burke, John, and Kaj Halberg. *Seed of Knowledge, Stone of Plenty: Understanding the Lost Technology of the Ancient Megalith-Builders*. San Francisco, CA: Council Oak Books, 2005.

Burkert, Walter. *Greek Religion*, trans. John Raffan. Cambridge, MA: Harvard University Press, 1985.

Butler, Alan, and John Ritchie. *Rosslyn Chapel Decoded*. London: Watkins, 2013.

Cahill, Thomas. *How the Irish Saved Civilization*. New York: Doubleday, 1995.

Callahan, Philip S. *Ancient Mysteries, Modern Visions: The Magnetic Life of Agriculture*. Austin, TX: Acres USA, 2001.

———. *Tuning Into Nature: Solar Energy, Infrared Radiation, and the Insect Communication System*. Old Greenwich, CT: Devin-Adair, 1975.

Carey, John. *Ireland and the Grail*. Aberystwyth, Wales: Celtic Studies Publications, 2007.

Carr, Harry, ed. *The Early French Exposures*. London: Quatuor Coronati Lodge No. 2076, 1971.

Chrétien de Troyes. *Arthurian Romances*, trans. William W. Kibler and Carleton W. Carroll. London: Penguin, 1991.

Clark, William W. *Medieval Cathedrals*. Westport, CT: Greenwood Press, 2006.

Claudy, Carl H. *Introduction to Freemasonry.* Washington, DC: Temple Publishers, 1931.

Connelly, Joan Breton. *The Parthenon Enigma.* New York: Random House, 2014.

Critchlow, Keith. *Order in Space.* New York: Viking, 1970.

———. *Time Stands Still.* New York: St. Martin's Press, 1982.

Curatola, Giovanni, ed. *The Art and Architecture of Mesopotamia.* New York: Abbeville Press, 2006.

Davis, Albert R. and Walter C. Rawls, Jr. *Magnetism and Its Effects on the Living System.* Smithtown, NY: Exposition Press, 1980.

DeGlopper, Donald R. "Religion and Ritual in Lukang," in Wolf 1974, 43–69.

de Hoyos, Arturo, ed. *Freemasonry's Royal Secret: The Jamaican "Francken Manuscript" of the High Degrees.* Washington, DC: Scottish Rite Research Society, 2015.

de Hoyos, Arturo, and S. Brent Morris, trans. and eds. *The Most Secret Mysteries of the High Degrees of Masonry Unveiled.* Washington, DC: Scottish Rite Research Society, 2011.

———. *Allegorical Conversations Arranged by Wisdom.* Washington, DC: Scottish Rite Research Society, 2012.

Devereux, Paul. *The New Ley Hunter's Guide.* Glastonbury, UK: Gothic Image, 1994.

———. *Places of Power: Secret Energies at Ancient Sites: A Guide to Observed and Measured Phenomena.* London: Blandford, 1990.

———. *Spirit Roads: An Exploration of Otherworldly Routes.* London: Collins & Brown, 2003.

Evans, Ann Llewellyn. *Shinto Norito: A Book of Prayers*. Victoria, CA: Tenchi Press, 2001.

Fideler, David. *Jesus Christ Sun of God: Ancient Theology and Early Christian Symbolism*. Wheaton, IL: Quest Books, 1993.

Geoffrey of Monmouth. *The History of the Kings of Britain*, trans. Lewis Thorpe. London: Penguin, 1966.

Gest, Kevin L. *The Secrets of Solomon's Temple*. Hersam, UK: Lewis Masonic, 2007.

Ghyka, Matila. *The Geometry of Art and Life*. New York: Dover Publications, 1977.

Gleason, William. *The Spiritual Foundations of Aikido*. Rochester, VT: Destiny Books, 1995.

Godwin, Joscelyn. *The Mystery of the Seven Vowels*. Grand Rapids, MI: Phanes Press, 1991.

Grand Lodge of Maryland. *Maryland Masonic Manual*. Baltimore, NH: Grand Lodge of Maryland, 1935.

Greene, J. Patrick. *Norton Priory: The Archaeology of a Medieval Religious House*. Cambridge: Cambridge University Press, 1989.

Greenough, J. B., G. L. Kittredge, A. A. Howard, and Benjamin L. D'Ooge. *Allen and Greenough's New Latin Grammar*. New Rochelle, NY: Aristide D. Caratzas, 1992.

Greer, John Michael, and Christopher Warnock, trans. *The Picatrix*. Iowa City, IA: Adocentyn Press, 2011.

Haeny, Gerhard, "New Kingdom 'Mortuary Temples' and 'Temples of Millions of Years,'" in Shafer 1997, 86–126.

Hahn, Robert. *Anaximander and the Architects: The Contributions of Egyptian and Greek Architectural Technologies to the Origins of Greek Philosophy*. Albany, NY: State University of New York, 2001.

Hamblin, William James, and David Rolph Seely. *Solomon's Temple: Myth and History.* London: Thames & Hudson, 2007.

Hancock, Graham. *Fingerprints of the Gods.* New York: Random House, 1995.

Hesiod, "Works and Days," in Dorothea Wender, trans. *Hesiod and Theognis.* New York: Penguin, 1973.

Hiscock, Nigel. *The Wise Master Builder: Platonic Geometry in Plans of Medieval Abbeys and Cathedrals.* Aldershot, UK: Ashgate, 2000.

Holmes, Urban T. *A New Interpretation of Chrétien's Conte du Graal.* Chapel Hill, NC: University of North Carolina Press, 1948.

Hughan, William James. *Memorials of the Masonic Union of A.D. 1813.* London: Chatto and Windus, 1874.

Huntley, H. E. *The Divine Proportion: A Study in Mathematical Beauty.* New York: Dover Books, 1970.

Hutchens, Rex R. *A Bridge to Light: A Study in Masonic Ritual and Philosophy.* Washington, DC. The Supreme Council 33°, 2010.

Huyler, Stephen P. *Meeting God: Elements of Hindu Devotion.* New Haven, CT: Yale University Press, 1999.

Iamblichus of Chalcis, *On the Mysteries*, trans. Thomas Taylor. San Diego, CA: Wizards Bookshelf, 1984.

ibn Khaldun. *Muqaddimah: An Introduction to History*, trans. Franz Rosenthal. New York: Pantheon Books, 1958.

Icke, David. *And the Truth Shall Set You Free.* Ryde, UK: Bridge of Light, 2004.

Jenkins, Philip. *The Lost History of Christianity.* New York: HarperOne, 2008.

Jones, Cheslyn, Geoffrey Wainright, Edward Yarnold, and Paul Bradshaw, eds. *The Study of Liturgy.* New York: Oxford University Press, 1992.

Kageyama, Haruki. *Arts of Japan 4: The Arts of Shinto.* New York: Weatherhill, 1973.

Kidder, J. Edward. *Japanese Temples: Sculpture, Painting, Gardens, and Architecture.* Tokyo: Bijutsu Shippan-Sha, 1964.

Kim, Joungwon, ed. *Korean Cultural Heritage, Vol. 2: Thought and Religion.* Seoul: Korea Foundation, 1996.

King, L. W. *Babylonian Religion and Mythology.* New York: AMS Press, 1976.

Knoop, Douglas, and G. P. Jones. *The Genesis of Freemasonry.* London: Quatuor Coronati Correspondence Circle, 1978.

Kruger, Kristina. *Monasteries and Monastic Orders.* Königswinter, Westphalia: H. F. Ullman, 2008.

Kuhn, Thomas S. *The Structure of Scientific Revolutions.* Chicago: University of Chicago Press, 1970.

Lambert, Malcolm. *Medieval Heresy.* Oxford: Blackwell, 1992.

Lawlor, Robert. *Sacred Geometry: Philosophy and Practice.* London: Thames and Hudson, 1982.

Layton, Bentley. *The Gnostic Scriptures.* New York: Doubleday, 1987.

Lemonick, Michael D. "So-Called Medieval Warm Period Not So Warm After All." Climate Central blog, http://www.climatecentral.org /news/so-called-medieval-warm-period-not-so-warm-15064.

Lemström, S. *Electricity in Agriculture and Horticulture.* London: The Electrician Publishing Co., 1904.

Lord, Evelyn. *The Knights Templar in Britain.* London: Routledge, 2013.

Lundquist, John M. *The Temple of Jerusalem: Past, Present, and Future.* Westport, CT: Praeger, 2008.

Lundy, Miranda. *Sacred Geometry.* Presteigne, Wales: Wooden Books, 2002.

MacNulty, W. Kirk. *Freemasonry: A Journey through Ritual and Symbol.* London: Thames & Hudson, 1991.

Malory, Thomas. *Le Morte d'Arthur.* New York: Modern Library, 1994.

Mannikka, Eleanor. *Angkor Wat: Time, Space, and Kingship.* Honolulu: University of Hawai'i Press, 1996.

Mbiti, John S. *African Religions and Philosophy.* Oxford: Heinemann, 1990.

McClendon, Charles B. *The Origins of Medieval Architecture: Building in Europe, A.D. 600–900.* New Haven, CT: Yale University Press, 2005.

Michell, John. *New Light on the Ancient Mystery of Glastonbury.* Glastonbury, England: Gothic Image, 1997.

———. *The View Over Atlantis.* New York: Ballantine, 1969.

Michell, John, with Allan Brown. *How the World Is Made: The Story of Creation According to Sacred Geometry.* Rochester, VT: Inner Traditions, 2009.

Miller, Helen Hill. *The Realms of Arthur.* New York: Scribners, 1969.

Nelson, John K. *A Year in the Life of a Shinto Shrine.* Seattle, WA: University of Washington Press, 1996.

North, John. *Stonehenge: A New Interpretation of Prehistoric Man and the Cosmos.* New York: Free Press, 1996.

O'Brien, Jacqueline, and Peter Harbison. *Ancient Ireland: From Prehistory to the Middle Ages.* New York: Oxford University Press, 1996.

Padovan, Richard. *Proportion: Science, Philosophy, Architecture.* London: Spon Press, 1999.

Parke, H. W. *Festivals of the Athenians*. London: Thames and Hudson, 1977.

Partner, Peter. *The Murdered Magicians: The Knights Templar and their Myth*. Oxford: Oxford University Press, 1981.

Patai, Raphael. *Man and Temple in Ancient Jewish Myth and Ritual*. New York: Ktav Publishing House, 1967.

————. *The Hebrew Goddess*. Detroit, MI: Wayne State University Press, 1990.

Pennick, Nigel. *Sacred Geometry: Symbolism and Purpose in Religious Structures*. Chievely, England: Capall Bann, 1994.

Pennick, Nigel, and Paul Devereux. *Lines on the Landscape: Leys and Other Linear Enigmas*. London: Robert Hale, 1989.

Persinger, Michael, and Gyslaine F. Lafreniere. *Space-Time Transients and Unusual Events*. Chicago: Nelson-Hall, 1977.

Plutarch, "The Life of Themistocles," in Plutarch's *Lives*, trans. Arthur Hugh Clough. New York: Collier, 1937.

Ralls, Karen. *The Templars and the Holy Grail: Knights of the Quest*. Wheaton, IL: Theosophical Publishing House, 2003.

Reed, Thomas Milburn. *Washington Monitor and Freemason's Guide to the Symbolic Degrees*. Seattle, WA: Grand Lodge of Washington, 1976.

Ritner, Robert K. *The Mechanics of Ancient Egyptian Magical Practice*. Chicago: University of Chicago Press, 1993.

Roberts, John M. *The Mythology of the Secret Societies*. New York: Scribners, 1972.

Robinson, John. *Born in Blood*. New York: Random House, 1989.

Russell, Jeffrey Burton. *Inventing the Flat Earth*. New York: Praeger, 1991.

Rose, Michael S. *Ugly As Sin: Why They Changed Our Churches from Sacred Spaces to Meeting Places and How to Change Them Back*. Manchester, VT: Sophia Institute Press, 2001.

Sallust. *On the Gods and the World*, trans. Thomas Taylor. Los Angeles, CA: Philosophical Research Society, 1976.

Schenk, Jochen. *Templar Families: Landowning Families and the Order of the Temple in France*. Cambridge, MA: University of Cambridge Press, 2010.

Schonfield, Hugh J. *The Essene Odyssey*. Shaftesbury, UK: Element Books, 2004.

Scullard, I I. H. *Roman Britain: Outpost of the Empire*. London: Thames & Hudson, 1979.

Shafer, Byron, ed. *Temples of Ancient Egypt*. Ithaca, NY: Cornell University Press, 1997.

Skinner, Stephen. *Feng Shui: The Living Earth Manual*. North Clarendon, VT: Tuttle, 2006.

Sonoda, Minoru. "Shinto and the Natural Environment," *Shinto in History*. London: Routledge, 2000, 35–52.

Souden, David. *Stonehenge Revealed*. New York: Facts On File, 1997.

Spawforth, Anthony. *The Complete Greek Temples*. London: Thames & Hudson, 2006.

Steiner, Rudolf. *Agriculture: A Course of Eight Lectures*, trans. George Adams. London: Biodynamic Association, 1974.

Stewart, R. J. *The Prophetic Vision of Merlin*. London: Arkana, 1986.

Stevenson, David. *The Origins of Freemasonry: Scotland's Century 1590–1710*. Cambridge, MA: Cambridge University Press, 1988.

ten Grotenhuis, Elizabeth. *Japanese Mandalas: Representations of Sacred Geography*. Honolulu, HI: University of Hawai'i Press, 1999.

Thompson, Laurence G. *Chinese Religion: An Introduction*. Encino, CA: Dickenson, 1975.

von Eschenbach, Wolfram. *Parzival: A Romance of the Middle Ages*, trans. Helen M. Mustard and Charles E. Passage. New York: Random House, 1961.

von Simson, Otto. *The Gothic Cathedral*. New York: Pantheon Books, 1962.

Wangu, Madhu Bazaz. *Hinduism*. New York: Chelsea House, 2009.

Watkins, Alfred. *The Old Straight Track*. London: Methuen and Co., 1925.

Weston, Jessie. *From Ritual to Romance*. Gloucester, MA: Peter Smith, 1983.

Wilkinson, Richard H. *The Complete Temples of Ancient Egypt*. New York: Thames & Hudson, 2000.

Wolf, Arthur P., ed. *Religion and Ritual in Chinese Society*. Stanford, CA: Stanford University Press, 1974.

Yamamoto, Yukitaka. *Kami no Michi: The Way of the Kami*. Stockton, CA: Tsubaki America Publications, 1999.

Youings, Joyce A. *The Dissolution of the Monasteries*. London: Allen and Unwin, 1971.

INDEX

GET MORE AT LLEWELLYN.COM

Visit us online to browse hundreds of our books and decks, plus sign up to receive our e-newsletters and exclusive online offers.

- Free tarot readings • Spell-a-Day • Moon phases
- Recipes, spells, and tips • Blogs • Encyclopedia
- Author interviews, articles, and upcoming events

GET SOCIAL WITH LLEWELLYN

Find us on Facebook
www.Facebook.com/LlewellynBooks

Follow us on twitter™
www.Twitter.com/Llewellynbooks

GET BOOKS AT LLEWELLYN

LLEWELLYN ORDERING INFORMATION

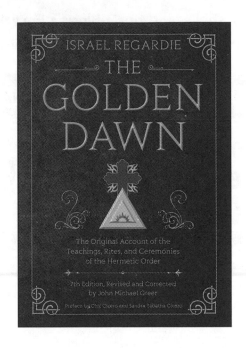

To order, call 1-877-NEW-WRLD

PRICES SUBJECT TO CHANGE WITHOUT NOTICE

Order at llewellyn.com 24 hours a day, 7 days a week!

The Golden Dawn
The Original Account of the Teachings, Rites, and Ceremonies of the Hermetic Order

Israel Regardie
7th edition, revised and corrected
by John Michael Greer

Over the three quarters of a century since it first saw print, Israel Regardie's *The Golden Dawn* has become the most influential modern handbook of magical theory and practice. In this new, definitive edition, noted scholar John Michael Greer has taken this essential resource back to its original, authentic form. Correcting errors and misprints, updating and adding missing illustrations, featuring a 20-page color insert, remedying omissions, and refreshing the design and typography, this definitive edition returns this modern masterpiece to its true stature.

An essential textbook in magical lodges and occult schools, *The Golden Dawn* includes initiation rituals, a complete system of Tarot, a ritual for invisibility, secrets of invocation and evocation, the mysteries of kabbalah, meditation techniques, Enochian magic, and much more.

978-0-7387-4399-8
7 x 10 • 960 pp.

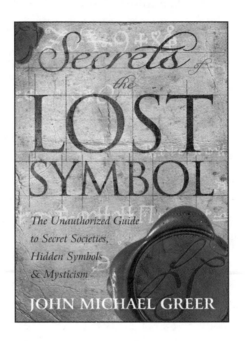

Secrets of the Lost Symbol
The Unauthorized Guide to Secret Societies, Hidden Symbols & Mysticism
John Michael Greer

Are mystic symbols embedded in Washington, D.C., landmarks? Was the Capitol's street layout designed using astrology and geometry? Did our Founding Fathers practice rituals in secret societies? What's the truth behind the mystical elements inside Dan Brown's blockbuster *The Lost Symbol*?

Formatted like an encyclopedia, this unofficial companion guide to *The Lost Symbol* is an essential resource for the millions of Dan Brown fans who want to know the facts behind the fiction. Discover the truth about Freemasonry, including its rituals, temples, and infamous members such as the legendary Albert Pike. Get the real story behind the Rosicrucians, the Key of Solomon, and ancient occult rites. *Secrets of the Lost Symbol* uncovers the forgotten histories of arcane traditions that have shaped—and still inhabit—our modern world.

978-0-7387-2169-9
5 x 7 • 240 pp.

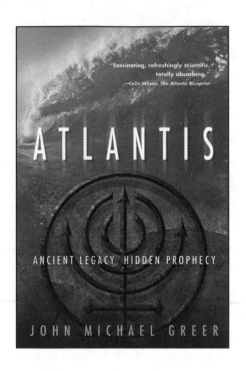

To order, call 1-877-NEW-WRLD

Atlantis
Ancient Legacy, Hidden Prophecy
John Michael Greer

Is there anything our modern industrial society can learn from the story of Atlantis, a legend that has endured for two thousand years?

From the dialogues of Plato to the modern age of Atlantology, esteemed occultist John Michael Greer traces the evolution of this controversial story about a great civilization drowned by the sea. See how this fascinating legend was reshaped by modern occultists and pioneers of the "rejected knowledge" movement. Greer also proposes his own revolutionary theory—based on Plato's accounts, human history, and geological science—of a civilization doomed by natural disasters at the end of the last Ice Age.

As the threat of global warming makes headlines today, Greer poses the ultimate question: is the legend of Atlantis a legacy of the distant past or a prophecy of our own future?

978-0-7387-0978-9
6 x 9 • 264 pp.

To Write to the Author

If you wish to contact the author or would like more information about this book, please write to the author in care of Llewellyn Worldwide and we will forward your request. Both the author and the publisher appreciate hearing from you and learning of your enjoyment of this book and how it has helped you. Llewellyn Worldwide cannot guarantee that every letter written to the author can be answered, but all will be forwarded. Please write to:

John Michael Greer
℅ Llewellyn Worldwide
2143 Wooddale Drive
Woodbury, MN 55125-2989

Please enclose a self-addressed stamped envelope for reply
or $1.00 to cover costs. If outside the USA, enclose
an international postal reply coupon.

Many of Llewellyn's authors have websites with additional information and resources. For more information, please visit our website:

WWW.LLEWELLYN.COM